T0274959

ESCAPING
THE
HOUSING
TRAP

CHARLES L. MAROHN, JR.   DANIEL HERRIGES

ESCAPING
THE
HOUSING TRAP

THE
STRONG TOWNS
RESPONSE TO THE HOUSING CRISIS

WILEY

Published by John Wiley & Sons, Inc., Hoboken, New Jersey.
Published simultaneously in Canada.

For general information on our other products and services or for technical support, please contact our Customer Care Department within the United States at (800) 762-2974, outside the United States at (317) 572-3993 or fax (317) 572-4002.

Wiley also publishes its books in a variety of electronic formats. Some content that appears in print may not be available in electronic formats. For more information about Wiley products, visit our web site at www.wiley.com.

Library of Congress Cataloging-in-Publication Data is Available:

ISBN: 9781119984528 (cloth)
ISBN: 9781394198306 (ePub)
ISBN: 9781394198313 (ePDF)

Cover Design: Paul McCarthy
Cover Art: Courtesy of the Author

SKY10072738_041224

Contents

Introduction

Take an evening walk around your neighborhood. As you stroll, count the windows of the homes you pass. If the lights are on, take a casual glance at what you can see from the outside. You don't need to snoop; just glance.

Housing is everything. It is the basis for our ability to meet most of our other needs and wants. It is our tether to a place and to a community. Home is where we make nearly all our most consequential plans. Our career trajectories, our close relationships, and our health all depend in part on what kind of housing we are able to secure and where.

Behind one of those windows, perhaps, is the place where somebody proposed to their sweetheart. Behind another may be a chair where someone sat and wept for hours after receiving tragic news. A college acceptance letter sits on a desk somewhere. A jury summons. Unpaid bills. An eviction notice. A letter from summer camp, or one from rehab.

Behind one of those windows, an elderly widow's live-in caretaker sweeps the floor. An office has been converted to a nursery. Somewhere there is a couch where an old friend looking for a new start has been sleeping. In one of those homes, somebody has made plans to start a business. Or move to another state. Or finally buy that motorcycle.

Ponder, for a moment, the irreducible complexity of the web of decisions that lead particular people to live out their most pivotal moments behind the particular windows of particular buildings. Let yourself be humbled by it.

Most of us, at the end of the day, have pretty simple aspirations. We'd like to live a good life in a place that is prospering. And though each of us will define "good life" a little bit differently, nearly everyone's conception of "good" is going to involve a home in which they are secure and comfortable.

This is the third in a series of books outlining the Strong Towns approach to the growth and development of cities and neighborhoods.

Central to this approach is the recognition that cities are complex systems. They are shaped by countless decisions made by millions of individuals over time, with interconnections that are challenging to trace or fully grasp. When attempts are made to simplify or ignore this inherent complexity in organizing urban life, challenges and disruptions arise.

The first Strong Towns book, *Strong Towns: A Bottom-Up Revolution to Rebuild American Prosperity*, reveals an epidemic of financial insolvency across North American local governments and outlines a citizen-led approach to growth and development that can make our communities financially strong and resilient. The second book, *Confessions of a Recovering Engineer*, describes the failures, in spiraling costs and a mounting crash death toll, of America's transportation system. It proposes a paradigm shift in how we plan and prioritize infrastructure projects. Both books, in large part, are stories of the failures of top-down institutions, and the promise of bottom-up alternatives.

There is massive complexity to the subjects covered in the first two books because of the human factor: our biases and fallibility, our capacity to make shortsighted decisions and convince ourselves of faulty priorities. However, both of those topics also have an element that is very discrete and quantifiable. Budget math is budget math. Asphalt is asphalt. Physics is physics.

Housing is more complex and arguably has the highest stakes of all.

In the early stages of developing this book, we would often mention to people that we were going to be coauthoring a book about the housing crisis. This tends to elicit nods of affirmation: "Oh wow, yes, what an important topic. Wait: which housing crisis exactly?"

You could probably survey 100 Americans and get 100 different answers as to what the "housing crisis" consists of. And if you had conducted this survey in 2009, you would have gotten a very different set of answers. Different still in 1975. Or 1933.

What you will not find is a lot of disagreement with the idea that there *is* a housing crisis. Virtually no one has ever responded by telling us that they don't think there's a problem. Indeed, the sense is widely and acutely shared across all strata of society that there is a profound problem with housing, and that sense is not new.

If you have a modest income and/or rent your home, the "what" of the crisis is probably not all that elusive to you. Today, we have a crisis of unaffordability. This problem isn't new, but its contours have expanded. The US Census Bureau reported in 2022 that nearly half of American renter households pay over 30% of their income in rent, an amount seen as likely to strain their personal finances and their ability to build up savings. Ownership is no easier. According to the Urban Institute, in December 2022 households earning the median US income could only afford to purchase 20 percent of US homes for sale. In some regions, homeownership is even more out of reach: in metropolitan Seattle, the figure was 7.6 percent. In Los Angeles, a mere 1.9 percent (Choi and Zinn 2022).

It has long been true that burdensome costs, substandard conditions, and the constant threat of displacement have shaped the housing experience for poorer Americans. Today, a broader sense of precarity extends to a lot more people.

"Precarity" is a more subtle issue than just "unaffordability." We use it to convey that many people who can, on paper, "afford" their housing are nonetheless being stretched or finding their lives disrupted in some way. The housing options available to them do not grant them stability and the means to freely make important life decisions.

A single parent raising a teenager in a high-crime neighborhood.

A 30-year-old living with her aging parents.

A 40-year-old far from his aging parents and unable to assist them with their health and mobility.

Someone who cannot afford to move to pursue a desired career.

Someone facing eviction who will be displaced from their neighborhood, and with it, from a community of shared culture, faith, or ethnicity.

Someone fleeing prejudice and discrimination who cannot obtain a home in a community where they will be accepted.

An elderly, disabled homeowner, with significant home equity but cash-poor, who cannot move without losing a vital support network of friends and neighbors.

A middle-aged couple mired in debt, who forgo vacations and visits to the doctor in order to make the mortgage payments.

A young couple, powerlessly watching their ability to purchase a home locally evaporate because of a decision to raise interest rates made a thousand miles away at the Federal Reserve.

Someone afraid to leave a troubled relationship because she does not know how she will afford housing on her own.

A couple who rent a house from a distant landlord, after losing their previous home to foreclosure following a period of unemployment and missed payments.

A college student living in his car.

People making uncomfortable trade-offs. A roommate they don't get along with. A punishing commute. Still living with an ex because neither can afford their own place.

All of those scenarios do not even include the direst of circumstances. As of January 2022, according to the National Alliance to End Homelessness, approximately 582,000 Americans were experiencing homelessness. About a quarter of those were chronically homeless. About 28% were people living in families with children (National Alliance to End Homelessness n.d.).

Approximately one in seven children born in large American cities between 1998 and 2000 experienced at least one eviction for nonpayment of rent or mortgage between birth and age 15 (Lundberg and Donnelly 2019). Among those born into deep poverty, the figure is one in four. Eviction can have spiraling consequences for health, for academic performance, and for the ability to secure housing in the future.

A widely circulated 2021 article in *Works in Progress* was titled "The Housing Theory of Everything" (Bowman, Myers, and Southwood 2021). It made the case that housing precarity is behind a range of issues that bedevil the wealthy Western world, from slowing economic productivity and innovation to rising inequality, from low birth rates to poor physical fitness. Why can't the wealthiest societies in the history of humanity figure out this housing thing?

The answer, in some sense, is that as a society, we don't want to.

The housing market is our source of shelter, but it is also the foundation of the American economy. Investments whose values are derived from home mortgages literally backstop the solvency of the entire banking system. This is a lesson we learned the hard way in 2008, and yet it remains true today. Not only the financial sector but millions of individuals' finances are dependent on equity in a house they hope will be an appreciating asset over time.

At the same time, we all need shelter. And there is no way for shelter to remain broadly affordable while home prices rise faster than incomes.

The tension between these two objectives may be clearer than ever. But we are no closer to identifying a simple way of resolving it. In May 2023, a *Newsweek* story titled "Housing Market Crash Fears Rise

Among Americans" summarized the results of a survey: "Americans seem conflicted about where they would like home prices to be heading: some 43 percent would prefer prices in their area to increase, while 41 percent would want to see them drop" (Carbonaro 2023).

We need housing prices to fall; we also cannot afford for them to fall. Thus, we are trapped.

It was not inevitable that we would find ourselves in this trap. In this book, we will explore the historical origins of our housing predicament. Based on this understanding, we will offer some rational responses: ways to begin extricating ourselves from a broken system.

There is a difference between a rational response and a solution. There is no simple way out of our housing trap, no magical fix that does not entail some societal disruption and some economic pain.

But we are not helpless. Within the financial and legal means of local leaders are avenues to reform regulations that stifle the production of housing, to curb the distorting influences of Wall Street capital on our towns and neighborhoods, and to cultivate a new groundswell of local, neighborhood-focused developers who can actually build the housing we need, where it is needed.

We can act upon these things immediately. Incrementally, we can begin to make local housing markets more responsive to local demand. Ultimately we will have a world of more plentiful, affordable, and varied housing options.

This book will challenge several common simplistic narratives about the housing crisis: those that assert, or imply, that it has either a single cause or a single solution.

Those who make such assertions often focus on only one facet of the issue. In this, they call to mind the Indian parable of the blind men and the elephant. It describes a group of blind men who set out to determine the nature of an elephant but arrive at vastly different conclusions. One man, touching only the trunk, concludes that the elephant resembles a large snake. Another, reaching out and finding the elephant's ear, concludes that it is more like a fan; the man who touches the leg likens it to a tree, and so forth. None of them produces an accurate mental picture of the whole animal.

The parable illustrates that people who have incomplete mental models of the world (which is to say, all of us) can arrive at vastly different and incompatible conclusions.

Our national discourse about housing is incoherent in part because we are touching different parts of the elephant. Those who set housing policy often do not understand housing finance. Those who focus on finance are often oblivious to the effects of land-use policy. These conversations—housing finance and land-use policy—occur in separate circles and are often insufficiently informed by each other.

The first third of this book will review the history of housing finance, from the creation of the modern home mortgage and the problems it was addressing at the time to the ways in which rising home prices have become ever more entangled with the health of the US financial system.

The second third of the book will address the public policy environment that governs housing as shelter, from local zoning and building codes to state laws governing development to federal affordable housing programs. All these things affect where homes are built, what can and cannot be built, and what political forces come to bear on these questions.

Understanding both will lay the groundwork for the third and final section, in which we discuss rational steps that local leaders can begin to take right now to make room for a new housing paradigm, one that is able to rapidly produce housing on a local scale in response to local needs.

In the history of how Americans are housed, a crucial hinge point is the society-wide paradigm shift we have labeled the suburban experiment. This is a term we have used extensively in our work at Strong Towns to describe an interconnected set of radical changes in how we build, finance, and understand cities. This shift occurred across the entire North American continent in a short span of time, beginning in the mid-20th century. There was effectively no control group.

The suburban experiment did not have a single cause. The mass marketing of the automobile made it possible to design communities around this revolutionary new transportation technology. Rapid industrialization had strained the social and physical fabric of American cities. And the Great Depression had destabilized the country's economic foundations.

In response to the Depression, we deployed massive government spending, and new systems of housing finance, planning, and regulation, across a continent. We did it in an effort to stimulate homebuilding and homeownership on a mass scale. The result was to take trends that had already begun, such as the building of suburbs and the creation of residential zoning, and give them rocket fuel.

Virtually everywhere, we went from towns built and modified over time by many hands to whole neighborhoods built all at once to a finished state. We began to build neighborhoods as monocultures, instead of eclectic mixtures of different kinds of homes and activities. And we began to design them differently, around the assumption that almost everyone would drive a car.

The suburban experiment also encompassed a shift away from building cities in proportion to our means, with an understanding that those means would increase over time. Armed with new financial tools, we would increasingly finance our cities and our homes through debt, obtaining a short-term sense of prosperity at the cost of long-term liabilities.

This experiment emerged from choices that were understandable at the time. They were mostly the choices of policymakers looking to solve large and immediate problems. But the suburban experiment did have an underlying ideology of sorts.

In his seminal work *Seeing Like a State*, the anthropologist James C. Scott (1999) identifies the defining ideology of technocratic states in the 20th century. Scott calls this ideology *high modernism*, and for a time it dominated elite thinking in governments both right- and left-wing, both democratic and authoritarian. High modernism consists of a strong belief in the scientific perfectibility of society. The high modernist seeks to render complex social phenomena discrete, legible, and measurable, in order to prescribe solutions through rational, scientific management.

The suburban experiment is America's high modernist revolution in city-building. We believed we could build a prosperous society on a new, never-tested template. We believed we could enhance access to one of humanity's most basic needs—shelter—by streamlining and standardizing our systems for providing it. We believed we could devise permanent solutions to problems that had bedeviled city dwellers forever.

The 20th century housing revolution was a three-legged stool: financial, regulatory, and cultural. Again, one can look at the motivations of those leading the charge in each realm, and it's not hard to find them understandable, perhaps even noble. They can be read as an effort to create broadly shared middle-class prosperity.

But nearly a century on, we can recognize that the experiment's goals are not being met.

Before the suburban experiment, the bar of entry to create housing was very low. Your home was relatively likely to be built by you, your family members and neighbors, or someone close to you in your community. However, much of the housing that existed was of very low quality. Every rung of the proverbial housing ladder existed, including situations like crowded, airless tenements that we would find intolerable today.

A regulatory revolution sought to guarantee basic standards of housing and neighborhood quality. Building codes, fire codes, and zoning codes were all invented and widely replicated toward this end. We can recognize the health and safety advances that this new city planning apparatus enabled.

These early planning reforms, however, soon outgrew their initial purpose. To bring legible order to America's cities and neighborhoods, we broadly outlawed many of the housing forms that had been basic building blocks of our cities. We curtailed many of the ad hoc strategies by which Americans had built wealth while simultaneously meeting their need for shelter. We wrote into law rigid, pseudoscientific, and often prejudiced notions of what a good home and a good community could be.

By the 1940s, zoning had been repurposed as the operating system by which we would build the new suburbia: a set of standardized housing monocultures amenable to streamlined planning and large-scale finance.

Today, we experience a world in which there are massive regulatory barriers to the production of housing. Those barriers are highest in affluent and desirable cities and neighborhoods. Far from guaranteeing the order and permanence promised by early zoning champions, the actual effect has been to destabilize our communities and to displace many Americans from living where, and how, they would like to live.

Culturally, the relationship between Americans and our neighborhoods has changed. The neighborhood was once the stage on which most of life took place. You were likely to live, work, and conduct commerce within a small radius, and as such you were a participant in the full range of the complex social life of your neighborhood.

Today, new residential bedroom communities are more often marketed as places of privacy and exclusivity. They are less likely to be physically and socioeconomically integrated with the broader community, and their residents experience them largely as consumers, not cocreators.

As consumers we expect to be catered to, and yet many share a strong sense that the building industry is *not* responsive to our wants or needs. There's a disconnect. Development, and developers, are widely unpopular. We recognize housing as necessary and may well recognize that many places do not have enough of it, yet the construction of new housing elicits ferocious protest at least as often as not. Many do not believe that development can deliver positive benefits for their communities.

In finance, we had a pre-Depression status quo in which debt was not easily available as a means of securing housing. Homeownership was not actually much rarer than today. But the path involved some improvisation, some making-do. Homes could be financed, but lenders were much more risk averse and limited in what they would offer.

A system engineered in large part to rescue the housing market from the depths of the Great Depression changed the game. The federal government began to insure the mortgage loans issued by commercial banks, allowing them to confidently make long-term loans with small down payments and attainable monthly installments. This innovation unlocked the possibility of homeownership for millions of middle-class Americans.

But the new system was not without a catch. Federal mortgage rules excluded many poorer and predominantly non-white neighborhoods from the benefits of this system, condemning these places to often catastrophic stagnation and decline. The same rules dramatically tipped the scales in favor of building new suburbs and away from revitalizing existing communities.

This experiment spread throughout American society at the same time as an unprecedented remaking of the physical fabric of our communities. Mass suburbanization subsidized by the building of highways would change the way many, eventually most, Americans lived.

The opening of the suburbs unlocked a one-time financial windfall for governments and citizens alike. For a generation of newly minted homeowners, it appeared virtually a law of the universe that home prices would only go up. Mayors and city managers looked at budgets determined by the values of those homes and concluded the same. The resources of postwar America must have felt inexhaustible.

The first homes in the planned postwar suburb of Levittown, New York, cost $6,990. In today's dollars, that is $91,515.76: cheaper than almost any home on the market today. But with each successive decade, the effort required to sustain the expectation that home equity gains will outpace general inflation has become greater. Successive waves of financial innovation have been aimed not at stimulating the supply or variety of housing but at increasing Americans' ability to take on debt to gain access to it. That debt, in turn, would become the basis for an ever-more exotic collection of financial instruments that extracted profit for investors out of the basic homeownership transaction.

The shock of 2008 did not force a total reset. Rather, the years since have seen home prices rise to levels even higher than the peak of the early-aughts bubble. This has been fueled by historically low interest rates and massive infusions of cash into the economy, as well as a decade of underbuilding. In the summer of 2023, the Case-Shiller Index of US home prices relative to incomes hit an all-time high (FREDd n.d.).

There is no way out of this trap that does not involve a painful correction. Housing prices are untenably high for millions of Americans, threatening the stability and prosperity of our lives. But anything more than a modest fall in home prices, in the near term, represents a threat to the banking system and the entire US economy.

The path to escaping the trap will require a building boom. But it won't be one that looks like the suburban building boom of the postwar era.

We need a lot more housing, in a more diverse range of places and forms than what is currently produced. Much of it will be small, and much of it will be carved out of existing homes and properties. We need a lower bar of entry, both for people seeking housing and for people creating it. We must reinvent the starter home, the bottom rung on the housing ladder, in a way that is appropriate to our era, not by seeking a return to the tenement conditions of a century ago.

In all of this, we can learn from the rapid yet decentralized process of growth that created many pre-suburban cities we still enjoy and admire today. These places were built by many hands, not few.

We must enable and cultivate a new generation of small-scale, incremental, citizen developers: people who can build in the communities they live in, where they have skin in the game, people who can work in the gaps and crevices of a neighborhood and make more out of less.

We need access to finance for these projects. We need communities of such developers who can share know-how and resources.

We also must re-jigger our planning apparatus, which has become an unwieldy tangle of rules that conspire to stifle even the smallest change to the existing physical character of many neighborhoods. The next increment of intensity, allowing for growth of the housing stock and evolution of the neighborhood, must be legal everywhere. Securing permission to do these projects must be fast and straightforward.

Every neighborhood must be allowed to grow and change. This means a cultural shift. We've been sold the promise of permanence: an illusion that we can be happy homeowner-consumers in endlessly appreciating homes in neighborhoods that look the same for decades.

The reality is that a place that is not changing is dying. We can wage a war against entropy, and we will lose it. Or we can recalibrate our cultural sensitivities to live with a certain amount of change, to relinquish a certain expectation of control.

If we can do this, there is much to gain. We will find that we can produce a world of far greater housing options and that this allows us to live richer lives. We will discover that we have more agency than we thought we did, that we can shape our communities to meet our needs, not the imperatives of an impersonal planning bureaucracy or a distant financial institution.

This will not look like a return to the past, which was never perfect or simple anyway. But it will involve a return to a recognition that cities are at their best when they are, as Jane Jacobs said, created by everyone. Genuine solutions to the problems we share cannot be orchestrated from the top down. But they can emerge over time from the work of many hands, pursuing separate objectives in a dance that is never fully choreographed.

This is how our cities, towns, and neighborhoods used to grow. In that respect, it's time to go home.

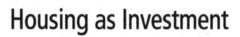

Housing as Investment

1

Is Housing Shelter or an Investment?

Securing shelter is a fundamental necessity for everyone. In Maslow's hierarchy of needs, the foundational level is rooted in the essentials of human existence. Basic life requirements include air, water, and food, in addition to the fundamentals of rest, clothing, and a place to shelter. When any of these essentials are absent, all other considerations naturally take a backseat as the immediate priority becomes obtaining these basic needs. It's not just a preference; it's a fundamental matter of survival.

The second level of Maslow's hierarchy is safety. Once a human's base needs have been met, it is natural to seek an increased level of security. Protection of oneself and one's property is urgent. There is also room here for things such as personal health, stable employment, and financial security.

A residence serves as more than just shelter; it enhances physical security and, under favorable circumstances, becomes a vehicle for accruing wealth and achieving financial stability. Homeownership often plays a pivotal role in ascending the initial rungs of Maslow's hierarchy.

The next step is love and belonging. The home plays a large role here as well. A home provides the place to raise a family and experience the intimacy of family life. Living in a place can provide a sense of connection to neighbors and a community.

Once a person has love and belonging, Maslow suggests the next level is esteem. Respect, status, and recognition are elements of esteem often reflected in a home. A housewarming party is a way to share good fortune with others. It's also a way to signal success.

At the pinnacle of Maslow's hierarchy is self-actualization, the pursuit of realizing one's full potential. While a home is not typically the catalyst for achieving self-actualization, the upkeep of a well-tended yard, engaging in occasional home improvement projects, or simply fulfilling mortgage payments can unexpectedly become avenues toward personal fulfillment.

The home is at the core of the American Dream because it is so many things to so many people. It's shelter. It's security. It's a store of wealth. It's a reflection of our status. It's where we live and experience life's most intimate moments. If we're lucky, it is the place we'll draw our final breath, surrounded by our loved ones, after a long life.

Housing serves us in so many dimensions, but what happens when these dimensions compete? When housing becomes a good investment for homeowners by reliably going up in value year after year, it impairs the ability of non-homeowners to purchase a home. When housing as a form of esteem or self-actualization leads homeowners to demand exclusionary zoning practices, it makes it difficult for needed housing to be built.

Economically, housing is an excludable good. If one person or family occupies a home, they can exclude others from making use of it. It is also considered a rival good. When a person or family occupies a home, that home is no longer available in the marketplace for someone else to occupy. This combination—excludable and rivalrous—makes housing what economists call a private good.

In theory, a free market will supply private goods in quantities and at price points to meet demand. Some essential private goods, such as food and clothing, the market provides in excess. The fact that some Americans go without food or clothing is not a function of supply breakdowns. There is ample food and clothing being produced, more than enough for everyone.

Housing is also an essential good, but it is not produced in excess like food and clothing. Quite the opposite; there is currently a shortage of housing in North America. This wasn't always the case, but today an increasing number of cities do not have enough homes to satisfy local demand.

In a marketplace, a shortage in supply of a private good will make the price of that good go up. A hamburger is a private good that, once it is consumed, is not available to anyone else. If there is a shortage of hamburger, the price will go up and people will shift to eating other things. In theory, this should prompt the production of more hamburger, bringing the price back down to a point where the market demand is met.

When someone buys or rents a home, they occupy it temporarily. At some point—it may be months or decades—that home goes back on the market. It isn't consumed the way a hamburger is. For people who own a home, and for those who own rental property, rising prices are a feature, not a flaw. Scarcity makes the private good they own more valuable.

Today in North America, there are two different, mutually incoherent conversations about the housing market. One is conducted by "housing" people and the other among "finance" people.

"Housing" people are primarily concerned with housing's availability as shelter across the spectrum of incomes and needs. Rising prices are reflexively understood as a negative thing. "Finance" people are primarily concerned with the performance of housing as an investment asset class. They may recognize the struggles experienced by many in obtaining housing, but rising prices are often the implicit or explicit goal.

"The housing market" does not mean the same thing to the two camps. To housing people it means the stock of homes available for sale or rent and the participants in those exchanges. To finance people the phrase "the housing market" often means the mortgage market, including secondary markets in financial derivatives.

At the end of the day, housing is shelter. It is the most basic of human needs. One might be tempted to assert, on moral grounds, that concerns over housing's role as shelter should automatically supersede sensitivities over housing's role as an investment. That isn't wrong, but it is oversimplified.

That is because housing as a financial product is the foundation of the American economy. To a disproportionate extent, the ability of people to have a job, obtain food, support their family, pay their taxes, and so much more is dependent on elevated housing prices. The converse is also true: falling home prices threaten the entire economy.

This is a tension that must be resolved, but there is no clear path to resolve it. There is a clear power imbalance, however, between those who benefit from high housing prices and those who are harmed by them.

Who Benefits from High Housing Prices?

Policy discussions about creating affordable housing often suffer from a fatal incoherence. The people having the conversation and the organizations they represent are generally harmed by a decrease in prices. The incoherence is that they want housing to become more affordable but without prices going down.

This is rarely stated openly, but it manifests in the policies put forth. Many of the least affordable cities have in place policies that aim to create a stock of dedicated affordable housing, albeit limited and inadequate, without disrupting the overall upward trajectory of prices. For example, inclusionary housing is the practice of requiring developers to include a percentage of below-market units as a condition of approving a development. In a sense, the more expensive units must be priced even higher to subsidize the below-market units. High prices are reinforced in the name of affordability.

To truly reduce prices through supply and demand mechanisms requires building a lot of new units. There is an institutional inertia against such an approach. That resistance needs to be acknowledged, not to shame but to understand why this challenge is so difficult. The list of those who benefit from high housing prices is long. It includes nearly everyone in a position to influence the production of new housing.

For example, local governments benefit from high housing prices. This is especially true for places that utilize the property tax. Cities often tout a declining tax rate as a sign of good fiscal management. When property values go up by a double-digit percentage, it allows local governments to raise more money at a lower tax rate. For taxpayers, there is less incentive to complain about local taxes going up $200 in a year where the property being taxed goes up by $20,000.

State and federal governments also benefit from high housing prices. States generally receive sales and income taxes. The federal government taxes income, both from the employee and the employer. As home values rise, it drives the kind of transactions that increase state and federal tax revenues. For the last couple of decades, this includes the cashing out of home equity for consumption spending.

Banks and insurance companies are obvious beneficiaries of rising home prices. Both hold mortgage-backed securities as part of their required reserves. When values are rising, those reserves become even more secure. If prices were to fall, it threatens their solvency in a way Treasury bills do not. An environment where home prices consistently rise increases the margin of error for financial institutions.

Developers and contractors are also routinely bailed out by appreciating home values. In fact, developers who mess up a project just need to wait for another year of appreciation to make up their lost margin. The fact that interest rates have been very low for the past two decades has made this kind of financial sloppiness more the rule than the exception.

In the broader market, pension funds and other conservative investors have placed trillions of dollars into housing. While they don't necessarily benefit from rising prices, falling prices do threaten their investments. These major financial institutions would be very resistant to policies that broadly lower home values.

As would the largest and most influential group: existing homeowners. It is obvious that it doesn't benefit someone to sell at a high price only to turn around and buy at a high price. Still, only a small percentage of homeowners move in any given year. The rest are generally content to have their net worth increase by thousands of dollars annually. They would be very cranky were the opposite to occur.

Line up all these constituencies on one side of the influence ledger. Who sits on the other side? Who doesn't benefit from appreciating home values? Renters; first-time homebuyers, especially young people and those without savings or equity to trade in; and the poor. It hardly needs to be said that these are less influential constituencies.

Even if we truly desire housing to become more affordable, we need to acknowledge that our personal incentives are mostly at odds with that goal. Put another way, individually, we have a vested interest in one approach (rising prices and growth), even though collectively we may express a desire for the opposite (broader affordability and housing stability).

It is impossible for housing prices to climb annually at rates greater than inflation while simultaneously having housing become more affordable. More than even an economics problem, this is a cultural challenge.

Understanding the Housing Market

Almost everyone wears shoes. For all practical purposes, shoes are essential clothing for most humans alive today. Shoes come in seemingly as many varieties as there are feet. In fact, most Americans own multiple pairs. While some struggle to pay for shoes, there are many different price points and ways of acquiring them. Our economy produces shoes in such abundance that we never experience a shortage. There is no shoe crisis or shoeless problem.

Pretend for a moment that this isn't the case. Imagine a shoe market that produces only two kinds of shoes: a high-end loafer and an elite-brand tennis shoe. The high-end loafers are produced by a few companies such as Gucci and Louis Vuitton. The elite-brand tennis shoes are produced by companies such as Nike and Adidas. They are named after famous sports figures.

A century ago, there was a shoe crisis. Shoes were abundant but very poor in quality. A financial crisis then caused people to lose their shoes, through no fault of their own. The federal government stepped in and provided insurance and subsidies to get the shoe market moving again. New shoes were produced in abundance. Prices were broadly affordable. Quality went up significantly.

Through a broad cultural consensus, two styles of shoe begin to dominate the market: high-end loafer and elite-brand tennis shoe. Federal subsidies are set up to promulgate these two choices. Local regulations are put in place to reinforce this preference. Everyone from large banks to local shoe salesmen find it lucrative to support the emergence of these two options.

In this imaginary world, anyone who wants shoes can still buy them. There is a market, and that market has multiple competitors. Yet those competitors are competing at only two price points. Both price points are rather expensive.

People who can't afford shoes at high prices buy used shoes. New shoes filter down to be purchased by poorer people. Over time, the prices for new shoes climb. More and more people compete for the used shoes that are available. Now the price of used shoes climbs, as well.

The federal government steps in to assist people buying new shoes. They set up direct and indirect subsidies. They encourage banks to assist shoe manufacturers. Local governments, too, get in on the act and provide their own set of subsidies to shoe corporations. People can now pay more for their Gucci loafers and Air Jordans, so prices soar. So do profits.

Shoe corporations can sell both styles of shoes as fast as they can produce them, but there is a limit to how fast they can be produced. Local permitting restricts the number of shoes that can be made. Rising prices have bloated supply chains, making everything more expensive. The extensive web of public and private capital vested in producing high-end loafers and elite-brand tennis shoes stifles innovation.

Political factions arise that advocate for the production of more high-end loafers, with some fraction offered at subsidized prices. Opposing factions arise to object to these plans. A used and ratty pair of Air Jordans is selling for twice as much as a new pair cost a decade earlier.

Speculators now buy new Gucci loafers without any intention of wearing them. They simply want to capture the price appreciation. Shoe prices climb higher and higher. Lots of people who want shoes can't get them. They go barefoot. Those who can buy shoes feel financially squeezed. Price increases are normalized, even expected. Many people are desperate to get any pair of shoes.

This all feels bizarre. What kind of mass insanity would have to occur for it to become normal that only two types of shoes were available for purchase, and those produced by only a handful of suppliers? In this imaginary world, how long would this go on until someone did the obvious thing and began producing penny loafers? At what point in this self-created shoe shortage would people simply start making their own shoes?

We have an abundance of shoes today, and so this entire scenario seems absurd. It is absurd. Yet our present housing crisis, which seems normal to us, would be absurd to anyone living a century ago. In the context of millennia of human development, we are the first culture to find ourselves with a chronic shortage of housing. We have grown used to something that is deeply abnormal.

In a little less than a century, housing has gone from being abundant but low quality to relatively good quality but now an elite product. We wiped out the starter rung on the ladder. We need a housing market that produces penny loafers again.

Can Housing Prices Go Down?

Economists have long studied a phenomenon known as the resource trap. Sometimes called the "paradox of plenty," the resource trap afflicts many countries that are rich in natural resources. For such places, having natural resources can be a blessing, but it can also be a curse.

The blessing comes from the jobs and opportunities the resources provide, such as opportunities to mine, drill, or log. The curse comes when the community becomes trapped in the resource economy, unable to grow beyond it.

This is easy for Americans to see in countries such as Venezuela or Saudi Arabia. Abundant oil has allowed their governments to persist, despite not meeting the needs of their people. Glitzy projects and occasional handouts have allowed them to limp along. High unemployment and low family wealth persists, despite the astounding riches extracted from the ground.

In a resource trap, quality of life becomes a cost to reduce. Jobs and wages are expenses to be trimmed. Opportunities for growth and investment are a distraction to the core goal of efficiency. In service of the resource being extracted, the economy becomes trapped in a predatory cycle, obsessively reducing society's overall standard of living just to keep things going.

America has created its own resource trap. Instead of oil or some other commodity, the resource Americans have ready for extraction is their wealth. That wealth used to be tied up in a family's home, an incidental savings plan capturing portions of a lifetime of labor. The home now is merely the drill bit used to gain access to that wealth.

The primary purpose of a house today isn't to provide shelter. That is such an old-fashioned, quaint way to think about housing. No, the primary purpose of a house is to create a piece of mortgage paper, a financial instrument that can be brokered, transferred, bundled, securitized, hypothecated, traded, collateralized, and gambled with.

It is a piece of paper that represents the future earnings of each of us. The more Americans are squeezed financially, the more of that wealth they become willing to access. The more they can access, the more they are prepared to pay for the ability to be a homeowner. The more they will pay, the higher home prices go.

We are trapped. This is a cycle that can only go in one direction. Housing prices may correct a little, but they can never be allowed to fall to a level that would be considered affordable. Dramatically falling home prices would wreck too many things. We experienced that in 2008.

America's housing market is stuck in a trap. It is a financial trap, of course. We have placed housing at the core of the financial system. Home prices can't meaningfully decline without threatening the entire financial sector.

It is also a regulatory trap. We built a regulatory environment to quickly propagate a new pattern of development. It builds new homes and businesses quite well but, once built, locks them in regulatory amber. All change, any natural evolution of a place, can be fiercely resisted.

Finally, it is a cultural trap. We have common beliefs and practices that are part of the culture of housing in America. To escape this trap, we need to move beyond those beliefs and practices. We need to create a new culture around housing. What housing looks like, where it goes, how it is built, and who builds it all need to be on the table.

Housing is shelter. It is one of the most critical human needs. Housing is also the greatest store of wealth—in some cases, the only store of wealth—for American families.

To escape the housing trap, we must overcome the basic contradiction that housing can be both affordable and a good investment, more than just a store of wealth.

2

Building the Trap

When considering homes in the early 20th century, modern Americans can be excused for thinking of them in glamorous terms. The Tudors, colonials, and bungalows that were popular a century ago are still stunning, especially when contrasted with the confusing architecture of today's suburbia. In desirable areas, these older homes often sell at a premium. The notion that "they don't make them like they used to" makes an effective marketing pitch for sellers because it seems so self-evidently true to buyers.

Yet homes built a century ago that are still here today are merely the small fraction of those that survived. Psychologists recognize survivorship bias as a cognitive fallacy that humans are highly susceptible toward. When we examine modern homes, we see a wide range of quality, from homes that are well built and stunning to those that are much more questionable. For older homes, the lowest quality are long gone. The only ones that remain—the ones we observe as representing the era—are those grand houses deemed throughout the decades as worthy of maintaining.

We shouldn't be surprised that most houses of the early 20th century were not well built. From a technical standpoint, almost all of them would be considered substandard today. Many of them would be un-occupiable, so far below housing codes as to be deemed a public nuisance. These homes were not built to last more than a couple of decades, let alone a century. We don't see them today because they were torn down, burned down, or abandoned to rot in place.

Modern Americans expect certain amenities, and pay extra for others, but nobody today considers indoor plumbing something extra. It's standard, yet it wasn't in the early 1900s. Indoor plumbing was available to the wealthy by the mid-1850s. As ventilation methods became more well understood, indoor toilets became more common. Even so, still more than a third of US houses lacked a flush toilet in 1940. Outhouses were common and, for multistory tenements, sanitation was often accomplished with privies over waterproof vaults built in the rear of the unit (Lutz 2011).

Water supply systems, originally built to assist in suppressing fires, provided drinking water to homes, becoming widely available on a parallel timescale. Hot piped water, bathtubs, and showers came to affluent homes first but eventually spread to others. The 1940 census indicated that nearly half of homes still lacked these facilities at that time. For tenements, it was common to have water supplied by communal, outdoor hydrants.

Electrification came to America's homes in the early decades of the 20th century. The largest cities were served first, with service being run to suburban areas and smaller cities next. Rural areas would lag behind, some for many decades. In 1907, only 8% of households had electricity. By 1920, that had grown to 35%. A decade later, at the beginning of the Great Depression, only two out of three American households had access to electricity (Woolf 1987). While retrofitting an existing home with electricity is far easier than adding indoor plumbing, all the machines and appliances that were byproducts of electrification changed the way internal space was utilized.

Also dramatic were changes in building materials and construction techniques. For much of American history, lumber was locally sourced, with carpenters making up for the lack of quality milling with extra hand-fitting labor. By the early 1900s, this rough lumber, as it was called, started to be replaced with lumber that was finished with greater precision. This meant that more lumber could be shipped per railcar, resulting in a dramatic reduction in shipping costs.

Between 1880 and 1920, it was common to have shipping costs be more—sometimes twice as much—than the price of the lumber sold at the mill. World War I created intense demand for finished lumber along with significant investments in railroad access to previously remote lumber mills. Suddenly, lumber switched from being a locally produced product to a national commodity. The competition created even more downward pressure on prices. This trend was further reinforced with the first national size standards, adopted in 1924. The result of these changes was a dramatic reduction in the total cost of lumber (Smith and Wood 1964).

In this time, Sears, Roebuck and Co. even sold complete home kits. A prospective home buyer could open the catalog, pick out the model they were seeking, order and pay for it, and then have it shipped via rail car and local transport to the project site. The company even marketed the homes as easy to assemble, so simple that someone with rudimentary carpentry skills could complete the task in just 90 days.

To deliver on the promise, Sears, Roebuck and Co. and other kit home competitors standardized many elements of home construction. They also began using products such as asphalt shingles and drywall to lower costs. One simplification technique called "balloon framing" made use of old growth timber to produce framing lumber that was 20 feet long or longer. Such long runs on exterior walls made framing easier, but it also made for perfect air ducts. When fires occurred, as they frequently did, balloon-framed homes burned very quickly, often so quickly the people inside had no chance to escape.

A century ago, the barriers for building and occupying a home were low, as was the quality of most homes. While there were transient people who lacked shelter, it was not difficult for even poor Americans to obtain some sort of dwelling to shelter in. In that way, Americans of the early 20th century resembled their ancestors from many centuries and even millennia prior.

Understanding the Traditional Development Pattern

In a very coarse sense, cities of the past were neighborhoods of affluent people surrounded by neighborhoods of poor people. This pattern takes on nuance, of course, especially in larger cities where neighborhood centers expand toward each other over time, but the general pattern is one of incremental investment building wealth, with that wealth emanating outward from downtowns and neighborhood centers.

This is because cities of the past were largely organic in their approach to development. Ponder a culture growing in a petri dish. Free of constraint, the culture grows incrementally outward, incrementally upward, and thickens up, growing incrementally more intense at its center. The complex, adaptive nature of pre-Depression American cities experienced growth in a similar way.

A settlement begins with a collection of modest investments; no more than shacks hastily assembled out of local materials. The land was cheap, and so the buildings built on them were correspondingly cheap. It would make little sense for a major investment to precede these little bets; it would be too risky. The success of the small and incremental was necessary to justify and support the success of the latter major investment.

That's because, as more of these little bets are constructed, as more people move to the little settlement, two things happened simultaneously to create the feedback loop that is the hallmark of complex, adaptive systems. First, land values rise, if only modestly, due to the increase in demand. Second, the hastily assembled structures start to decline, to fall apart and need major repair.

That combination—rising land values and declining structure integrity—creates a natural redevelopment pressure. The more incremental growth there is, the more valuable the underlying land becomes, particularly in the center of the settlement where properties are the most accessible. As the shacks fall apart, people purchase and redevelop them with higher-value materials, structures more aligned with the higher land value.

Over time, these feedback loops create the petri-dish effect. The edge grows incrementally outward through modest little bets while the center continues to naturally thicken up, each sequential building becoming more substantial and ornate than the one it replaces. In this organic framework, a traditional neighborhood can grow from hasty settlement to Manhattan, which is, in fact, exactly what occurred in New York City.

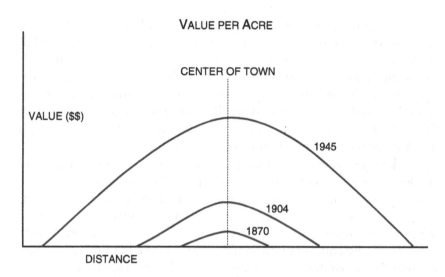

VALUE PER ACRE

As a complex, adaptive system, the traditional style of development evolved into existence due to its many advantages. Financially, this pattern is quite stable and, in fact, has all the hallmarks of antifragility, a term coined by Nassim Taleb (2014a) to identify systems that grow stronger when subjected to stress. During times of prosperity and times of want, periods of growth and periods of stagnation, cities built on the traditional development pattern grew stronger and more prosperous, largely because they had something to offer everyone.

For the very affluent, there were stable, established properties in the core of each neighborhood that provided not only prosperous places to live but where significant investments could be made with confidence. These are blocks that had matured past the start-up phase. They had demonstrated their value and their readiness for the next increment of serious investment. The social and cultural incentives aligned with the financial incentives to nudge the neighborhood to the next level of maturity, something that benefited the entire city.

On the edge of town, the personal incentives were different but no less aligned with the prospects of the city. This was start-up territory, where relatively cheap property could be acquired and modest structures built, often with easily accessible materials. In a modern sense, we can optimistically think of these as starter homes, buildings that could be added on to or reconstructed over time as means allowed. Less generously, we could describe them as the equivalent of a tar paper shack, an ad hoc form of building common outside of the world's richest countries. The chosen interpretation would depend a lot on the trajectory of the neighborhood.

For someone with nothing yet looking to build something, the edge of town offered tremendous opportunity. Land was affordable. Regulation was nonexistent. A home, a shop, or some combination of the two could be built relatively easily, providing both shelter and opportunity. If the community continued to grow, the edge neighborhood matured. That organic petri-dish effect would accrue wealth to formerly start-up properties that were now closer to the wealthy center and further from the expanding edge.

It's seductive to feel nostalgic about this effect, especially since modern American development patterns lack this kind of wealth-building potential for upstarts, not to mention the poor. Yet, for all its dynamism, the traditional development pattern wasn't a guaranteed winner. Sometimes edge neighborhoods failed. Other times, growth stalled, and the community would stagnate. There is a fine line of perception that separates the start-up neighborhood from the slum.

Even where an edge development did succeed, it generally meant living for years, sometimes decades, in something akin to a neighborhood of tar paper shacks, hoping that feedback loop of land values and structural decline would eventually reach your family's investment. That's a significant sacrifice for a chance at wealth creation.

From the perspective of the modern American, the tar paper shack on the edge of town is completely unacceptable. A newly planned block or neighborhood full of them would be nearly unimaginable. In our affluence, it is ironically easier for today's Americans to accept a degree of homelessness, even tent encampments, as an unfortunate, but necessary, reality of modern life than to entertain allowing something with the semi-permanence of a neighborhood of tar paper shacks.

That is understandable, perhaps even a shade of admirable. At our best, we aspire to have our neighbors live in homes that are safe, sanitary, and dignified. Yet this desire comes at a cost. It ups the ante, the entrance fee, that someone must pay to secure housing. It raises the bar of entry to full participation in our society.

The primary insight of *Strong Towns: A Bottom-Up Revolution to Rebuild American Prosperity* is that complex, adaptive systems "imperfectly harmonize many competing priorities simultaneously over time." There is a give-and-take between different objectives, with no cultural priority being perfectly achieved without some sacrifice to other things we find important.

In pre-Depression America, housing within cities was abundant and cheap. There was a low bar of entry to obtaining shelter, even a starter investment. Yet that housing was often of dubious quality. It was frequently unsanitary, unhealthy, overcrowded, even dangerous. Such low-quality housing was abundant in every city, and it was undignified, especially for a nation of rising affluence and global stature.

Over the second half of the 19th century up until the Great Depression, Americans in the progressive movement fought against such low-quality housing. Their reforms ultimately changed the way we do housing today, dramatically improving housing quality while also harmonizing competing interests in ways they likely never anticipated.

The Progressive Movement's Housing Reforms

Improving the quality of housing was a top progressive priority from the Civil War all the way through the Great Depression. Successful reforms of this era generally took the form of government mandates to landlords and housebuilders, establishing minimum building standards, fire codes, and zoning regulations.

For example, in 1901, the New York legislature passed the Tenement House Act, which built on progressive legislative successes in the prior century. The Act expanded minimum standards for ventilation, the number of windows, the location of bathrooms, the number of fire escapes, and other health and safety features of multifamily buildings.

Prior to the Act, bathrooms for a tenement house were often located outside and were shared communally by tenants. Now, every apartment is required to have a private bathroom, which has to be located inside the apartment. The Act also went after loopholes in prior legislation. Before the Tenement House Act, New York's mandates for fire escapes were frequently met by installing small windows between units, openings found to be quite unhelpful during a real building fire. The new law mandated *external* fire escapes at a rate of one for every two units.

The Tenement House Act specifically prohibited the "dumbbell tenement," which was a popular design of the time. Prior housing reform legislation mandated a minimum level of access to light and air, which the dumbbell design met by having a narrow internal shaft between units. This gave the architectural plans a dumbbell shape and the occupants little in the way of light and air. Windows would now need to open onto a street or courtyard, not a gimmicky flue of stagnant air built an arm's length between two neighboring units.

Another mechanism for improving housing quality was the adoption of building codes. These began as model codes for cities to adopt, put together at the behest of the insurance industry. The earliest model code in the United States was the National Building Code, published in 1905. It was assembled by the National Board of Fire Underwriters after many of their members experienced huge insurance losses the year prior in the Great Baltimore Fire.

The primary objective of the National Building Code was to stop the spread of fire between buildings. It included requirements for fire walls where buildings had a wall in common, specified roofing materials, and placed limits on the number of windows used on fire-resistant walls, among other requirements. The code was adopted by many major cities across the United States.

The Building Exits Code was published in 1913, and updated in 1927, by the National Fire Protection Association, an organization founded by multiple insurance companies, a pipe manufacturer, and some sprinkler installers. The code focused on ensuring adequate egress from buildings. This was an urgent issue after a series of tragedies, including the Triangle Shirtwaist Factory fire in 1911, which claimed the lives of 146 female garment workers, who were unable to escape the building as the doors in the stairwells and exits were locked.

An organization calling itself the Pacific Coast Building Officials put together the Pacific Coast Building Code. It would be repackaged as the Uniform Building Code (UBC) in 1927 by a California-based group calling itself the International Conference of Building Officials. The UBC was the first comprehensive building code not only addressing issues of health and safety but providing standardized industry requirements for many facets of construction. It was widely adopted in cities west of the Mississippi, replacing a hodgepodge of local building codes. For over nine decades, the UBC was routinely updated to reflect changes in the industry. It was replaced entirely in 2000 by the International Building Code.

Progressive reforms also included the introduction of zoning laws and other land use regulations. Early zoning codes separated land uses into separate districts in an attempt to reduce overcrowding and keep unwanted uses from encroaching on more desirable areas. This not only meant separating industrial, commercial, and residential activities. It also soon came to mean drawing distinctions among types of residential development.

In practice, unwanted uses in a neighborhood often meant unwelcome people. Many early zoning codes explicitly sought to exclude the poor, racial minorities, and immigrants from well-to-do neighborhoods by excluding the types of housing those groups tended to occupy.

A landmark Supreme Court case, *Village of Euclid v. Ambler Realty Co.*, affirmed the constitutionality of zoning in 1926. We will look more closely at zoning in later chapters of this book.

When examined historically, all these reforms seem not just reasonable but urgent given the poor housing conditions at the time. And while the progressive movement was often inspired by the plight of the poorest and more disadvantaged (though not always), the reforms they championed to address the crisis in housing quality did much to improve living conditions for all Americans, wealthy and impoverished alike.

Cities adopted these reforms piecemeal in the decades leading up to the stock market crash of 1929. Yet, following the onset of the Great Depression, these new rules, regulations, and processes went into a form of regulatory hibernation as building slowed and the nation went through broad economic dislocation. In city halls, internal champions for the progressive new approach would emerge but, since few new homes were being built, minimal field testing of these ideas took place. The regulatory framework would reemerge half a generation later under a very different set of conditions than it originated in.

Housing Becomes a Financial Product

Until the Civil War, Americans had few mechanisms to buy a house. Home purchases were largely cash transactions. Banks wouldn't lend average people money for a house. That changed with the National Bank Acts of the 1860s, a series of laws that established a national banking system to help fight the war. A side effect of these laws was the creation of the individual mortgage.

These early mortgages were very different than those available to modern Americans. They required a large down payment, often 50% of the value of the home. Their duration was also much shorter, often five years or less, with interest-only payments due monthly. A balloon payment for the entire principal was due at the end of the term.

This structure balanced the risk to the bank and its depositors with the investment of the homeowner. Local banks in the late 1800s operated the simple way many of us erroneously believe banks operate today. They accepted deposits in return for interest and safekeeping. They then lent out those deposits to secured creditors in exchange for interest and a promise to pay back the principal.

These banks were hyper-local undertakings. They were also extremely conservative; banks that took a lot of risks with depositors' money didn't survive long in a pre-bailout age of bank runs and financial volatility. The large down payment was one way of ensuring skin in the game, providing a significant buffer of equity should the bank need to seize a property. The short duration of the loan provided similar protection against volatility.

A banker can't project inflation rates, interest rates, and other critical market measures decades into the future. If required to make *and then hold* a 30-year loan, a local bank would need to charge unrealistic amounts of interest to protect itself against loss. It would need to charge predatory rates to secure their return within the first few years of the loan. A five-year loan with a balloon payment balanced the bank's need for security and return of capital with the capacity of the mortgagee to make payments.

This balance came under extreme pressure after the stock market crash in 1929 and the Great Depression that followed. The individuals who lost their jobs and were unable to make monthly payments went first. Their homes were foreclosed on. The banks who did the foreclosing were not in the home ownership business and so they sold the homes to recoup their losses. With high unemployment and extreme levels of economic distress, those homes were sold into a depressed market. That put further downward pressure on prices.

Next in line were people forced to sell their homes to pay off debts. They were trying to avoid economic ruin, but they, too, sold into a depressed market, one with more sellers than buyers. These distressed sales put yet more downward pressure on home prices.

Then the balloon payments started to come due, tipping the housing market into a downward spiral. A new loan required the borrower to have 50% equity. With home prices falling, that equity was no longer there when the balloon came due. Homeowners with jobs, savings, and the capacity to continue to make mortgage payments were unable to roll over their loans unless they could come up with large amounts of cash to make up the difference. Many could not.

Suddenly, through no fault of their own, Americans were being foreclosed on simply because their balloon payment came due in a depressed market. More foreclosures meant more distressed sales in a declining market, an undesirable feedback loop that only led to lower prices and yet more foreclosures.

The Great Depression was deeply disorienting for those living through it. Even today, economists debate the causes. Those living through it had no common narrative to explain what was happening to them. More importantly, there was no consensus vision for how to respond. The entire New Deal project of the Franklin D. Roosevelt administration was an attempt to try a lot of things to discover what worked.

The first thing they tried to stop the foreclosure crisis and the downward spiral of home values was to establish the Home Owners' Loan Corporation (HOLC). Established in June 1933, in the early days of the New Deal, the HOLC provided refinancing for homeowners who were struggling to make mortgage payments.

The agency purchased mortgages that were in default or in danger of foreclosure. The agency then worked with the property owner to refinance the mortgage with a lower interest rate and longer term, typically 20 years. HOLC also introduced the concept of amortization, where the monthly payment wouldn't be only interest but would include a principal payment. This allowed homeowners to increase their equity over time and eventually retire the loan completely.

The HOLC was not a bank. It was a government agency. Yet it functioned much like a bank, mustering private capital through the issuance of bonds and then investing that capital in mortgages that yielded a return. It could offer lower interest rates to borrowers and competitive returns to investors because HOLC bonds were considered a safe investment, especially during turbulent economic times.

As part of ensuring its loans were, in fact, safe investments, the HOLC directed the creation of "residential security maps." These maps, which would later be referred to as "redlining maps," were intended to guide the HOLC's lending decisions by providing information about the perceived risk of default in different neighborhoods. The maps used a color-coding system to rate neighborhoods based on perceived risk. The highest-rated neighborhoods were coded green, while the lowest-rated neighborhoods were coded red.

Neighborhoods that were coded red were considered the riskiest and were generally excluded from HOLC lending programs. This was no modest nuance. For example, 52% of 1930s Kansas City was redlined and designated as hazardous, neighborhoods the HOLC described as being "characterized by detrimental influences in a pronounced degree, undesirable population or an infiltration of it" (Marohn 2020). In Kansas City, the "undesirable" population was mostly Black but also included some recent working-class immigrants from places such as Italy and Belgium.

The Home Owner's Loan Corporation stepped in to arrest the damaging feedback loop of foreclosures and declining home prices in some neighborhoods, mostly the mature neighborhoods of white, middle-class Americans. In other places, those occupied by minority populations and the poor, HOLC stood by and allowed the decline to continue. The agency would stop using these maps in 1940, when they ceased making new loans, but the private sector would continue to use them for decades afterward, to devastating impact on the wealth and prosperity of minority and disadvantaged populations.

Twelve months after the creation of HOLC, the Federal Housing Administration (FHA) was established as part of the National Housing Act of 1934. Where the HOLC took distressed loans off the books of local banks, the FHA intervened to get those banks back to writing new mortgages.

The primary mechanism the FHA used was mortgage insurance. With this insurance, the FHA guaranteed a portion of a new mortgage loan, protecting the lender from default and allowing them to offer the borrower more favorable terms. The insurance paid out in the event of default, in which case the FHA would pay the lender the amount of the guarantee. The lender would then use the foreclosure proceeds to recover what they could of the remaining debt.

The FHA's mortgage insurance protected banks, but it was sold to borrowers. To qualify, a borrower needed to have a stable income, a good credit history, and a down payment of at least 20% of the home's purchase price. In these instances, the borrower could qualify for a 30-year, fixed-rate mortgage. The FHA limited the size of the mortgages it would insure so only middle-class households would benefit from the government's support.

Mortgage insurance still required local banks to hold the home loan on their own books, potentially through to maturity. This was still problematic. A 30-year, fixed-rate mortgage is a long-term product, but a depositor's cash at the bank has the shortest and most fickle of all possible terms. For banks, borrowing short-term at variable rates and lending long-term at a fixed rate is a high-risk path, one that frequently ends in insolvency. Even with mortgage insurance, local banks struggled to originate home loans.

Local banks also often lacked the capital to issue new loans. A bank's capacity to lend is limited, to some degree, by the amount of deposits on hand. Once a mortgage is created, a bank needs to secure more deposits in order to make another loan. Mortgage insurance made loans less risky, but it didn't give the bank more capital to work with.

To address these problems, in 1938, Congress amended the National Housing Act to establish the Federal National Mortgage Association, commonly known as Fannie Mae.

Fannie Mae's purpose was to buy FHA-insured mortgages from local banks. The government-sponsored entity not only took these long-term loans off the hands of local lenders; in doing so it gave those banks more capital to issue new mortgage loans to homebuyers. Local banks could now issue mortgages with the confidence that, so long as the mortgage met the FHA underwriting requirements, there was a guaranteed buyer that would take it off their books, when that might be needed.

In a few short years, housing finance went from a hyper-local undertaking to a nationally supported endeavor. By purchasing and refinancing distressed loans, the federal government arrested the damaging feedback loop in home prices and stabilized the housing market. By insuring new mortgages and by directly purchasing qualified mortgages, the federal government capitalized the housing market and allowed it to start functioning again.

While some will argue that a free market should be allowed to plumb the depths of despair in order to correct itself, it is difficult to argue that these interventions in the mortgage market weren't both necessary and helpful, particularly given the cultural anxiety and social instability of the 1930s. It is impossible to predict what would have happened had these New Deal interventions not occurred.

What is clear is that the tools that helped arrest housing decline in the Great Depression worked even better to create a housing boom after World War II. By 1939, the housing trap had already been built. It would take decades, many of them economically robust and glorious, for that trap to be fully set.

Stabilized and Ready to Grow

Consider how the housing market interventions of the 1930s affected the ability of a theoretical family to purchase a theoretical home valued at $100,000.

The most significant New Deal change was lowering the down payment. Instead of needing to come up with $50,000 to purchase that $100,000 home, a household now only needed to put $20,000 down. It is difficult to overstate the impact of a lower down payment.

Obviously, a 20% down payment is much easier to attain than 50%, but putting that dollar amount into monthly payment equivalents shows just how much easier. A 50% down payment required a family to save or acquire 12.5 years' worth of payments before they could purchase a home. At 20%, that ante amount falls to 3.5 years' worth of payments.

Lowering the required down payment made it easier for people to enter the mortgage market. A prospective homeowner still needed to be able to build some level of wealth before they were eligible to participate in home ownership, but it was not nearly as onerous a task near the end of the 1930s as it was at the beginning. Lowering down payments is a strategy that would be used multiple times in the coming decades.

Mortgage insurance helps banks by limiting their overall risk. That allows those banks to then offer mortgages with lower rates of interest. That also helps homebuyers.

And when Fannie Mae became a ready purchaser of qualifying loans, residential mortgages transformed from a risky product that required a high rate of return to something with a much more manageable level of risk for a local bank.

In a distressed market, lower interest rates and longer repayment windows reduced monthly payments, alleviating financial stress for homeowners. For the theoretical $100,000 home, shifting from a 20-year to 30-year mortgage lowers payments from $670 per month to $590 at an 8% interest rate. Then, lowering the interest rate to 6% further reduces the monthly payment to $480. In this theoretical example, that's a 30% reduction in monthly payment from these two strategies alone.

Of course, the nature of mortgages was also transformed through amortization, allowing homeowners to build equity over time. While the pre–New Deal interest-only loan might have a lower monthly payment, the mortgagee would have just as much debt when the balloon payment came due as they did when they began making payments. With the new fixed-rate, 30-year mortgage, a borrower that made all payments would ultimately own their home free and clear.

By the beginning of World War II, home mortgages had become financial products easily recognizable by the modern homeowner.

Note that the median home prices in the 1930s were a small fraction of the $100,000 used in this theoretical example. This example is a baseline that will be carried into the next two chapters to show the extent that the emergency tools developed in the New Deal were expanded, modified, and enhanced to spike home prices upward.

	Buying a House in 1930	Buying a House in 1940
Theoretical home price	$100,000	$100,000
Required down payment	$50,000	$20,000
Mortgage term	5 years	30 years
Interest rate	8%	6%
Monthly payment	$335	$480
Balloon payment	$50,000	$0

Robert Shiller is an American economist, academic, and Nobel laureate known for his contributions to the fields of financial economics and behavioral finance. He is currently a professor of economics at Yale University.

Shiller is perhaps best known for his work on the dynamics of asset prices and the efficient markets hypothesis. He has written several influential books, including *Irrational Exuberance*, which explores the role of psychology in financial markets and in identifying speculative bubbles. In that book, Shiller explores US trends in housing market data, along with an exploration of numerous housing bubbles, with a dataset going back to 1890. This data is still updated monthly and is available for download (Shiller n.d.).

Case Shiller Home Price Index, January 1900 to January 1950

During the early part of the 20th century, there was volatility in the housing market that is captured in Shiller's data. Year-to-year fluctuations higher and lower of 10% or more were very common from 1900 to the onset of World War I. The standardization of lumber helped lead to a reduction of prices by roughly 25% once the war effort kicked in. Home prices stayed in that depressed band, with some volatility during the early years of the Great Depression, up until the end of World War II, when they began an upward push.

By 1945, housing prices were still 16% lower, adjusted for inflation, than they had been in 1900, but that was about to change. The housing trap was now built. It would now be deployed in a way that dramatically increased home prices, a wave of exuberance that made 1945 a low point in price that has not been experienced since.

3

Setting the Trap

Kansas City, Missouri, developer J.C. Nichols was a visionary. His ideas on growth and development shaped post-war suburbanization across North America. Nichols was a founder of the Urban Land Institute (ULI), a nonprofit organization dedicated to enhancing cities through private sector–led development. ULI continues to award the J.C. Nichols Prize for Visionaries in Urban Development in his honor.

On November 18, 1948, Nichols gave a speech to the National Association of Real Estate Boards at a gathering in New York City. The speech was called "Planning for Permanence." It was a bold vision for a new version of the American city, one that sought to replace the messy and chaotic struggles of prior generations with a permanent prosperity now seemingly attainable in the wake of World War II.

According to Nichols, Americans had long endured the chaotic "fleeting and shifting uses of property" in urban areas. He urged his colleagues to build homes and neighborhoods that instead would endure. As had the progressives of the early 1900s, Nichols demanded that Americans have more intentional planning of their cities. Planners, developers, and other local leaders need to "anticipate all aspects of urban life" so the places they built would last for "a century or more."

Using the familiar rhetoric of war, Nichols called on developers across the continent to "attack" the city-building approaches of the past. "We are the men to lead the attack," Nichols said in the opening moments of his speech.

Nichols's words reflect the dominant mindset of the post-war era. It was a combination of disdain for the accepted wisdom of the past along with a boundless, naive optimism for what could be accomplished by empowering men of vision and action. This was the mindset of a generation that had not only lived through economic depression but had prevailed against the dual threats of Nazism and imperialism, defeating them with an aggressive, top-down mobilization of people and industry.

In 1948, America stood alone as the only major industrial power not decimated by war. It had the world's reserve currency, held the Western world's gold, was pumping more oil out of the ground than Saudi Arabia, and had vast undeveloped spaces ready for exploitation.

In Nichols's view, such an America, having now seen in the mobilization for World War II what is attainable through proper planning and coordinated action, could "build a country desirable and fit for our children and our children's children" simply by adopting a mindset of building for permanence.

If such a permanent prosperity was to be possible, Americans needed to relinquish old ways of thinking. The organic evolution of neighborhoods and the messy churn of their many uses could no longer be tolerated. Instead, neighborhoods would be built all at once, to a finished state, instantly delivering on their ultimate promise.

Mechanical Permanence as an Antidote to Organic Messiness

In his speech, Nichols framed past American successes in heroic terms. The talk had tales of pioneers that "braved hostile Indians, conquered endless plains [and] crossed barren deserts." Nichols spoke of people (of European descent) advancing across the frontier, founding settlements as they went. His suggested acts of heroism sound absurd, sometimes even offensive, to modern ears. Yet they made an important, albeit ahistorical, point for the audience.

These early Americans didn't expect their settlements to be permanent. How could they? They were too busy trying to survive. Today, we can do better.

Listening to Nichols, one is prompted to pity these prior generations for the futility of their efforts. By his narrative, 19th- and early-20th-century Americans occupied "hurriedly built, mushroom settlements." They did the best they could with what they had, but most of the settlements they built were "soon to decay and be abandoned; a few to become great cities."

There is no sense from Nichols that these great cities are the by-product of an organic process, one that includes a degree of decay, even abandonment. When a city grows incrementally, a neighborhood matures through a process that includes decline and redevelopment. This is a feature, not a flaw, but Nichols described it as a "tragedy."

Furthermore, Nichols laments that the common culture accepts the organic approach as "inevitable" or, worse, as "evidence of normal growth." For Nichols and his peers, that attitude needed to change. Americans needed to see the messiness of the pre-Depression development pattern as unacceptable. Instead of a chaotic process of maturing, just do it right the first time.

"Let us not be content to build up and tear down," Nichols said.

Nichols challenged the assembled crowd of developers, "How can we rest on our oars—largely accept conditions as they are . . . be proud of our past achievements—when billions of dollars of loss occur annually in the unnecessary building up and tearing down of large sections of our American towns and cities?" A new kind of developer could save society billions and bring about broad prosperity, with a new approach.

Progressive reforms of prior decades and New Deal responses to the Great Depression meant the tools needed to plan for permanence were now widespread. In the speech, Nichols called for distinct residential zones for small homes separate from zones for larger homes. Everything was to be "carefully allocated in respective areas" with well-planned transitions between them. Golf courses, parks, parkways, and other buffers would be designed to create "seams of protection for residential areas."

Neighborhoods planned to have "ample playgrounds" and "adequate park areas." Access is by "quiet, carefully planned, curving minor residential streets designed to discourage through traffic."

According to Nichols, all neighborhoods "must have elementary and high schools, libraries, shopping centers, churches with community activities, fire stations, utility and municipal facilities." These will all be carefully located, well spaced, and planned for expansion.

Nichols also got into very specific details for what prosperity looked like on the ground. He called 25-foot residential lots "old-fashioned" and said new lots should be at spacious widths of "60 feet or more." He called for "two feet of off-street parking space for each foot of floor space" in shopping areas. He said cities needed to zone ample amounts of land for future expansion.

There was even a spirit of egalitarianism. Nichols suggested his approach would create "good living in neighborhoods of modest homes as in areas of large homes." Ideally, everyone could eventually have a slice of permanent prosperity.

"Light, air, sunshine, pleasing, harmonious architecture, open spaces . . . Here are the real heartbeats and sunbeams of urban life. Home ownership is on the march this very hour. Let us work to make our country a land of happy, contented homeowners."

Taken as a whole, Nichols's vision is a marketing brochure for America's suburban experiment. Optimizing all areas of life has long been the unrealistic dream of the utopian. For Nichols, that dream was now possible, and it was developers that would make it happen. After the War, the ideals of the progressive movement found their most vocal champion in the very big business mindset they spent decades opposing.

Yet the Nichols marketing brochure wasn't selling a development approach as much as it was promoting a national investment strategy. Building for permanence requires lots of capital, the kind that is long-term and patient. The inverse of that insight is also true; making multi-decade investments requires confidence in the stability of the outcome.

Permanence can only be attained with long-term investments while long-term investments cannot be made without the promise of a plausible degree of permanence.

Neighborhoods needed to be built once, built right, and assembled in a way that secured their future. No bank could provide long-term financing if the neighborhood was in a constant state of flux. There could be no ongoing chaos of buildings reimagined, reworked, and replaced. No start-up slums maturing over time into stable and prosperous neighborhoods.

Local governments needed to be able to finance major infrastructure investments. They had to build water supply systems, stormwater management systems, and sewage disposal systems. They needed to finance the roads, streets, sidewalks, and bridges. Unlike pre-Depression developments, these new public investments needed to be made *before* the neighborhood had matured and *before* a sufficient tax base was established.

Municipal officials were not going to make such gambles unless they were assured, and could assure their voters, that what was being built had permanence. They had to plausibly believe they weren't gambling but were making sound, long-term investments in the community.

Businesses also needed to have confidence in the stability of this new approach. It's one thing to start a small business and grow it incrementally over time, expanding as success and capital allowed. An entire shopping plaza as a neighborhood amenity is something completely different. It needed to be built, to a finished state, *before* the patrons had fully materialized. The shops must include recognizable brands to provide the latest in lifestyle accessories. And those tenants needed to sign the kind of lengthy leases necessary to finance such an undertaking. None of that was possible without the promise of stability.

Most importantly, families needed to take on extended mortgages. They needed to buy homes built to a finished state in neighborhoods delivered as a completed package. They needed to believe that committing to a long-term debt instrument was a good investment. Large numbers of families needed to buy into a new model of stasis. They needed to believe in the possibility of permanent prosperity.

As Nichols extolled in his speech, "The home, the most precious possession in life—the real heritage of a free people—will have permanent value, and desirable, healthful and inspiring surroundings for many generations, where homes will grow old graciously."

No more messiness. No more chaotic change. No more unpredictable evolution of neighborhoods over time. The promise to the new homeowner was simple: sign the mortgage and experience an ideal lifestyle along with the promise of stable financial value. You and your home can grow old graciously together. Build wealth together. A permanent prosperity.

Repeat this at scale, and America's cities could become machines of growth. With Nichols's vision, there is no more fear of sliding back into a second Great Depression. No more anxiety over social unrest or economic dislocation. Everyone willing to work hard could have a home and old-age security (at least those society allowed to assume a mortgage).

"Here is where we can lick socialism and communism," Nichols said.

After World War II, housing as an investment became the key to social stability, economic growth, and wealth creation. It was the critical component of building a middle class. Housing as an investment was now the economic engine by which America would come to dominate the world.

For a moment in time, permanent prosperity felt possible.

The First Generation of America's Suburban Experiment

Debt is a way to move future earnings forward in time. With debt, a person can spend money today that they will make in the future. The further into the future earnings are tapped, the more money is available to spend today.

A 30-year mortgage takes three decades of future earnings and pledges them to a present expense. The trade-off is logical from the point of view of the person taking on the mortgage. A home is a long-term investment; not many people can afford to pay cash for a home. Using a mortgage allows a purchaser to amortize the price of that investment over a long period of time. Buying a home thus becomes a generational commitment to building wealth.

For an economist, however, a mortgage has a different connotation, especially for a new home. That new home isn't an investment; it's consumption. That consumption adds to the size of the economy. The money spent on the new home doesn't sit in the home or in a financial instrument called a mortgage. It goes to work immediately in the form of multiple transactions.

All the materials that go into the new home are paid for when the home is built. That means all the people who harvested the wood, processed it into lumber, and transported it to the job site get paid for that work. The people who own the land and grow the wood get compensated for their capital and labor. The investors who lent all these people money to perform those tasks are also made whole.

Take the supply chain for lumber and multiply it across all the various industries that go into creating materials for a new home— the windows, wiring, plumbing, roofing, and many more—and the three-decade commitment of a home purchaser has an immediate and extraordinary impact on the broader economy.

Now consider the people who build the home. All the carpenters, plumbers, electricians, insulators, roofers, and on and on who work on the home receive wages for their labor. They receive that pay immediately, not over decades. That money recycles back into the economy as they go about their lives, creating what economists call a multiplier effect.

As military and industry demobilized at the end of the Second World War, all that wartime spending vanished. Economists and politicians worried America was going to slide back into another Great Depression. New home construction was the perfect economic stimulus to offset the decline in military spending. By purchasing a new home and assuming a mortgage, families unlocked decades of their future earnings and put them to work immediately growing the economy.

To make this work, the financial tools developed during the Great Depression were extended and repurposed. Instead of saving the housing market from collapse in a deflationary spiral, Americans after World War II deployed the same government support approaches to expanding the housing market. In doing so, they discovered that the tools that worked to stem decline worked even better to juice the overall economy.

This began with the Servicemen's Readjustment Act of 1944, commonly known as the G.I. Bill of Rights. Among other things, the Act established a housing assistance program for veterans returning from World War II. In a way that recurs across many housing initiatives, the program began modestly and expanded over time.

For example, the G.I. Bill originally provided a loan guarantee of 50% of the home's value, up to $2,000. The maximum loan length was 20 years. These provisions were soon expanded to guarantee up to $4,000 with the loan lengthened to 25 years. In 1950, the 50% guarantee increased to 60% with a maximum guarantee of $7,500 on a 30-year mortgage. Increasing loan guarantees and extending loan lengths meant more long-term capital put to immediate work growing the economy.

The original program targeted returning veterans during a two-year economic readjustment period. That window was soon expanded to 10 years. This made the program a general benefit of military service, not a one-time readjustment initiative. That benefit was later extended to unmarried widows of those killed during their service.

This further solidified the philosophical shift from one-time economic readjustment to housing assistance as an ongoing service benefit.

The original Act required an appraisal that reflected the "reasonable normal value" of the house. This phrasing was widely interpreted to denote the prewar value of the home. Due to the Great Depression, established neighborhoods had a history of depressed home values, an impediment to generous appraisals. No such limitation existed in the new suburban neighborhoods. The new suburbs were the primary beneficiaries of this interpretation.[1]

In the decade after the end of World War II, the Servicemen's Readjustment Act, along with the subsequent amendments, facilitated $33 billion in home loans to veterans. That was 4.3 million home loans, roughly 20% of all new homes built during that time (National Archives n.d.).

The National Mortgage Association Charter Act of 1954 rechartered Fannie Mae. The federal government had originally capitalized Fannie Mae with taxpayer money. The new Act directed the Government Sponsored Entity (GSE) to start phasing out taxpayer investment. Instead, the private lenders that Fannie Mae purchased mortgages from were required to contribute to the entity's equity. Fannie Mae still purchased FHA and VA approved mortgages, but at least 3% of the transaction now involved Fannie Mae issuing banks an ownership stake in Fannie Mae instead of cash (Congressional Research Service n.d.).

On the way to being privatized, the new Fannie Mae was paradoxically expected to be a more active tool for economic policy. The Act directed it to "stop a decline in mortgage lending and home building." Another provision directed Fannie Mae to aid families dislocated by federal slum clearance and urban redevelopment projects. Authority was given to the president of the United States to accelerate Fannie Mae involvement on a project-by-project basis.

Fourteen years later, Fannie Mae was split up and reorganized again. The Housing and Urban Development Act of 1968 turned Fannie Mae into a for-profit, shareholder-owned company, albeit one

---

[1] Data for the prior four paragraphs came from a document called "Legislative History of the VA Home Loan Guarantee Program" published by the Department of Veteran's Affairs https://www.benefits.va.gov/homeloans/documents/docs/history.pdf.

with a government guarantee for its debt (Congressional Research Service n.d.). The Secretary of Housing and Urban Development (HUD) retained oversight on the issuance of stock and debt. Fannie Mae was directed to allocate a "reasonable portion of its mortgage purchases to mortgages on low- and moderate-income housing."

The 1968 Act also created the Government National Mortgage Association (GNMA or Ginnie Mae), a government-owned corporation within HUD (Congressional Research Service n.d.). Ginnie Mae was given the authority to purchase only government-backed mortgages.

The Act also introduced another change that would come to profoundly shape the housing market as we know it today. It gave both Fannie Mae and Ginnie Mae the authorization to issue mortgage-backed securities (MBSs). Ginnie Mae was allowed to provide insurance for privately issued MBSs, so long as they consisted of government-backed mortgages. This was the beginning of what today is known as mortgage securitization.

In the simplest form, Fannie Mae and Ginnie Mae purchased federally backed mortgages from local banks. Fannie Mae (a private-sector company, with government backing) and Ginnie Mae (a publicly owned company) then grouped those mortgages together into an offering. They then sold shares in that offering, called a security, to the public. These securities were purchased mostly by savings and loan associations (S&Ls), a form of bank that specializes in real estate. The S&Ls, in turn, received their capital from the bank deposits of individuals and families.

A carpenter building a home could take a portion of their earnings and deposit it in the local S&L. The S&L would pay the carpenter interest on that deposit. The S&L would then take the money they had on deposit and buy an MBS from Fannie Mae, Ginnie Mae, or a private bank where the MBS was backed by Ginnie Mae. That MBS might include a small slice of the carpenter's own mortgage, a federally guaranteed loan the carpenter received from the same S&L where they made the deposit, a loan the S&L then sold to Fannie Mae, Ginnie Mae, or whatever bank had created the MBS.

This feels complicated because it is. It creates a set of far-flung relationships and interdependencies that are not as discernible as those present in traditional local banking. Before the Great Depression, a carpenter made a deposit at a local bank. That local bank then took that money and lent it as a short-term mortgage to someone who was a neighbor of the carpenter, someone living in the same community. None of these transactions were insured. If a bank made bad loans in the community, the carpenter would likely know. So, then, would everyone else. Such a poorly run bank would lose its depositors long before the loans had a chance to go bad.

That wasn't a perfect system, and the Great Depression demonstrated the limitations of such a hyper-localized financial approach, but it had one critical aspect that the evolving system of post-war mortgage finance lacked: direct accountability. In 1930, the carpenter could witness their savings being put to work. By 1970, the carpenter's savings could be directly funding part of their own mortgage and not only would the carpenter not know nobody would know.

By centralizing the mortgage market, the United States was able to rapidly expand mortgage credit. The resulting spending allowed the country to not only avoid a second Great Depression after demobilization but to grow its way out of the financial hole it was in at the end of World War II. It also dramatically expanded home ownership, building a broad middle class in the process.

Between 1945 and 1970, the gross domestic product (GDP) grew 371% while public debt expanded by only 43%. This allowed the debt-to-GDP ratio—a measurement of the country's ability to handle its public debt—to shrink dramatically, from a dangerous 114% at the end of World War II to a manageable level of just 35% in 1970.

The improved financial capacity of the public sector was a direct result of the expanded use of mortgage credit in the private sector. Between 1945 and 1970, mortgage debt exploded by 1,134%, from 16% to 41% of GDP. The housing market was now the foundation of the economy. Keeping it going was the top priority.

This was evident in 1970 when the S&Ls began experiencing distress due to rising interest rates. Taking on short-term deposits and then lending that cash out long-term by purchasing mortgage-backed securities was a risk pre-Depression banks could never have taken. With Fannie Mae and Ginny Mae, the federal government had intentionally created the market for this kind of gambling. S&Ls were playing by the new rules.

While rising short-term interest rates increased the amount they needed to pay out to depositors, it had no impact on the fixed amount they received from the long-term MBSs they held. This imbalance threatened S&Ls solvency.

In response, Congress passed the Emergency Home Finance Act. It established the Federal Home Loan Mortgage Corporation, known as Freddie Mac. Like Fannie Mae, Freddie Mac is a for-profit, shareholder-owned company with government backing of its debts and liabilities. Freddie Mac was created to purchase mortgages from S&Ls, bundle those mortgages, and sell them as securities. This was meant to give the S&Ls cash to write more loans. With interest rates rising, it also served as a mini bailout of the S&Ls, allowing the thrifts to replace lower yielding loans with loans that were higher yielding.

The Emergency Home Finance Act took another dramatic step in expanding the mortgage market. It authorized Fannie Mae and the new Freddie Mac to buy and sell mortgages not insured by the federal government. These so-called "conventional" mortgages were loans that hadn't gone through the conservative vetting process established decades earlier by the FHA. Since the Great Depression, the secondary mortgage market had always had a very risk-averse foundation. Now, during a minor crisis, that conservative foundation began to be undermined.

In 1971, Freddie Mac issued the first mortgage-backed security made up of conventional loans. A descendant of this practice, the subprime mortgage-backed security, would be at the center of the 2008 financial crisis.

The Second-Generation Implications of Permanence

During the first two-and-a-half decades after World War II, millions of American families moved into well-designed neighborhoods, each detail a testament to a life of permanence and prosperity. What unfolded after that is not a narrative of perpetuated bliss but a tale of how time, entropy, and the unyielding commitment to an unchanging ideal can lead to an unanticipated battle against decline. As the intricacies of neighborhoods built for permanence are explored, a nuanced story of maintenance, distress, and the unforeseen consequences is uncovered that challenges the very foundations of the suburban experiment.

A family moves into a new home in a new neighborhood. Everything is just as the marketing brochure suggests. The homes are beautiful with all the modern amenities. The shopping areas are brand-new with all the latest things a family desires. The parks are gorgeous and fully outfitted. The schools are brand-new and have the best features money can buy. All the streets and sidewalks and light fixtures look just right.

Not only does everything look good, but it feels right. Any family living in the new neighborhood is going to be surrounded by families living a similar lifestyle. Middle-class families are with other middle-class families, everybody at roughly the same income level and at a similar place in life. All "those people," however one may wish to define that, are nowhere in sight, a fact that (incorrectly, but convincingly) attests to the hard work, intelligence, and proper values of those living in the new neighborhood.

Everything about this arrangement self-affirms the success of the people living in it. But that is on day 1. What happens when it ages? When happens when a couple of decades of entropy take its toll on a place designed for stasis? What happens to a neighborhood where permanence is the foundational understanding of its existence?

Neighborhoods built all at once, to a finished state, experience an echo of maintenance. Unlike neighborhoods that are assembled incrementally and then mature over time, a neighborhood predicated on permanence will have a period—perhaps a couple of decades—where everything is shiny and new. After this, everywhere and all at once, decline will start to set in.

Every home in the neighborhood was built within a few years of every other home. When the shingles on one roof reach the end of their life span, all the shingles on all the roofs are also reaching the end of their lifespans. A leaky roof can be patched, but only so much and for so long. Eventually, the shingles need replacement, or the home will go bad. A new roof is quite expensive.

If it was merely a matter of everyone fixing their roof every two to three decades, that might be manageable. Unfortunately, every house in the neighborhood eventually needs repainting. Like the failing roofs, this needs to happen to all the homes in the neighborhood at roughly the same time.

Every sidewalk starts to crack and fail at the same time. All the appliances, fittings, and hinges were installed at the same time, age at similar rates, and fail simultaneously across the entire neighborhood.

In the ideal scenario, every family living in the neighborhood has the means and resources to not only continue to pay their mortgage and their local taxes but also to perform all the maintenance necessary to keep the neighborhood looking like the marketing brochure. That might be the case in the most affluent neighborhoods, but in most places, there will be families that simply can't keep up.

Maybe they have suffered the loss of a job, an unexpected illness, or some other bit of misfortune. They put off repainting the house a few years longer than they should have. They let weeds grow through the cracks in the sidewalks. They put plywood over the window that got broken last summer.

These are very normal things, but the more times they happen, the more the neighborhood begins to diverge from the marketing brochure. The promise of permanence begins to be undermined. Idyllic stasis is no longer an experienced reality.

Unfortunately, the promise of permanence has also limited the menu of options for responding to distress. As will be discussed in later chapters of this book, a neighborhood of single-family homes is a neighborhood of single-family homes. There is no mechanism—regulatory or financial—for such a place to become, for example, a neighborhood of duplexes. The organic renewal process common in prior generations is no longer an option.

And while it is theoretically possible for someone to purchase a single-family home in decline, within a neighborhood that is also in decline, and make a significant investment to reestablish the perfection of the original marketing brochure, why would anyone do that? They wouldn't. Instead, they will just buy a new home in a new neighborhood, one where the marketing brochure still has credibility.

Like a crumbling dike struggling to hold back a flood, living in a neighborhood built for permanence becomes a battle against entropy, a fight against the kind of disorder that the expenditure of time demands. Time destroys the notion of permanence. The regulations, financial incentives, and cultural expectations built around selling permanence undermine organic efforts at renewal. Without permanence or renewal there is only one option left on the menu: decline.

Pride and peer pressure might persuade some people to sacrifice savings, vacations, or other spending to prioritize maintenance of their homes. A homeowner's association might bring formal pressure to do so. Local governments can intervene with minimum maintenance standards. These efforts buy time, but the arrow points in only one direction. Decline is inevitable because no other long-term option exists.

The same decline that happens to an individual home also manifests in the broader neighborhood. That brand-new park is now a couple of decades old, the equipment well used, if not completely outdated. The same with the school. Everything from the carpet to the technology is old, while the newer neighborhoods have all the latest on offer. A home buyer with ample resources is unlikely to purchase a home in an older neighborhood when they can move a few miles up the highway and buy a home in a place where everything is newer, shinier, and better.

In the older neighborhood, the streets and sidewalks that the developer built and gifted to the city decades ago are falling apart and in desperate need of maintenance. Suddenly, revenue from the tax base that came at such a low initial cost is found to be inadequate for the task. Same with the underground utilities and drainage systems. Cities can't charge hookup fees or access charges the second time around. The price tag for treading water is not only greater than anticipated but also more than the neighborhood can afford.

Faced with broad and growing decline, higher local taxes, increased utility fees, and reduced public services, those that can afford to leave the neighborhood do the obvious thing: they move. This leaves behind those of lesser financial means to struggle against atrophy. This is the opposite of what Nichols said would happen when he suggested "homes will grow old graciously" along with their owners.

The suburban experiment was designed to skip over the messy process of incrementally assembling a neighborhood, but those steps are necessary if the neighborhood is to grow strong and endure. Neighborhoods built all at once go bad all at once. At the end of the first generation of this experiment, the housing-led growth machine began to break down.

A generation that had lived through the Great Depression, World War II, and an unprecedented economic expansion in the two-and-a-half decades after the war now had to find a way to deal with the problem of systematic neighborhood decline. It was a problem they didn't anticipate. If anything, it was a problem they thought they had solved.

The Trap Starts to Close

Conventional wisdom held that there is an inverse relationship between unemployment and inflation. When the economy grows, greater demand for goods and services causes prices to climb (inflation). This encourages businesses to hire more employees (falling unemployment). During a recession, the opposite happens. Reduced demand for goods and services causes prices to decline (deflation). This induces businesses to retrench and lay off workers (rising unemployment).

This relationship broke down in the 1970s. The economy stagnated while prices and unemployment rose in tandem. This is a phenomenon now known as stagflation. Stagflation is not only bad for the economy but also a disaster for the housing market.

During stagflation, interest rates rise in response to inflation. If a bank is going to lose 5% of their purchasing power each year due to inflation, they are going to demand more than 5% per year in interest when they loan money. Otherwise, there is no return. No return for long enough means no bank.

The need for interest rates to keep up with inflation is especially true for a 30-year mortgage. A mortgage is a debt instrument where the bulk of the repayment happens decades in the future. For a local bank, that is a lot of risk. If a bank issues a mortgage at 5% and interest rates later rise to 10%, the resale value of that 5% mortgage goes down significantly.

For example, consider a $100,000 mortgage. At 5%, that mortgage will return $5,000 in interest in its first year. At 10%, the mortgage will return $10,000 in the first year. If a bank owns a $100,000 mortgage at 5% and interest rates rise to 10%, their best move is to sell the 5% mortgage and seek a new homebuyer to issue a new, higher-rate mortgage.

If the 5% loan is a qualified mortgage—if it meets the FHA standards—then that's not a problem. The federal government established Ginnie Mae to be the sucker at the card table, to absorb the lower-interest loan as part of their portfolio. Ginnie Mae will buy the 5% loan at full value and take the lower returns for the next three decades. That's a gift the federal government agreed to give banks to get them to play in the long-term mortgage market.

Fannie Mae and Freddie Mac might have interest in buying the 5% mortgage but, by the 1970s, they are both for-profit entities. Unlike Ginnie Mae, they aren't expected to be suckers at the card table. If one of them buys the loan, they aren't going to pay $100,000 for it. If the going interest rate is 10%, they are going to pay something less than $100,000 for a loan at 5%.

What this means is that, if you're a local bank, you sell to Ginnie Mae or you immediately lose money. That's for a qualified loan.

If the 5% mortgage is a conventional loan—it doesn't meet the FHA standards—then Ginnie Mae is not allowed to buy it. Fannie or Freddie might purchase it, but they will only do so at a reduced price. In other words, the bank trying to sell the mortgage is going to take a loss. Selling at a loss is bad for business.

Rather than sell at a loss, the local bank could try to hold the 5% loan to maturity. In this scenario, the bank is hoping that interest rates fall. In the meantime, depositors will demand more than 5% interest to keep their money at the bank, forcing the bank to bleed capital by paying out more interest than they receive. Either that, or the bank will maintain low payouts and lose their depositors. Whichever they decide, holding onto a low-interest mortgage is a direct path to insolvency.

For banks invested in mortgages, rising interest rates create a whole lot of bad options. In the 1970s, rising interest rates squeezed bank balance sheets. Banks didn't want to hold mortgages. They were also reluctant to write new mortgages for any loans they weren't guaranteed to be able to offload. This pullback was deflationary.

Many who can afford the $540 monthly mortgage payment for a $100,000 loan at 5% will struggle to make the $880 monthly payment for the same mortgage at 10%. In fact, most people buy homes based on the monthly payment they can afford. For those who could get a mortgage, rising interest rates reduced how much they could pay for a home. This was also deflationary.

All this downward pressure meant that housing prices dropped during the first half of the 1970s. This also spooked banks. Lower down payment requirements for mortgages meant the bank's margin for error had shrunk substantially. On a new mortgage, a 10% market correction might wipe out all of a homeowner's equity.

As stagflation took hold, interest rates climbed, and the first generation of post-war housing stock aged into decline, banks suddenly, but logically, did not want to lend to homebuyers.

Corrections are a natural part of a business cycle. After two-and-a-half decades of housing growth and price appreciation, a market correction is normal. The post-war growth machine, fueled by an unprecedented expansion of credit in the housing market, started to sputter.

Yet people needed jobs. And they needed homes. They needed shelter. A 1973 study on America's housing needs by the Joint Center for Urban Studies at MIT and Harvard concluded that, despite decades of an unprecedented housing expansion, 13.1 million American families, nearly one in five, were "housing deprived" (Joint Center for Urban Studies of MIT and Harvard 1973).

For those committed to J.C. Nichols's vision of permanent prosperity, the rationale was there to expand the housing playbook further, doubling down on the financial experiment that had seemingly worked so well.

That is exactly what Congress did. The Housing and Community Development Act of 1974 was passed to help banks struggling with inflation and higher interest rates. In the Act, Congress authorized Ginnie Mae to acquire conventional mortgages, those that didn't meet the FHA underwriting standards. This was to happen whenever the president of the United States found that inflation was having a "severely disproportionate effect on the housing industry."

The Emergency Housing Act of 1975 provided additional relief to banks. It made payments directly to banks on behalf of struggling homeowners. It provided additional insurance to banks to entice them to take on riskier loans. The act also expanded Fannie Mae's ability to purchase conventional mortgages for multifamily properties and individual condominium units.

This all had the desired effect. After bottoming out near the end of 1974, house prices shot up to, and then beyond, post-war highs. On the way to a peak in 1979, Congress continued to make it easier for people to borrow money. They expanded mortgage insurance, reduced down payments, expanded the types of housing that were eligible for federal support, raised the maximum loan amounts, and placed an emphasis on expanding credit to people who otherwise could not afford to purchase a home.

In 1979, Freddie Mac's private debt was, by law, given the same standing as federal government debt. This meant that institutions could lend freely (and lucratively) to Freddie Mac and use the GSE's promise to pay as the highest form of collateral. Suddenly, the American mortgage became a foundation stone for the entire banking system.

In this new market, it was obvious to all that good things happened when housing prices went up and bad things happened when housing prices went down. The lesson was clear: for the good of the economy, housing prices could not go down.

The federal government needed to be in place to backstop banks that worked in the mortgage market. They needed to assume responsibility for any souring mortgage loans these banks might have on their books. They needed to intervene, when called on, to keep capital flowing into the mortgage market.

For banks, it was not yet a full "heads we win, tails you lose" scenario. Getting there would require an even bigger crisis.

The Savings and Loan Bubble

At the end of the 1970s, the already high inflation rate began to climb. At the beginning of 1979, it was at 9.1%. Eighteen months later, inflation peaked at 15.9%. In response, the Federal Reserve raised interest rates dramatically. The fed funds rate went over 19% twice in 1981. It stayed over 10% during most of the first half of the decade.

Predictably, the housing price bubble created in the 1970s surge in lending began to dissipate. The entire cycle of bank stress that played out in the prior decade repeated, only on a greater scale. S&Ls were the most vulnerable lenders. By 1982, the S&L industry was insolvent by $150 billion (Black 2005, 5).

In this case, insolvent did not mean out of business. The insolvent S&Ls continued to operate, accepting depositors' cash, using that money to make loans and purchase securities. A bankruptcy occurs when the Federal Savings and Loan Insurance Corporation (FSLIC), which insured the depositors from loss, stepped in on the depositors' behalf to take over the trust. The investors in the S&L then lose their investment, depositors are made whole (up to insurance limits), and the trust is restructured in a way that allows it to operate as a solvent institution. This process is designed to protect depositors, taxpayers, and the financial system.

The industry was insolvent by $150 billion, but the FSLIC had only $6 billion in insurance proceeds on hand to address the insolvencies. Since the US Treasury stood behind the federal insurance funds, addressing the S&L shortfalls meant the federal budget deficit— already at an unprecedented and controversial $110 billion in 1982— would more than double.

As S&L regulator William K. Black wrote in *The Best Way to Rob a Bank Is to Own One*, "No one wanted to recognize that contingent liability" (Black 2005). The Republican Reagan administration had promised tax cuts and a balanced budget. The Democratic Congress did not want to cut popular programs. The industry had no desire to admit its insolvency.

Most importantly, as Black writes, "Americans loved the S&L industry because S&Ls made loans to people, not corporations, and made possible the American dream of owning a home." Home prices needed to go up, not down. Americans needed the S&Ls to make that happen.

The aligned desire of nearly everyone to overlook the S&L industry's insolvency set the stage for large-scale financial fraud, culminating in the S&L crisis and bailout of the late 1980s. The hope among legislators and regulators was that the S&Ls could grow their way back to solvency. Deregulation was the consensus path to achieving that end.

Legislation and regulatory discretion reduced the amount of capital that S&Ls were required to hold in reserve. This allowed them to lend more, but it also reduced their margin for error. At the same time, they were granted broader authority to branch out beyond residential mortgages and make new, and ultimately riskier, loans. To quell the fear of insolvency starting a bank run, deposit insurance was raised from $40,000 to $100,000. This made it easier for S&Ls to attract deposits (Robinson 2013).

The Housing and Urban-Rural Recovery Act of 1983 provided, among other things, federal insurance for alternative mortgage products, including adjustable-rate mortgages. The following year, the Secondary Mortgage Market Enhancement Act of 1984 dramatically expanded the market for private mortgage-backed securities by making those rated AA or above the financial equivalent of US Treasuries.

If a nationally recognized statistical ratings agency rated a mortgage-backed security as AA or AAA, that security could be held by an S&L or private bank as their required reserves. This was in lieu of holding Treasury bills. Since an MBS was almost guaranteed to pay a greater return than a Treasury certificate, the market for mortgages was now set to become insatiable.

Prior to 1984, home ownership and the housing market it provided were the *figurative* foundation of the economy. Now, with mortgage-backed securities set to guarantee the solvency of every financial institution, home ownership and the housing market were on their way to becoming the *literal* foundation of the economy.

Unsurprisingly, this didn't stabilize the S&L industry. Instead, it encouraged a go-for-broke strategy of investing in riskier and risker projects, with taxpayers on the hook to cover losses. Housing boomed to unprecedented levels, reinforcing the notion that home ownership is not only a sound way to obtain shelter, but it is also a great investment. As fraud grew, well-run institutions were crowded out by nefarious actors. The latter—unconstrained by the need to run a solvent institution—were able to offer better terms to depositors and borrowers alike.

To add to the risk, insolvent S&Ls were allowed, even encouraged, to buy other insolvent S&Ls. With an accounting trick called "blue sky," the combined entity would be solvent and highly profitable, at least on paper. In fact, the more insolvent the S&Ls involved, the greater the paper profits.

This made a lot of people wealthy. They, in turn, found it to their benefit to be generous to politicians and others, those whose continued acquiescence made the whole pyramid scheme possible. To that end, the 1984 Act also preempted some state attempts to limit "blue sky" transactions.

It wasn't until the late 1980s, when more than 1,000 S&Ls had failed, that Congress stepped in to address the industry's problems. The Financial Institutions Reform, Recovery, and Enforcement Act of 1989 cleaned house. The primary S&L regulator, the Federal Home Loan Bank Board, was abolished. So was the FSLIC, whose insurance responsibilities were given to the Federal Deposit Insurance Corporation (FDIC).

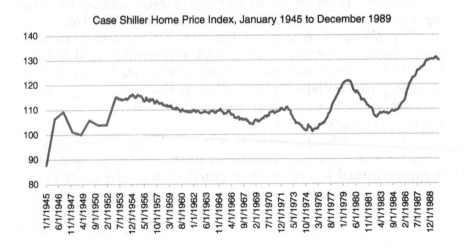

Case Shiller Home Price Index, January 1945 to December 1989

Deregulation had failed. In its place, decentralization became the new focus for experiencing economic growth, particularly in the housing market.

To that end, one part of the 1989 Act restructured Freddie Mac. It directed the GSE to provide aid to the secondary market for mortgages of low- and moderate-income families, so-called subprime mortgages. The Act also directed various regulatory agencies to establish standards for real-estate appraisals and then establish a state-based system of licensing and certifying appraisers. These two reforms metastasized to be the core of the next great financial crisis.

At this point, the financial trap was set. All that was needed was time.

4

Trapped

On September 3, 2001, *Forbes* contributor Stephane Fitch wrote an article titled "What If Housing Crashed?" The article explored warning signs that America was in a housing bubble. Fitch suggested that the bubble was beginning to correct. He cited changes in the market including rising inventory levels, extended listing times, and price drops.

Fitch notes the common belief among Americans that "stock prices fluctuate, but house prices just go straight up." He then asks, "Could this assumption be wrong?" (Fitch 2001).

Fitch wasn't the only one in the investment world pondering this question. Two months earlier, Josh Rosner, managing director at the research consultancy Graham Fisher & Co., wrote an analysis of the housing market. Its prescience has since made it well known. Titled "Housing in the New Millennium: A Home Without Equity is Just a Rental with Debt," it made a strong case that the housing market was overvalued (Rosner 2001).

Rosner starts his analysis by citing the National Partners in Homeownership (NPH). The NPH was a collection of over 50 public and private organizations working together to reach "all-time high national homeownership levels by the end of the century." This collaboration included government regulatory entities such as the US Department of the Treasury and the Federal Deposit Insurance Corporation. It also included regulated businesses, such as America's Community Bankers and the Mortgage Bankers Association.

"It was almost unprecedented for regulators to partner this closely with those that they have been charged to regulate," Rosner noted.

The NPH called for significant reductions in mortgage down payments. This goal was to remove barriers for Americans who had poor credit or struggled to save for a down payment. During the 1990s, two NPH partners, Fannie Mae and Freddie Mac, reduced down payment requirements on mortgages they purchased from 10% to 3%. In 2001, they eliminated the need for a down payment altogether.

This had a dramatic impact on the amount of equity, or skin in the game, that homeowners had. In 1989, only 7% of home mortgages originated with less than 10% down payment. By 1999, half of all mortgages had down payments of less than 10%, and 1 in 20 had no equity or negative home equity. To offset their increased risk, Fannie and Freddie required borrowers to purchase private mortgage insurance (PMI) for loans with low homeowner equity. This is an insurance policy that protects the lender in case a borrower defaults. Private insurers such as American International Group (AIG) provided these policies.

This made PMI a critical part of the financial system, but as Rosner notes, the PMI market was simultaneously becoming opaque. Instead of writing policies based on an individual evaluation of risk, bulk mortgage purchasers were buying their PMI policies in bulk. This lowered insurance costs for borrowers, but it also squeezed the margins of insurance companies. "Longer term, the financial stability of the PMI companies may be negatively impacted as their margins decline," Rosner wrote. Seven years later, negative impacts to insurers such as AIG would be at the center of a financial crisis.

Another NPH innovation was the broad adoption of underwriting software. The traditional process for underwriting a mortgage was extensive and personal. The new software approach instead relied on a credit score. This allowed borrowers with good credit scores to take on more debt than they could with traditional underwriting.

Frank Raines, the chairman of Fannie Mae, claimed that "lower income families have credit histories that are just as strong as wealthier families." According to Raines, Fannie Mae expanded their purchasing of loans with ultra-low down payments by 40 times in the 1990s.

With equity reduced, and with riskier borrowers now a larger percentage of the mortgage pool, mortgage pool, the lender's small margin for error shrunk even more. This increased the importance of the already critical appraisal process. Yet Rosner was raising major alarms on appraisals. He suggested that, over the prior decade, the appraisal process had been severely compromised. Serious conflicts of interest were now commonplace.

For example, instead of the traditional practice of randomly assigning an appraiser from a blind pool, Rosner notes that it was now common for appraisers to be "hand-picked by agents and brokers." This created tremendous pressure to "hit the bid" by appraising the property high enough to allow the purchase to move ahead. Appraisers that didn't play along risked losing business to those that would.

Rosner's report is well known because of its prescience. The problems he identified in 2001 didn't cause an immediate market correction. Instead, as he suggested might happen, the housing market continued to expand. But the problems he identified only grew worse over the subsequent years.

As an investment analysis, Rosner's report focused on impacts to the broader market. American median family income had stagnated for most of the prior two decades. Nonetheless, the ability to extract equity from a home allowed families to increase consumption. Rosner wanted to know: "Is there enough equity in the home to stimulate the economy?" For investors, this is the key question. How long can this housing-fueled party last, and how painful will it be when it ends?

Those were not the questions for many homeowners, or even prospective homeowners. The irony of the 1990s was that, under the guise of making home ownership more accessible, home purchasers were simply able to pay more for the same housing. Then, with housing prices going up, they were able to take the equity they gained from that appreciation and supplement their stretched incomes.

It was a feedback loop that many investors, economists, and politicians were grateful for. It covered up a lot of other stresses. Yet while a higher percentage of Americans owned homes at the end of the 1990s than at the beginning, they weren't wealthier.

Household debt-to-income ratios increased 15% during the 1990s (FED 2018). In 1989, consumer debt to liquid assets was 60%;

by 1999 it grew to 96% (Rosner 2001). Debt fueled the economy, and home equity was a huge source of that capital.

Here is the Case Shiller Home Price Index from the end of World War II up to the month when Fitch wrote the article for *Forbes*. Both he and Rosner were observing unprecedented home price appreciation. By 2001, levels were significantly higher than even the S&L bubble.

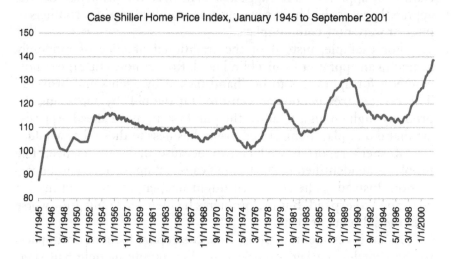

In his *Forbes* article, Fitch noted that Americans, and by extension the American economy, were addicted to increases in home prices. He asked, "What happens when those prices stop increasing?"

Fitch's article was published eight days before the September 11, 2001, terrorist attacks.

The Subprime Crisis

One month after the September 11 terrorist attacks, US President George W. Bush urged Americans to get back to normal. "We cannot let the terrorists achieve the objective of frightening our nation to the point where we don't conduct business. Where people don't shop" (Bush 2001).

In prior wars, America's leaders called on citizens to sacrifice. For example, in World War II, gasoline, sugar, butter, and coffee were some of the items rationed. President Bush called for Americans to keep shopping, to keep consuming. This said more about the precarious nature of the economy than the country's cultural mood.

Before September 11, the economy seemed to be sliding into recession. The fallout from the end of the 1990s technology bubble had the NASDAQ market index down 40% from its all-time high. Enron, at one point the seventh largest US company, had collapsed in a fraud scandal. Over the first half of 2001, the Federal Reserve cut the discount rate from 4.5% to 3%.

The terrorist attacks destroyed the World Trade Center in Manhattan, a complex at the center of the global financial system. In the aftermath, economists and policymakers feared a painful economic retrenchment. Anxious Americans might pull back as the country prepared to fight an irregular war against an ambiguous enemy. Any warnings of a housing bubble, however well founded, were a fringe concern.

A week after September 11, the Federal Reserve lowered the discount rate to 3%. By the end of the year, it would be at 1.25%, on the way to a low of 0.75% in November 2002. Lowering interest rates is like reducing financial gravity. The weight of debt burdens declines, and money begins to seep into places it otherwise wouldn't go.

For the next four years, the US financial sector embarked on a frantic search for yield. For example, pension funds need a return on the trillions of dollars they invest. They also need that return to be safe; they can't gamble with people's retirement savings.

If a pension fund needs an annual return of 7%, and Treasury notes are paying 1% or less, where does a safe return come from? One source was mortgage-backed securities (MBS), which might be yielding 4% in comparison. With an MBS rated AA or AAA, the pension fund can use a little bit of leverage (borrowed money) to magnify the gains. The safe rating allows them to do this in good conscience.

What worked for pension funds also worked for banks, retail investors, and others seeking greater returns. This is, after all, what the strategy of lowering interest rates is supposed to do. Get money off the safe sidelines and into the broader economy to stimulate growth.

Federal legislation allowed banks to use AA- and AAA-rated MBS to meet their reserve requirements. The more AA- and AAA-rated MBS banks bought, the more top-tier reserves they held and the more credit they could issue.

When a bank originates a mortgage, it sells it on a secondary market. The purchaser bundles it with other mortgages and sells slices of that bundle as an MBS. The issuing bank might hold the mortgage for only a day or two before selling it. A bundler might have it for a month before they pass on the risk to others by selling the MBS.

A family could buy a home and, before they make their first mortgage payment, portions of that payment, and all subsequent payments, will be promised to potentially hundreds of different investors.

There weren't enough traditional mortgages to meet this demand. There weren't even enough conventional mortgages. As fast as the banking industry could create a mortgage, the secondary market was ready to purchase it. To meet the demand for mortgage paper to bundle, the industry turned to subprime mortgages.

A subprime mortgage is a mortgage loan issued to someone who doesn't qualify for a traditional or conventional home loan. This could be for reasons that are easy to explain. A young homebuyer who has a stable job but lacks a credit history. Or someone with an irregular pattern of earnings, such as a self-employed small business owner or an artist paid in periodic lump sums. It could also be because they can't afford to buy a house. The underwriting process is supposed to discern between those who can and those who cannot afford to buy a home.

Yet with insatiable industry demand for mortgage paper to bundle, and with risk so easily transferred to others, the entire mortgage process—from underwriting all the way to the purchase of an MBS—became perfunctory. Seemingly anyone could buy a home by taking out a mortgage. Housing prices soared.

Much like the S&L crisis, bad financial practices drove out the good. An appraiser consistently willing to "hit the mark" by providing a generous appraisal saw more referrals than appraisers who were scrupulous. The appraiser willing to go along with the higher price had their generous mark affirmed by rising home prices.

Banks and closing companies could check all the boxes of the underwriting process by relying on information provided by home purchasers. Much has been made of the no-income, no-job, no-asset mortgages, called NINJA loans, but the same incentives that existed for appraisers also existed here. If a bank or closing company insisted on deeply investigating all the claims of applicants, the realtors would take their clients elsewhere. Not surprisingly, the less scrupulous loan processors came to dominate the market.

The new mortgages were quickly passed along to bundlers. The loan processors pocketed the closing fees while passing on the risk associated with holding the mortgage. Since subprime mortgages carried a higher interest rate, bundlers were willing to pay even more for them.

Many of the subprime loans used adjustable-rate mortgages (ARM). These are home loans with interest rates that can change periodically based on fluctuation of market rates. The initial interest rate is typically lower than that of fixed-rate mortgages, making ARMs appealing to borrowers in the short term. This was particularly true when banks offered very low teaser rates for the first 12 or 24 months.

When the teaser rate period ended, the monthly payment on the loan reset to a much higher amount. It was very common for ARMs to be refinanced when the initial teaser rate adjusted. This effectively made them short-term loans. Compared to, for example, a safe and secure five-year Treasury bill, an MBS of ARMs paid a much higher rate of interest. This made them very desirable for banks. An MBS of subprime ARMs, even more so. The bundlers paid a premium for them.

The banks that bundled the loans likewise experienced a race to the bottom. By the early 2000s, bundling conventional mortgages into an MBS was straightforward. A collection of 30-year fixed mortgages, with substantial down payments and high credit scores, bundled into an MBS, would easily earn a AAA rating.

Innovation came through the bundling of lower-rated, subprime mortgages. This move required the ratings agencies to play along. Bundlers argued that adding a few subprime loans into the mix created no additional risk to the MBS so long as the portfolio was geographically diversified. Subprime loans in California might default, but that wouldn't have any impact on those in Florida.

Like the appraisers and the loan originators further upstream, the ratings agencies, even individual analysts, that played along were the ones invited to do more ratings. A generous mindset came to dominate the market.

This was helpful when the bundlers began to develop more exotic mixes. For example, bundling multiple MBSs together created a security called a collateralized debt obligation (CDO). The CDO had slices rated AA and AAA but also riskier components that were lower rated, such as BBB.

The riskier slices could then be combined into a new CDO, something called a CDO-squared (a CDO of CDOs). This gave the ratings agencies a chance to take a second look. If the new CDO-squared had enough geographic diversity, it could still gain a AA or even a AAA rating. These bundles of bundles of risky mortgages were now considered as safe as Treasury bills.

Lubricating all these transactions was the insurance industry. If there was any question about an MBS or a CDO, an insurance company, someone like the American International Group (AIG), sold a policy providing guarantee of payment.

Without a history of widespread mortgage defaults, insurance premiums for MBSs were low. With the housing market booming, providing insurance was highly lucrative. Once again, the least scrupulous players became the market makers, with everyone else needing to match their terms or lose market share.

The demand for mortgages was so great that the industry created a product called a synthetic CDO. The term "synthetic" denotes something that imitates a natural product. In this case, a synthetic CDO imitated the performance of a real CDO. This allowed an infinite number of mortgage-related products to be created from a limited number of underlying mortgages.

From top to bottom, the 2000s housing bubble feels like an orgy of consensual half-truths, deceits, and outright frauds. In many ways, it was, but it also solved a critical problem. The housing bubble kept a fragile economy growing. What was expected to be a deep recession in the early 2000s was, instead, an economic boom. This was broadly seen as a universal good.

Through an unprecedented expansion of credit, the housing bubble allowed an enormous amount of future wealth to be pulled forward to the present and spent. That fact made it easier for policymakers to justify the housing bubble, despite it making homes far less affordable for Americans. It also made it easier to ignore what was happening to Americans, especially to the poor and most vulnerable, who participated in the bubble by being prey to financial predators or sat it out while housing prices and rents rose faster than incomes.

People still needed a place to live. They still needed shelter. Those families attempting to live judiciously, to make a prudent investment in a home, had to compete with those who joined in the mania. Many who shouldn't have purchased a home were enticed to play along. Those who could afford to play the game were pushed to extend themselves beyond prudence. Some homeowners became speculative investors, purchasing multiple properties solely for the price appreciation. In hindsight, the line between participant and victim becomes blurry.

Between 2000 and 2005, the median home price in Southern California grew by 117%, from $241,350 to $524,020, an increase of more than $280,000, or $56,000 per year (Hung and Tu 2008). In 2005, the median household income in Southern California was $53,600 (EDD n.d.). In other words, the median homeowner made more from home appreciation than the median family earned in income. And, with the ability to do a cash-out refinance or simply take out a home equity loan, much of that appreciation could be accessed to increase family spending, even to pay the mortgage.

Return to the theoretical home price scenario modeled in Chapter 2. The theoretical $100,000 house in 1940 had a monthly mortgage payment of $480. Take away the effects of inflation, changes to household income, larger homes, changes in construction techniques, and other factors that influenced home prices between 1940 and 2005 and focus solely on finance.

Apply the financial conditions of 2005 to the $480 per month mortgage payment from 1940. How much more could a family pay for a home in 2005 if they can only afford that same $480 per month mortgage? With an adjustable-rate mortgage at a 2.5% teaser rate, where the home appreciates by 15% annually and half of that appreciation is cashed out to help pay the mortgage, how much could a family pay for the same 1940s home, all other things held constant?

The answer is $279,500.

	Buying a House in 1940	Buying a House in 2005
Monthly payment	$480	$480
Mortgage term	30 years	30-year ARM
Interest rate	6%	2.5% teaser rate
Required down payment	$20,000	$0
Annual appreciation cashed out (50% cash out of 15% appreciation)	$0	$7,500
Theoretical home price	$100,000	$279,500

Seventy-five years of financial innovation and government support applied to the housing market allowed the family that would have been foreclosed on in the Great Depression to pay 280% more for the same home in 2005. American homeowners had come full circle, from humble beginnings pursuing housing as basic shelter to participants—some reluctant, some eager—in the bubble mania of housing as speculative financial instrument.

In June 2005, the chair of the Federal Reserve, Alan Greenspan, told members of the Congressional Joint Economic Committee that a bubble in home prices for the nation "does not appear to be likely." This was wishful thinking. Greenspan did acknowledge there were "signs of froth in some local markets" but asserted that it was not a widespread phenomenon.

Like most economists, Greenspan believed that there was no correlation between local markets. The housing market in Florida was not related to that in California. He believed the same of Texas and Minnesota. People buy and sell homes in a local market. Prices reflect the supply and demand dynamics of that locale.

Yet markets were now almost completely correlated. What happened in Florida was also happening in California, and what happened in Texas was also happening in Minnesota. This is because the market in housing was no longer driven by local supply and demand. The dominant force in the housing market was now the financial sector's demand for mortgage paper.

The sale of a house was merely incidental to what really mattered: the creation of a financial instrument called a mortgage, the basis for a daisy chain of high-demand financial products. The AA and AAA collateral at the foundation of every bank had morphed into a financial bomb primed and ready to go off.

In 2001, Stephane Fitch challenged *Forbes*'s readers to ponder what might happen when housing prices stopped increasing. The answer started to be revealed in the months immediately following Greenspan's 2005 congressional testimony.

Home value appreciation slowed. Without equity to cash out, it became more difficult for homeowners to refinance. This was particularly true for subprime loans. When teaser rate ARMs on these fragile subprime loans reset at higher prices, many mortgages went into default. Foreclosures began to rise. Reminiscent of the 1930s, banks sold repossessed homes into a slowing market. This caused further deceleration. Eventually, home prices began to fall.

In February 2006, Ben Bernanke took over as chairman of the Federal Reserve. A month later, he testified to Congress. He said that the housing sector had been mired in a deep slump for more than a year. He claimed that problems in the subprime market seemed "likely to be contained" (Bernanke 2007). That year, the Case Shiller Home Price Index reached a peak and began dropping.

Bernanke made similar remarks a little over a year later. In May 2007, at a conference put on by the Federal Reserve Bank of Chicago, he acknowledged the likelihood of increases in mortgage delinquencies and foreclosures. The chairman said that Federal Reserve governors "do not expect significant spillovers from the subprime market to the rest of the economy or to the financial system"(Jacobe 2007).

The situation continued to deteriorate. The investment bank Bear Stearns collapsed in March 2008. In July, Countrywide Financial, the nation's largest originator of mortgages, was acquired in a fire sale by Bank of America. In September, Fannie Mae and Freddie Mac were placed under government control. A fragile Merril Lynch merged with Bank of America. The insurer American International Group was effectively nationalized by the federal government. Then, Lehman Brothers entered bankruptcy. Financial markets were reeling.

The George W. Bush administration hastily assembled a $700 billion bailout package for Congress to approve. The president is reported to have said, "this sucker could go down," referring to the US economy (Goldenberg 2008). Talking points around the bailout package suggested that, without immediate approval, there would be a run on all banks and no money in any ATM within 48 hours.

Drama reached a crescendo when Treasury Secretary Henry Paulson, former chief executive at Goldman Sachs with a personal fortune estimated at the time to be $700 million, got down on one knee and begged the Speaker of the House, Democrat Nancy Pelosi, to save the bailout package from defeat. "Please don't blow up this deal," Paulson is said to have begged (Goldenberg 2008).

Many have suggested in hindsight that these dramatics were overblown, but there is good reason to believe that the central actors really thought *the sucker could go down*. After all, if a crash in housing prices reversed the bubble gains of the prior decade, every MBS would experience precipitous decline. Since every bank held MBSs as reserves, every bank in America would experience tremendous financial distress. Many, perhaps most, would fail under those conditions.

It was not a joke to suggest that, without a bailout, there would have been no money in the ATMs. This is what it means to be trapped.

On October 3, 2008, the Emergency Economic Stabilization Act of 2008 passed Congress and was signed into law. The law created the Troubled Asset Relief Program (TARP). Housing prices continued to fall, but the financial sector stabilized. What came to be known as the "subprime housing crisis" or simply the "housing bubble" began to recede.

The Case Shiller Home Price Index shows the unprecedented valuations reached during this financial bubble.

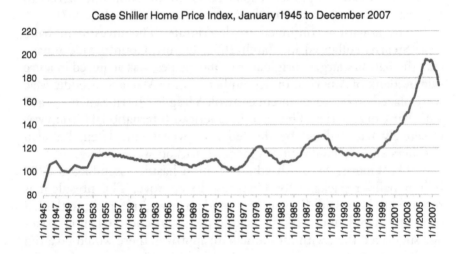

Case Shiller Home Price Index, January 1945 to December 2007

The Road to Recovery?

There is a famous saying in financial circles that is generally attributed to billionaire investor Warren Buffett. "Only when the tide goes out do you learn who has been swimming naked." When easy money stops and financial conditions tighten, those investors holding the riskiest, most fragile positions are exposed.

In 2008, the list of investors swimming naked was long. Among them were America's banks, big and small. Their reserves were investments believed to be the most secure, including AA- and AAA-rated mortgage-backed securities. By the end of the year, it was clear those beliefs were wildly wrong.

Any bank would have to recognize a huge loss if they sold one of their MBSs. Holding an MBS might subject them to even greater future loss. Mark-to-market regulations required banks to accurately value their portfolios, but with the market for MBS broken, the true mark was unclear. Banks could not even calculate how insolvent they were. Credit markets froze.

The TARP program directed the US Treasury Department to purchase or insure "troubled assets," the euphemism used for mortgage-related financial instruments that banks needed to unload. The idea was that, by allowing the Treasury to make these purchases, prices would stabilize, even rise, and the assets would no longer be troubled (Congress 2008).

That plan was abandoned very quickly. Treasury officials realized that these complicated trading instruments could not be fully understood, let alone properly valued. Also, the list of assets needing purchase vastly exceeded the money allocated. The Treasury had brought a knife to a gun fight; by keeping the knife under wraps, they could pretend it was a gun.

A month after TARP was established, the Treasury Department pivoted. Instead of buying troubled assets, Treasury opted to make direct investments in eight banks. Dramatically, the CEOs of each of these banks were gathered and forced to accept the money, whether they needed it or not. This was a tactic to avoid cascading bank runs. The most fragile banks couldn't be identified when everyone received support. Troubled assets remained in place.

By the end of 2008, the discount rate was all the way down to 0.5%, kicking off an extended period of what came to be known as zero interest rate policy (ZIRP). It would be more than six years before interest rates moved higher (FREDa n.d.).

Adding to ZIRP's massive distortion of financial gravity was the Federal Reserve's Quantitative Easing (QE) program. It was announced the same month as the TARP pivot. With QE, the Federal Reserve purchased MBS directly from Fannie Mae and Freddie Mac. They were able to do this by expanding their balance sheet, creating their own reserves. A less sophisticated way to describe this is "money printing," a prerogative of financial systems often judged by history as incompetent or despotic.

With QE, the Federal Reserve was able to do what the Treasury Department with TARP could not: create a market for MBS by buying them in unlimited quantities. They bought them from Fannie and Freddie, who continued to buy them from everywhere else. This essentially laundered the market's questionable securities until prices stabilized. In 2010, commercial banks collectively owned MBS valued at $1 trillion (FREDb n.d.) while the Federal Reserve, using QE, owned $1.1 trillion (FREDc n.d.).

This was all initially done in the service of market stabilization. At some point, the goal of stabilization morphed into a new goal: recovery.

In much the same way that the financial tools developed to stop decline in the Great Depression worked to create the post-war expansion, the extraordinary measures taken during the subprime crisis were repurposed to expand the housing sector and the economy along with it.

Yet what exactly did it mean for the housing sector to recover? The period between 2000 and 2008 is called a "housing bubble." Even the country's most senior economic officials use that term. So how exactly does an economy recover from a bubble? What is it that is being restored?

After the subprime crisis, home prices never returned to an historic normal, let alone became depressed. At its lowest point, the Case Shiller Home Price Index was still higher than the level Stephane Fitch and Josh Rosner called a bubble back in 2001. There was a crash in prices from an unprecedented high, but there was never a depression in home prices.

Here is the Case Shiller Home Index, updated through the end of 2022.

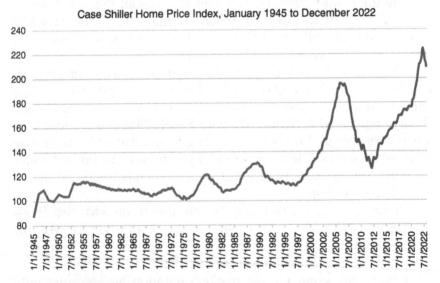

Case Shiller Home Price Index, January 1945 to December 2022

A financial bubble is, by definition, unsustainable. A post-bubble recovery in the housing market, one that restores it to unsustainable levels, feels like madness. It is the kind of approach a society would pursue only if there were no other choice. The post-crash re-creation of the 2000s bubble demonstrates just how dependent on housing the American economy is.

Mortgage-backed securities still sit at the heart of the banking system. The origination, bundling, and trading of mortgages remains a major source of income for the financial sector. Homes are still the greatest source of wealth for American families. They are a dominant source of revenue for most local governments. Home construction and related industries employ millions. In so many ways, the housing market is the American economy.

A threat to the housing market, therefore, is a threat to the entire economy. With the systems in place today, there is no way for housing prices to broadly return to even 2001 levels, let alone any type of post-war normal, without massive economic disruption.

We can have a growing economy, with low unemployment, but with a financial bubble in housing that makes it broadly unaffordable. Or we can have housing decline to pre-bubble levels and experience another Great Depression.

Either way, without a change in approach, a growing percentage of Americans will find it difficult to obtain shelter.

What Comes Next?

The tide has not yet gone out on this renewed bubble. The many complex factors that created it are yet to be revealed. As with any financial bubble, in real time there are many theories as to its cause along with a fair number of denials. What is undeniable is that the housing trap creates a market now dominated by moral hazard. Investors in housing products worry little about the risk they assume. They have witnessed the lengths officials will go to ensure that housing prices don't fall.

The warping of financial gravity that QE and an extended period of ZIRP created is impossible to fully assess. There are some obvious signs, however, of a radical shift in the makeup of the marginal buyer.

A home is worth whatever the highest bidder is willing to pay for it. This bidder is the marginal buyer. During the 2000s bubble, the marginal buyer was often a subprime borrower. Their bid reflected a belief that rising prices would provide growing wealth and the opportunity to refinance when cash became tight. They drove the market.

Everyone else wanting a home needed to be willing to match their willingness to pay.

Following the 2008 crisis, subprime borrowing was curtailed. The recovery bubble needed a new marginal buyer. A new market maker. In a 2012 speech to the National Association of Homebuilders, Federal Reserve Chairman Ben Bernanke suggested a way forward. "With home prices falling and rents rising, it could make sense in some markets to turn some of the foreclosed homes into rental properties," the Chairman said (Bernanke 2012). Wall Street investors did just that.

In *Underwater: How Our American Dream of Homeownership Became a Nightmare*, reporter for the *Wall Street Journal*, underwater homeowner, and reluctant landlord Ryan Dezember describes the new gold rush for foreclosed properties to rent. The idea of centrally managing a portfolio of rental properties had once seemed impossible, but technology such as smartphones and tablets, along with advances in cloud computing, "enabled investors to conduct an unprecedented land grab and profitably manage thousands of far-flung properties" (Dezember 2020).

Dezember describes monthly auctions in places such as Atlanta being called "Super Tuesday" by Wall Street–backed bidders. Billions of dollars' worth of homes were transferred from the foreclosed to investors in auctions to bulk buyers. They competed mostly with each other; typical homeowners were sidelined. Dezember reports that Blackstone, a Wall Street private investment bank, was "buying as much as $150 million worth of houses in a week."

Investors in rental properties made money in two ways. The first was through appreciation. Gravity-warping low interest rates meant investors could be patient waiting for the market to turn around. In fact, the more properties purchased for rent, the tighter the housing market became and the better this strategy worked. Institutional investors with privileged access to capital could dominate a market, outbidding all local competition. This fostered conditions that accelerated the appreciation of their portfolios.

The second was through rental income, although not in a traditional sense. Historically, a tenant may pay a landlord by running next door with cash or slipping a rent check under the door. Being late on rent meant confronting an angry landlord. Raising the rent meant a conversation with an anxious tenant. This relationship should not be overly idealized, but it did have a human dimension.

The new investment bank landlords have no such social friction. In fact, the algorithmic approach used by institutions to arbitrage complex financial securities is used to establish optimum rental pricing. The optimum price isn't the price that keeps a unit full or people sheltered. It is the price with the highest return on capital.

The highest return on capital comes from a tight market, where rents are increased to the maximum level before tenants start to filter down to lesser units. Rents also need to be high enough to price out the most difficult tenants, a strategy that reduces overall management costs.

Over time, institutions honed their skills at managing rental properties in bulk. As the number of foreclosed homes declined, these institutional investors moved higher up the property food chain. The real estate news site Redfin reported that, by the end of 2021, nearly a third of investor purchases were for mid-priced homes (Anderson and Bokhari 2022). In the first quarter of 2022, the marginal buyer for one in five homes was an investor (Anderson 2023).

Rising home prices and rents, combined with ZIRP conditions, eventually brought home builders back into the market. With the holding cost of capital artificially low, builders—like landlords—could always afford to hold out for the premium price they needed. Along with a new wave of suburban single-family homes, the 5-over-1 building swept the country, appearing in seemingly every market a permit could be obtained.

A 5-over-1 building is a great Wall Street product. It is five floors of inexpensive wood-framed construction over a single-story concrete podium. The standardized construction approach means they are easily bundled and securitized on a secondary market. They can be customized to target any price point, from working class to luxury. They are not built to endure multiple life cycles but instead to be fully depreciated by the end of the financing period.

Again, for multifamily housing such as the 5-over-1, a tight market is a feature, not a flaw. With a housing market more sensitive to investment capital than local supply and demand conditions, this product—and the various downstream financial instruments derived from it—will continue to be built until capital costs become tighter.

Even then, there will be tremendous resistance to price reductions. A 5-over-1 as a rental unit is built with a construction loan and then sold to investors utilizing a commercial debt instrument. Much like the mortgage back in the 1930s, that commercial debt instrument needs to be rolled over periodically. With each rollover, the multifamily structure is revalued.

The valuation of a multifamily 5-over-1 isn't a function of the quality of construction or the amenities. It's a function of rents. A luxury building with no tenants is essentially worthless while a decrepit building consistently filled will have great value.

For example, a builder constructs a multifamily building. It is initially valued at $1 million based on the anticipation that tenants will pay $1,000 per month for each unit. Once built, the units sit empty because people are unable to pay $1,000 per month. To fill the units, the price will need to drop to $500 per month. What that means is that the building is now worth half of what it was initially valued. When refinancing happens, the owner of the building will need to come up with cash for the difference or lose the building.

Yet, with interest rates near zero, that owner can keep the rental price at $1,000 per unit, theoretically sit there with an empty building, and wait for market rents to rise to meet the mark. There is no real cost to service the debt and, thus, no real pressure to move off the proforma rental price.

The owner may even bring in tenants with offers like a two-year lease at $1,000 per month with the first 12 months free. This is effectively $500 per month, but in the world of extend-and-pretend Wall Street finance, the lease is written at $1,000 per month (with a teaser). In financial circles, there are widespread rumors of vacant units and this kind of incentive-laden lease being written. With no way to track this, there is no way to know for sure.

The only way to uncover this economic distortion is to return gravity to the capital markets by allowing interest rates to rise. An increase in the holding costs for vacant property will force a resolution to this stalemate. The tide will go out and expose those swimming naked.

Whatever inventory is currently sidelined will be brought into the market through foreclosures or a diminishment of profit expectations. Foreclosure will probably include the failure of some investment banks. Whether that will trigger another round of QE, interest rate manipulation, and bailouts is unknowable.

Inexplicably, Fannie Mae and Freddie Mac remain in conservatorship more than a decade and a half after they were nationalized. The two entities continue to purchase loans, including subprime loans. As such, they continue to dramatically shape the housing market, assuming an unknown amount of risk in support of rising home prices.

On paper, Fannie and Freddie both returned to profitability in 2012. They finished paying back the federal government for the bailouts by the middle of the Trump administration (Schroeder 2019). Profits continue to go to the Treasury, with that money used for things unrelated to housing, such as the 2021 infrastructure bill (Haynie 2023). Efforts to end the conservatorship have stalled.

A global pandemic in 2020 seemed like it might be a triggering event, one that might burst the recovery bubble. Instead, home prices soared as people began to move around, buying homes in remote locations as pandemic lockdowns morphed into a new work-from-home normal. Interest rates, which had been inching up, went back to ZIRP as another round of QE stimulus went into effect.

During the COVID-19 pandemic, inflation, the much-anticipated outcome of loose fiscal and monetary policy, broke out of assets such as stocks and housing and into the broader market. The price of everyday goods rose at rates not experienced since the 1980s. The subsequent rise in interest rates brought into stark relief the absurdity of long-term mortgages as an investment vehicle.

When interest rates fall, the investment value of a 30-year fixed rate mortgage goes up. Someone owning a bundle of mortgages paying 6% annually is going to want to hang onto them when new mortgages are being made at 3%. Yet those are the exact conditions when the borrower refinances, terminating the 6% payment in exchange for a lower-yielding loan. The investor has no recourse but to give up their prized asset.

The opposite happens when interest rates rise. Someone owning a bundle of mortgages paying 3% annually is going to want to trade them out when new mortgages are being bundled at 6%. That is exactly when homeowners hunker down. Few people committed to paying a 30-year mortgage at 3% seek to refinance when rates go to 6%. Again, the investor is stuck, this time with lower-yielding paper.

Mortgages are at the foundation of our financial system, yet they are the worst kind of investment. The reason investors accept such bad payoff asymmetry is because the federal government is committed to keeping housing prices elevated. Investors buy mortgages because mortgages are a safe bet.

Housing prices may adjust downward slightly over a short timeframe. They may even drop dramatically if markets temporarily spin out of control. Either way, there will always be a coordinated effort to reinflate the housing market. There must be; if the housing market fails, the financial system fails. That is the lesson from 2008. It is even truer today.

Prices can't go down. Not in any meaningful way. This makes the next innovation in housing finance somewhat predictable: the 50-year mortgage. While demographic trends suggest there will be upward pressure on wages over the coming decade or more, there remains a massive affordability gap for the next generation of homebuyers.

The 50-year mortgage, fully backed by the federal government, financed through Wall Street investment banks, will lower monthly payments enough to allow desperate Americans in their 20s and 30s to buy homes from desperate Americans in their 70s and 80s, all while keeping prices elevated and the financial sector secure.

In a century, we have come full circle. In the 1930s, financially sound homeowners sought short-term loans from fragile local banks. In the 2020s, national too-big-to-fail banks seek long-term mortgages from fragile homeowners. If a home without equity is like a rental with debt, we are poised to turn Americans into a nation of debt-laden renters.

Housing as Shelter

5

Zoning Lockdown

The Illegal City of Somerville

Somerville, Massachusetts, is a thriving city. It has, in spades, the attributes that the median city planner and real estate professional alike will tell you are in great demand and short supply in 2020s America: *walkability, vibrancy, sense of place*. Adjacent to central Boston, Somerville is known for top-tier educational institutions, a robust arts and culture scene, and lively civic squares surrounded by locally owned shops and restaurants.

Unsurprisingly, the city's attractive lifestyle comes at a price. As of this writing, there are dozens of homes for sale in Somerville listed for over one million dollars.

Such a price ought to be a clear signal that there is ample market demand for a place like Somerville. According to economic theory, developers should respond by building more housing in Somerville, and by creating more blocks and neighborhoods that resemble the most in-demand parts of Somerville.

There is only one problem: they largely can't. In 2015, Somerville's city planners undertook a study to find out which of the city's existing residential properties conformed to Somerville's own zoning code. The number of fully zoning-compliant lots in the city of 80,000 people was a surprise to everyone: there were only 22 (Hertz 2016).

The city of Somerville, it turned out, had declared itself illegal. There was no single reason for this but a combination of requirements working in tandem. These included rules about building height, lot size, density, and the positioning of buildings on a lot. Nearly every property was in violation of one or more.

Somerville's zoning code was clogging the city's planning bureaucracy and choking its growth. It was legal to continue to use an existing building for a use that had been in effect before the code was created. But as soon as a property owner wanted to undertake so much as a routine expansion—a front porch, a back deck, a finished basement—they were liable to trigger a complicated and costly set of inspections and requirements (McMorrow 2014). And anyone seeking to build a new building would encounter even more limitation on where it could be and what they could do.

It would be one thing if this situation were an oddity, a case of bureaucracy run amok or unusually incompetent city staff. But "illegal neighborhoods" are not uncommon. An estimated 54 % of homes in San Francisco are in buildings that could not legally be built today (Mapbox n.d.). Even in Manhattan, which has among the most permissive standards in the US for density and height, 40% of buildings are nonconforming (Bui, Chaban, and White 2016).

It would be another thing if Somerville's zoning reflected some sort of informed consensus that the city's historic form is not up to standards of adequate habitation, in the same way that a car manufactured in 1970 would not meet today's safety or emissions standards. But no one is making this argument, and the prices of those historic homes would seem to refute it.

And yet the *kind* of place that Somerville typifies is, in fact, illegal to reproduce almost anywhere in America. That kind of place is the kind we built everywhere under the traditional pattern of development that prevailed before the Great Depression. It is compact and fine grained, a city where needs can be met on foot. It has a varied mix of homes, businesses, and modest apartment buildings on tightly spaced lots.

Such places, today, are mostly cities under glass, frozen in time. We have almost entirely stopped building more of them or expanding on those that exist.

Yet surviving "illegal" buildings are all around us. They are not unfamiliar or exotic to modern Americans. Older neighborhoods are peppered with residential structures that predate modern zoning and would be illegal to replicate today. Within them, all sorts of Americans go about their lives peaceably.

Somewhere, perhaps near you, an extended family lives together in a duplex to share both housing expenses and childcare. A working-class family rents an apartment in an area where they could not afford to buy a home, securing access to a safe neighborhood with good schools.

Today, duplexes are illegal to build in most American neighborhoods.

Somewhere nearby, an aging parent or a 20-something couple live in an accessory dwelling unit (ADU) behind a larger home. You may know these backyard cottages as mother-in-law units, granny flats, casitas, carriage houses, garage apartments—a variety of vernacular terms reflecting the diverse circumstances in which these arose organically as a prior generation's practical solution to housing needs.

Backyard cottages, like duplexes, are illegal to build in most American neighborhoods today. Where they still exist because their construction predated the zoning code, they are *legally nonconforming*: a clinical bit of planner-ese that evokes the tone in which a 1950s sociologist might have spoken about deviant subcultures.

Many of the neighbors of these buildings have likely never given a single thought to their illegality. The dissonance between our zoning codes and our cities as they actually exist is a little-understood feature of American planning.

Most Americans have heard of zoning. But to the extent that they know anything about it, it's what they know from games such as *SimCity* or *Cities: Skylines*. That is, zoning is part of the basic order of the city: a simple, universal, and presumably sensible regulation put in place to protect the character of our neighborhoods. Zoning, we are told, is the reason your home is unlikely to be menaced by a smokestack.

Most countries around the world have zoning in some form, but the North American version is quite exceptional. It is unique in the rigidity with which it separates different uses of land into distinct, mutually exclusive districts. It is also unusual in the primacy it gives to one form of housing: the detached single-family house.

If zoning began as a tame creature, today it is a huge, multi-headed hydra. It is an enormous and unruly beast that has grown beyond the designs or imagination of its early proponents. And zoning constitutes a massively distorting influence on the shape of our cities and towns, including where we build housing, what we build, and who gets to build it.

The Roots of American Zoning

Land-use planning has existed as long as there have been cities. For most of history, though, its focus was on defining the shape of the public realm, rather than regulating the private. The ancient Greeks and the Chinese Zhou Dynasty established street grid systems. The Spanish Law of the Indies, used in the creation of colonial settlements in the Americas, dictated the orientation of city blocks to maximize shade and airflow, and provided for a central square fronted by civic and religious buildings.

There is some early precedent, as well, for regulation of the use of private land. But its scope was typically narrow. Imperial Rome regulated the location of brickyards and cemeteries (Hirt 2014). A sixth-century treatise by the Byzantine architect Julian of Ascalon called for the prohibition of taverns, brothels, and baths in proximity to residential homes, as well as restrictions on activities that could cause fire, smoke, or odors. But for the most part, the management of land use in pre-industrial cities was left to private agreements between neighbors.

Pre-modern land-use laws tended to be limited in their scope, and the state limited in its powers of enforcement. The industrial revolution of the second half of the 19th century, however, threatened the viability of this laissez-faire approach.

Industrializing US cities grew unfathomably quickly. Chicago in 1850 was a frontier settlement of 30,000. By 1890, it was a metropolis of one million inhabitants; by 1930, it had grown to three million. This occurred in a largely decentralized fashion, as individual builders followed simple templates copied over and over, with minimal oversight.

We built housing rapidly, but much of it was cramped, unhealthy, and unsafe. And it existed in the context of neighborhoods undergoing rapid, chaotic change. This elicited two responses that directly led to the rise of zoning.

One was an attempt by the well-to-do to insulate themselves from the chaos of the industrial city. By the 1880s, new commuter suburbs built along streetcar and railroad lines provided the earliest test runs for the prospect of "planning for permanence" that J.C. Nichols would later articulate. These places often advertised that residents' quality of life would be secured through deed restrictions prohibiting uses of property that were perceived as disruptive or detrimental. These included shops and apartments.

The other response was the series of progressive housing reforms discussed in Chapter 2. At first, reformers set their sights on correcting the most unsafe and unsanitary conditions found in the apartments of the working class. The work of photographer Jacob Riis drew national attention to the cause after publication of the 1890 book *How The Other Half Lives*. It galvanized support for the public-health movement that would lead to New York's 1901 Tenement House Act.

But this reformist zeal soon found other purposes. Increasingly, there was a push to crack down on communal and rental living arrangements that many of the early zoning proponents found *morally* objectionable. These reformers waged a deliberate war on multifamily housing in the earliest decades of the 20th century. They largely won it. They used zoning and building codes as their tools. Many of the key figures were the same progressive public health reformers who had worked on the tenement laws.

What many of the earliest zoning laws explicitly targeted was a set of commonplace strategies for securing housing in America's booming cities. These strategies had not arisen as a matter of public policy; they were emergent and adaptive responses. They were imperfect and often uncomfortable, but they were copied en masse because they met people's need for shelter.

These strategies included boarding houses and residential hotels, lodging in private homes, and various innovative forms of small-scale multifamily construction and homeownership. Almost all of them would be widely illegal in US neighborhoods by the 1930s.

The Birth and Death of the Triple-Decker

In the late 19th and early 20th centuries, a wave of migrants from both rural America and overseas flooded into the cities of New England, looking for work in the region's mills and factories. Somerville, which had a population of just under 15,000 in 1870, would by 1920 be home to six times as many residents. In New England, the housing solution that arose to serve such burgeoning urban populations was not the tenement but the triple-decker.

The triple-decker is a distinctively New England housing type. It is a three-story, wood-framed house consisting of three stacked apartments, each typically with a small balcony. The interior units have nearly identical floor plans, thus resulting in kitchens and bathrooms stacked on top of each other for ease of plumbing and ventilation. Some are basic boxes, while others have ornamentation characteristic of the Victorian and Queen Anne styles popular at the time.

Triple-deckers sprouted by the tens of thousands in cities including but not limited to Boston, Providence, Lawrence, Worcester, and Woonsocket. According to the New England Historical Society, 16,000 triple-deckers housing 192,000 people were built in Boston alone between 1880 and 1930 (New England Historical Society n.d.).

The triple-decker was a "small-d" democratic housing solution, in that it was inexpensive and uncomplicated to build. Most were not built by professional real estate developers but by a combination of skilled tradespeople, mill and factory owners, and immigrants. These homes quickly became the preferred option of immigrants to New England because they were an affordable first rung on the ladder to homeownership, at a time when obtaining a mortgage for a single dwelling was prohibitive for those without significant savings.

The owner of a triple-decker would typically live in the ground-floor unit and house relatives in the second unit, allowing a family to share housing resources and reduce expenses. The third floor would be occupied by a paying tenant, and the income stream would make ownership of a triple-decker a viable proposition for a working-class owner.

As a working-class housing solution, the triple-decker was a vast improvement over the New York tenement. According to the New England Historical Society, "An ambitious clerk or mechanic who earned an average of $25 a week could rent for $20–$25 an apartment with a parlor, dining room, kitchen and bathroom. It also had a stove, hot water, two bedrooms, two porches, heat, electricity and hardwood floors."

Triple-deckers, however, almost immediately provoked the ire of the New England establishment, and campaigns began to restrict their spread.

Some of the complaints were aesthetic. In 1900, the Worcester Board of Trade called the triple-decker "a blot on the landscape . . . like an enormous dry-goods box on our sightly hills." Other criticisms cited safety concerns including the very real risk of fire (as was the case with much of the housing of that era).

Much of the criticism, however, also contained overt or thinly veiled anti-immigrant sentiment. A 1917 article in *Providence* magazine assailing the "three-decker menace" asserted, "The newcomers to Providence find an environment perhaps more kindly to the weak, but less kindly to the strong. The newcomers have lower standards. Are we raising these standards or are ours sinking toward their level?"

In 1912, a Massachusetts state law allowed cities to ban any "wooden tenement" in which "cooking shall be done above the second floor" (Sperance 2021). By 1920, dozens of municipalities had banned the construction of new triple-deckers. In 1923, Providence passed its ban. By the 1930s, the construction of triple-decker homes had almost completely ceased in New England.

The backlash against triple-deckers had a public-safety element, but that was no longer primary. Of equal and perhaps greater impact was simply the fact that many found triple-deckers, or their residents, to be unsuitable neighbors.

The "Lodger Evil"

Lawrence Veiller, who had been the main framer of the New York State Tenement House Act in 1901, was a leader in the housing reform movement. In 1911, Veiller formed the National Housing Association (NHA), which sought to produce model housing and zoning regulations for cities to adopt. He set his sights on his perennial nemesis of urban population density, declaring in 1912 that "the lodger evil is the root of our room overcrowding problem."

It was common at the time for American households to take in a lodger or boarder. In the 19th century, as many as half of urban Americans spent part of their lives either as lodgers in others' homes or as hosts of lodgers in their own. In 1850, according to census records, a lodger was present in 35% of households in the central cities of metropolitan areas of 50,000 inhabitants or more. By 1900, this figure had fallen to 21%, but the practice remained a common strategy for affording housing in America's bursting cities.

Lodgers were most often unmarried young men, frequently immigrants who had come to America in advance of their families and would stay in the homes of families of the same ethnic groups (Beito and Beito 2016). Lodgers would occupy basements, attics, and spare rooms. The frequency of these arrangements varied by ethnic group but was most common among Eastern and Southern Europeans.

Lodging was an adaptive, usually short-term strategy to reduce rent burdens and increase household savings. Both contemporary and modern evidence show that households with lodgers tended to have greater savings at the end of the year and that the practice was associated with higher rates of homeownership later in life among ethnic groups including Poles, Slovenes, and Italians. By the 1930s, foreign-born individuals owned a majority of the homes in New York City (Beito and Beito 2016).

To Veiller and like-minded reformers, on the other hand, "the lodger evil" was seen as not merely a source of unhealthy overcrowding, but a contributor to crime and sexual immorality. And proposals to curb this "evil" soon evolved into a much more sweeping attack on multifamily housing.

Residential Hotels / SROs

Another housing option targeted by progressive reforms was the residential hotel, or single-room occupancy (SRO) boarding house. By 1900, these had proliferated in American downtowns, offering mostly working-class laborers a basic room with a bed, access to a communal kitchen or dining hall, and most importantly, affordable access to the amenities and jobs of the city.

Veiller saw these, as well, as hotbeds of immorality. "The bad effect upon the community of a congregate form of living is by no means limited to the poorer people," he wrote in 1905. "Waldorf-Astorias at one end of town and 'big flats' at the other end are equally bad in their destruction of civic spirit and the responsibilities of citizenship."

Building codes passed in the early 20th century largely prohibited SRO arrangements and prevented the renovation of existing residential hotels. Zoning prevented the hotel model from expanding to new neighborhoods. Many of these buildings—now "illegal" relics—were ultimately demolished. In *Homeless*, Gerald Daly writes that Chicago lost 23,000 SRO units in the decade between 1973 and 1984—the equivalent of demolishing 100 public housing towers.

Zoning as a Tool of Economic Exclusion

Early zoning proponents understood how zoning could be used to effectively ban certain housing typologies without having to ban them, simply by making them prohibitively expensive to build. Veiller recommended the use of fire codes for this purpose, because "zoning legislation will no doubt be fought strenuously and perhaps defeated." No one would question the importance of fire safety regulations, even when they were used to achieve other aims:

> [D]o everything possible in our laws to encourage the construction of private dwellings and even two-family dwellings, because the two-family house is the next least objectionable type, and penalize so far as we can in our statute, the multiple dwelling of any kind. . . . If we require multiple dwellings to be fireproof, and thus increase the cost of construction; if we require stairs to be fireproofed, even where there are only three families; if we require fire escapes and a host of other things, all dealing with fire protection, we are on safe grounds, because that can be justified as a legitimate exercise of the police power. . . . In our laws let most of the fire provisions relate solely to multiple dwellings, and allow our private houses and two-family houses to be built with no fire protection whatever. (NHA Proceedings 1913, 212)

The legacy of this strategy remains evident today. The model building codes used by virtually every US city include one code for most residential and commercial buildings, and a separate, simpler code exclusively for one- and two-family structures.

Frank Backus Williams, a collaborator of the famed city planner John Nolen, expressly recommended in a 1916 report that cities use land-use planning as a route to economic exclusion:

> She can indirectly create certain residential districts from which all but one family houses and others from which all but one and two family houses are measurably excluded. This she can do by making such height and area requirements as will render it unprofitable, at the price of land prevailing in the district, to build anything but the desired type of residence. (Nolen 1916)

Soon, it would not be necessary to achieve this effect indirectly. The first residential zone reserved exclusively for single-family homes was established in Berkeley, California, in 1916, in its Elmwood neighborhood. Elmwood's developer, Duncan McDuffie, was explicit about his desire to exclude Black residents from the neighborhood as a goal, but the actual text of the zoning code contained no reference to race. McDuffie understood that a neighborhood of single-family homes would be unaffordable for most Black families at the time.

A year later, the US Supreme Court ruled in *Buchanan v. Warley* that zoning could not be used expressly to achieve racial segregation. But Berkeley's code was safe, because its racial intent was implicit, not stated. Similar stories underlie many zoning codes implemented around the country in the following years and decades, ostensibly to protect quality of life, but at least in part as a pretext for racial and socioeconomic exclusion.

Single-family zoning received its national legal test in 1926 when the Supreme Court heard *Village of Euclid v. Ambler Realty Co.* At issue was whether the city of Euclid, Ohio, by implementing a single-family residential zone, had unfairly reduced the value of Ambler's land. The Supreme Court sided with Euclid and indicated that zoning ordinances would generally be upheld as long as some connection to the public welfare could be argued. Infamously, the court's opinion contained the assertion that "very often the apartment house is a mere parasite, constructed in order to take advantage of the open spaces and attractive surroundings created by the residential character of the district."

As a result of *Euclid v. Ambler*, the term "Euclidean zoning" was born, referring to the practice of designating zones of a city for single, exclusive uses.

At the time of the ruling, at least 425 American cities had zoning codes. Soon, the number would be in the thousands.

Zoning and the FHA

Zoning was influenced by the biases of planners at the time, which favored homeownership and low-density development. But it would soon be greatly influenced as well by the financial innovations occurring in response to the Great Depression.

The Federal Housing Administration incorporated requirements related to zoning into its guidelines for mortgage underwriting. This put a great deal of pressure on cities to adopt zoning ordinances that matched the FHA standards so that banks would issue loans in their neighborhoods.

Among the lending standards adopted by the FHA by 1939 were highly specific land-use requirements with no carefully studied or scientific basis. To insure a mortgage on a house, the FHA required that lot coverage not exceed 30% of the net area of an interior lot or 40% of the net area of a corner lot. It stipulated that lot width should exceed at least 50 feet, which was twice as wide as many urban lots at the time. And it indicated that "a dwelling should be located on its lot so that no wall of the principal building was at any point less than fifty feet from the building line on the opposite side of a street, less than fifteen feet from a rear lot line, or less than three feet from a side lot line unless the dwelling was built to the lot line," according to research by Andrew H. Whittemore (2013).

The FHA preferred single-use to mixed-use developments. FHA guidelines stipulated, "The neighborhood shall be homogenous in character and shall offer reasonable security against decline in desirability for residential purposes due to encroachment of inharmonious land uses, such as commercial or industrial occupancies. . . . A bungalow surrounded by apartment buildings, or an apartment building in a neighborhood of detached houses . . . would be a questionable risk." The FHA overwhelmingly denied mortgages in areas that were unzoned or contained a mix of uses.

By 1936, 40% of all single-family construction in the US was insured by the FHA. This was a powerful lever for the spread and standardization of zoning. Cities that didn't adopt zoning consistent with FHA lending guidelines would threaten the ability of their residents to secure low-cost mortgages. And this fact tended to outweigh the objections of critics who argued their property values or freedom of choice would be threatened by the new restrictions.

Standardization was the name of the game. Zoning codes were often simply duplicated from one community to another, rather than any attempt made to adapt them to local conditions. It is not uncommon today that you can open the zoning code in a rural Midwestern area and find language such as "allow for the adequate penetration of sunlight and air into the property." Such language, curious in application to a farmhouse, made perfect sense in the context of New York tenements in which it was actually created.

What had been a tool to address the genuine public health concerns posed by those tenements, and then a range of nuisances (both real and perceived) associated with urban living, was now being repurposed as the institutional architecture, the underlying operating system, of America's grand suburban experiment.

The rapid spread and standardization of zoning, especially single-family residential zones, put the existing, evolutionary patterns of cities under glass. Neighborhoods would now be frozen in amber, unable to grow to a higher level of intensity. New neighborhoods on the suburban fringe would be built according to highly regimented templates.

The zoning codes that proliferated in the 1930s and beyond showed a strong preference for superficial order. It is this tendency in planning that Jane Jacobs would decry two decades later in *The Death and Life of Great American Cities*. Jacobs explained how the superficial disorder of a dense and eclectic urban neighborhood often masked a complex underlying order: a deep set of social relationships contingent on the ways that people interacted in physical space. It was this that modern planning and zoning threatened to destroy.

The artificial order imposed by zoning, unlike the emergent order already present, had little scientific basis or relationship to local needs. But from a different perspective, its standardization has become an end in itself.

Recall the disconnect between two basic conversations about housing in America. Housing is our source of shelter, our way of meeting basic needs from safety to belonging. But housing is also a financial instrument, and an engine driving the entire economy.

Zoning is very well adapted to a world in which housing serves that latter purpose. It facilitates the efficient production of many transactions in residential real estate, each of which is legible to a financial industry that will then bundle and securitize millions of loans.

A standard set of rules, producing a housing monoculture, allows for economies of scale in planning and development on a level unseen in history. It allows for the mass-produced suburbs that we turned to building in the postwar era. And it allows for the fulfillment of J.C. Nichols's promise of permanence. Or rather, it provides for the near-term appearance of having fulfilled that promise, in brand-new neighborhoods designed for stasis and homogeneity.

Locking Down the Core Cities

By the end of the 1960s, almost every city of any size in America had a zoning code. The pressure to do so to access federal grants and mortgage financing was decisive, and city councils often voted to take up zoning without much scrutiny or fanfare. (Notably, one of the few places to put zoning to a popular vote was Houston, Texas, where voters decisively rejected it in 1948 and 1962. Houston remains the only large US city to not have zoning, although it regulates land use in other ways.)

In older cities whose built form predated the era of zoning, zoning tended to be less restrictive than in new suburbs. Although many standardizing assumptions were implemented, zoners made concessions to the on-the-ground reality of these places, which typically included a complex mixture of land uses and building types. Many cities continued to allow multifamily dwellings in older residential neighborhoods.

Soon, however, even these neighborhoods would face a wave of tightening restrictions. Most often, these so-called "downzonings" were efforts to stem decline and protect the investment of homeowners.

The first few postwar decades were a rough time for American cities. Nine of the ten largest US cities (all but Los Angeles, which contains vast suburban areas within its borders) and countless smaller ones declined in population in the 1950s, as middle-class residents decamped to new suburban homes. Many of these buyers were returning servicemen eligible for low-interest, zero down payment FHA mortgages thanks to the federal GI Bill. In practice, this lending was rife with racial discrimination: in the New York City suburbs, fewer than 100 of over 67,000 mortgages insured by the G.I. Bill were taken out by non-whites, according to Ira Katznelson (2006).

Meanwhile, many of the urban neighborhoods populated by people of color were subject to redlining, the practice of denying loans to borrowers in certain geographic areas deemed to be risky and thus unsuitable for investment. Beginning in the 1930s, the short-lived federal Home Owners Lending Corporation (HOLC) produced maps of dozens of American cities identifying these areas using a color-coded letter grade system, from A ("Best") to D ("Hazardous"). The FHA adopted these maps and used them to restrict where it would offer mortgage insurance. Banks, in turn, used the maps to guide mortgage lending.

In theory, these areas were chosen based on a sober assessment of financial risk to the lender. In practice, the criteria were often explicitly racial. Majority Black neighborhoods were almost always deemed "hazardous." Neighborhoods populated by poor, often ethnic, whites were also often redlined. So too were neighborhoods characterized by the kinds of land use at odds with the FHA's prescriptions for zoning: eclectic, dense, mixed-use.

Pause as well, and understand the immediate effect of being a homeowner in one of these declining or hazardous areas. Once redlined, there was virtually no market for your home. You could only sell to people who could pay cash because anyone who needed a mortgage couldn't get one. To say this destroyed property values is an understatement that fails to convey the damaging feedback loop of disinvestment and predation that followed.

Neighborhoods that had been redlined or were losing population saw little new development. Those who did buy and redevelop properties were investors, often unscrupulous and predatory ones. Low-quality rentals proliferated as well-off homeowners became fewer. In this environment, things that were largely the symptoms of neighborhood decline could be easily mistaken for the causes.

Homeowners in urban neighborhoods often adopted a defensive posture and sought to use zoning as a bulwark against the spread of social ills. And they associated these ills with the physical features they recognized as common to places in decline. Multifamily housing was one of those features. This led to a wave of downzoning efforts.

Downzoning, or reducing the allowed level of development in an area, was not one national movement with a single set of motivations. It was, however, an identifiable trend that accelerated in the 1970s. An example from Minneapolis is illustrative. The Lowry Hill East neighborhood sits adjacent to downtown Minneapolis. It has long been characterized by apartment buildings interspersed with stately homes, and its population is mostly renters.

In 1975, the Lowry Hill East Neighborhood Association succeeded in getting virtually the entire neighborhood downzoned to R2: a zoning category allowing only single homes and duplexes. The R2 designation was applied to existing apartment buildings as well. According to a neighborhood spokesperson, the hope was "that the properties would, if reconstructed, be redeveloped as single- and two-family homes" (Edwards 2016).

A quote from the neighborhood newsletter, in a series of clippings shared online by independent Minneapolis journalist John Edwards, reveals the hold-the-line mindset of the organizers who pushed for downzoning: "We will not allow our neighborhood to become low quality, high profit, accelerated depreciation tax write-offs for non-caring landlords, not the planned obsolescence slum ripe for more urban renewal cemetary [*sic*] architecture."

By the end of the 20th century, new apartments were prohibited in most American neighborhoods, urban and suburban alike. This included many neighborhoods such as Lowry Hill East that *had* existing apartment buildings still standing.

Lowry Hill East's homeowners had largely won their battle against redevelopment. But as growth returned to Minneapolis in the 21st century, the neighborhood would face a new problem: high housing costs and little room to add new supply.

During the decades of mass suburban flight, the limit on supply imposed by restrictive zoning was not keenly felt in urban housing prices. Housing demand was so meager in the depopulated inner cities of the Midwest and Northeast that much of it sat abandoned.

The story more recently has been very different. Since the 1990s, most large cities' population decline has halted or reversed. Nearly every US city has at least some urban neighborhoods that command a market premium.

In this context, the chickens of prior downzoning efforts come home to roost. According to Laura Foote, executive director of YIMBY Action (we will talk more about YIMBY in Chapter 7), "When economic growth pushes up against the net of bad housing policies, that's when you start to see a crisis as people get pushed down and pushed out."

Today, there are far more neighborhoods in America that are up against the net—that *cannot* grow at all—than those that are allowed to.

Dwell on the implications of that for a minute. "In most places, it is illegal to add housing," sounds outlandish on its face, but it is a literal statement of fact.

In most large cities, the share of residential land subject to single-family zoning ranges between 70% and 90%. In many suburbs, it is even higher. In these places, you cannot add homes, on a net basis. You can perhaps renovate or replace a home on a one-to-one basis, but you cannot turn one home into two, or four, or ten.

These neighborhoods are frozen at their current number of households, no matter how much the surrounding city transforms. No matter how many jobs are created. No matter how desirable the area is or how high rents get. No feedback loop is allowed to operate in which the success of a place manifests in the thickening-up that was common to neighborhoods under the traditional development pattern.

Downzoned and Pushed Out

If there's a place in North America that is the polar opposite of Somerville, Massachusetts, it just might be Victorville, California. Somerville is in verdant New England; Victorville is in the Mojave Desert. Somerville is densely packed; Victorville is spread out. Somerville has the Old World feel of much of the urban Northeast. Victorville is a quintessential Sunbelt suburb: miles and miles of tract homes in shades of beige, accessed by wide arterial roads whose intersections harbor big-box shopping centers. Very little is accessible without driving.

Victorville has no precious natural resources, no native industry. It lacks the mild climate of the Pacific Coast. It's not near fertile farmland. It owes its existence not to any natural advantages but to zoning decisions made decades ago in other communities, including Los Angeles, 84 miles away.

Victorville has one reason to exist: it has undeveloped land. Lots of it. Since 1980, Victorville has grown from a population of 14,000 to nearly 140,000. A bedroom community, it functions as a pressure release valve for the housing demand and high costs of the adjacent urban area.

As a bedroom community, Victorville strains the bounds of practicality. Two-thirds of employed Victorville residents commute more than 25 miles to work. This entails crossing a literal mountain range, either to reach the Inland Empire region, or to go further west to Los Angeles proper. At 39.3 minutes, Victorville has one of the longest average commute times in the nation. For these residents, the high cost of transportation—time, gas, maintenance, insurance—is still outweighed by the relative affordability of homes in Victorville, where the median sale price in August 2023 was $420,000, versus (for just a few examples) $625,000 in Riverside, $715,000 in Chino, and $959,000 in Los Angeles.

In the 1950s and 1960s, greater Los Angeles was a machine for converting orange groves to subdivisions at a staggering rate. During these years, however, incremental development continued apace in Los Angeles proper. LA was already, famously, a car city by this point, and much of what was built were relatively un-photogenic constructions: small, boxy buildings called dingbats, featuring apartments on a second story with car parking underneath.

Younger and faster growing than the old cities of the Northeast, Los Angeles did not experience the kind of urban decline and depopulation common to so many places in this era. But it did experience a backlash to development from established homeowners.

UCLA researcher Shane Phillips has documented the gradual locking down of Los Angeles. In 1960, the city had a zoned capacity of roughly four times its actual population. What was then a city of 2.5 million could have housed 10 million if every residential parcel were to be built to the maximum legal number of housing units. Throughout the 1970s and 1980s, downzoning campaigns were successful in many neighborhoods. By 2010, Los Angeles had a population of 4 million and a zoned capacity of only 4.3 million. In many individual neighborhoods, the population was *equal* to the zoned capacity. There are few to no vacant lots, and no legal form of redevelopment could result in a net gain in housing units.

Los Angeles was locked down. Sites where housing could legally be added had become a scarce resource. And like anything scarce, they exploded in price.

Build and No-Build Zones

Metropolitan Los Angeles today, like essentially all US metro areas, follows a basic pattern. In the majority of neighborhoods, essentially no new housing is built. Within this sea of stasis are small islands of intense development activity.

That activity comes in two forms. At the outermost fringe of the urbanized area, we find areas of mass-production suburban homebuilding. Within the existing cities, we find pockets of dense urban redevelopment, where most homes built are in large apartment buildings.

No-build zones predominate in nearly any region you choose to look at. In Hennepin County, Minnesota, which includes Minneapolis and many of its suburbs, more than 75% of all homes and apartments built in a recent five-year stretch, from 2014 to 2019, are in just 11% of the county's neighborhoods.

In an area experiencing less growth, it's even more lopsided. In Cuyahoga County, Ohio, a region of 1.2 million people that's home to Cleveland, just 21 out of 443 total neighborhoods—under 5%—accounted for 75% of the new homes built.

It cannot be overstated what a radical departure this geography of build and no-build zones is from the historic norm. Constant evolution was a defining characteristic of pre-suburban American cities. New neighborhoods were emerging at the urban fringe, but at the same time existing neighborhoods were undergoing steady change.

Today, there is no such steady change, only a binary choice between stasis or radically transformative change. Within established cities, a handful of neighborhoods where denser and taller development is legally permitted have been assigned the unenviable task of absorbing an entire region's worth of housing demand.

To understand the implications of this picture, imagine a pot with the lid on tight, containing water that has been brought to a vigorous boil. If you crack the lid ever so slightly in one corner, you will release a powerful rush of steam. If, on the other hand, you lift the lid off the entire pot, the steam will be distributed across a much larger area, and it will not escape with nearly as much force.

Allowing development only in small portions of cities concentrates demand and induces large increases in the cost of land in those areas. It all but ensures that the housing that is built in the "build zones" will be expensive and the impact of development disruptive and jarring.

At the risk of too many water metaphors, we can understand the effect of restrictive zoning another way. Consider a wetland: a marsh or swamp. Wetland ecosystems, by nature, have a large capacity to absorb excess water delivered by storms. The water distributes itself through countless tiny channels and is absorbed by vegetation and soils.

If we think of this wetland as a region's housing market, and the water as demand—people who need homes—then what zoning has done is erected an extensive series of dams and diversion channels. The effect of this is to flood certain areas, while others dry up entirely.

These floods are difficult to manage and prevent. Inevitably, much of the natural complexity and resilience of the ecosystem is lost.

In strictly zoned cities, where there is high demand for housing, spillover effects become rampant. If housing cannot be built in neighborhood A for all the people who would like to live in neighborhood A, then some of them will settle for the next-best option nearby. They will potentially "flood" neighborhood B with home seekers who will bid up rents and prices and compete against longtime residents for housing.

These floods may spread until people are priced out of a costly region altogether. A place like Victorville, which exists to house those barely maintaining a foothold in the SoCal housing market, is one consequence. But 84 miles and two mountain ranges away from Los Angeles is by no means the farthest that the spillover effects of its housing shortage can be felt.

In the late 2010s, small cities in the interior West began to experience large housing crises. Stunning run-ups in the cost of homes in places such as Boise, Spokane, and Bozeman are attributable, at least in part, to an influx of Californians, whose dollar goes further outside of California. Home prices in historically affordable Sunbelt metro areas such as Phoenix and Orlando also surged to record highs at the close of the 2010s.

The highest housing costs used to be concentrated in a handful of coastal metropolitan areas. Now, extreme unaffordability has spread like a rash from the coasts into the interior of the country. The spillover effects of no-build zones mean that housing scarcity in the most expensive cities has become the whole country's problem.

The Missing Middle

In Chapter 1, we introduced a thought experiment about a shoe market in which there were only two kinds of shoes being manufactured, both expensive and high-end products. There are basically only two residential products being built at scale in North America today. One is the master-planned suburban subdivision, dominated by single-family homes built by production builders using copy-paste floor plans. The other is large-scale apartment housing, especially the quintessential 5-over-1 building. These are housing monocultures. They are to the mix of housing types found in traditional cities what a tree farm is to a forest.

There is an entire range of small-scale multifamily housing, in between single-family houses and large apartment buildings, that has become a virtual non-entity in new construction. This range includes everything from a duplex or triple-decker to a small walk-up apartment building, nestled on a single urban lot, with perhaps a dozen apartments. Less commonly, it includes arrangements such as cottage courts and pocket neighborhoods: small homes arranged around a shared courtyard or other common space.

Collectively, this set of small-scale multifamily options is now known as the missing middle, a term coined by the planning firm Opticos Design. By broad definitions, missing-middle housing constituted fewer than 10% of the units built in the US in the 2010s.

Not only was the missing middle not missing before 1940; it was ubiquitous. It was the basic residential building block of the American city. It was the triple-deckers of New England, the workingmen's two-flat of Chicago, the brownstones of Brooklyn, and the painted ladies of San Francisco. All of these combined the possibility of small-scale development and homeownership with affordable rental options for those who could not buy their own home. Interspersed with these structures, and sometimes within them, were commercial spaces hosting neighborhood-serving businesses that people could access on foot.

The missing middle became ubiquitous because it is a sweet spot for affordable home construction in cities. When urban land becomes expensive as a neighborhood matures, a missing-middle building allows the cost of that land to be spread across multiple households. At the same time, these buildings can be constructed in roughly the same way as a single-family home, unlike larger apartment buildings, which require more expensive materials and more advanced building and design techniques.

The missing middle thus minimizes the combined cost of land and construction for a wide range of urban contexts. (At very high land prices, larger apartment buildings become the more economically viable option, which is why major cities' downtowns began to fill with multistory apartment buildings by the early 20th century.)

The missing middle has gone missing largely because of zoning. It is uniquely burdened by the one-size-fits-all rules applied to most North American neighborhoods.

One reason for this is that development entails fixed costs, such as those associated with regulatory compliance. These include application fees when petitioning for zoning variances or exceptions; utility hookup fees; transportation impact fees and required studies; and the costs associated with delay in the permitting process, a period during which the developer must maintain control of a piece of property and pay any taxes on it but cannot begin to build. All of these fees and holding costs fall most heavily on a small-scale developer, whereas a large-scale builder can defray them across many more units of housing.

The other reason the missing middle has gone missing is that the different elements of a zoning code tend to interact in complex ways to render development on a piece of land infeasible. By the time you have complied with building setback requirements (distance from the edges of the lot), height restrictions, floor area maximums, and added the mandatory number of parking stalls, there is often not enough room left on the lot to accommodate a viable multi-unit building.

Parking mandates are a particular kiss of death. Almost all cities require somewhere between one and two parking stalls for every residential unit. Enclosed parking is costly to build; surface parking eats up precious land.

Put bluntly, it is all but impossible to build a triplex or fourplex on a standard urban lot if you must also provide four or six off-street parking spaces. The most practical solution is to tuck the parking underneath the residence in a ground-level garage. However, such buildings will run afoul of height limits in the zoning code in many cities.

It is in ways like this that zoning rules out whole categories of useful housing that might otherwise be built.

Did Zoning Cause the Housing Shortage?

It is debatable to what extent an overall shortage of housing can be blamed on zoning. At the national scale, it is hard to make the case. Long-term trends in US homebuilding show a peak in new construction in the 1970s, followed by fluctuations in the rate of new housing starts until the 2008 financial crisis. At the inflection point that is 2008, homebuilding fell by nearly 80% from the pre-recession peak. The recovery since then has been slow: 9.8 million homes began construction nationwide in the 2010s, fewer than in any of the last six decades.

The underbuilding of the 2010s is a huge explanatory factor in recent soaring home prices. It is also one that is obviously not driven by zoning but by larger economic factors. Nothing changed systematically about the zoning of American cities in 2008.

What is undeniable, though, is that zoning constitutes a hard cap on housing availability in a lot of *specific* locations that would otherwise be in very high demand and experience very robust growth. These locations are well-located, desirable neighborhoods in every city, but also in some cases entire cities or even metropolitan areas. It is hard not to conclude that zoning has meaningfully constrained the growth of a region such as greater San Francisco or Boston.

We must reject the notion that one factor is "to blame" for housing shortages or high prices. The problem is complex and multicausal. But any full accounting of the present housing crisis must include a central role for a century of zoning policy.

A decade of low interest rates and other policies driving economy-wide asset inflation would have sent prices higher in regions big and small, centrally located and remote, regardless of America's land use policies. And this is indeed what we have witnessed in the years since 2008. However, these trends have undeniably been exacerbated by uneven patterns of development and underdevelopment and by pervasive spillover demand from locations that are, essentially, closed access. Like the breaching of a dam, these spillovers propel floods of cataclysmic money.

Zoning creates local scarcity, and local scarcity creates spillovers. Zoning makes the overall landscape of housing demand and supply much frothier and spikier than it would otherwise be. And this spikiness is a gift to those who would speculate on real estate.

In an America of broadly distributed incremental growth, we would see less difference in housing costs (either in absolute terms or relative to local incomes) between high-cost and low-cost regions. We would see less such divergence between neighborhoods in the same city. And we would see fewer opportunities for investor money to slosh in and radically transform a neighborhood.

In an America where the bar to entry to produce housing was lower, and where it was legal and feasible to incrementally add to the housing stock of any neighborhood at any time, we would see a housing supply that was more elastic and more responsive to local demand. Under these circumstances it becomes much harder to locally sustain a speculative bubble in rents or real estate prices.

Can We Escape from Zoning Lockdown?

In software engineering, there is a concept called *technical debt*. It refers to the high cost of retrofitting code that has become bloated and complicated over time to make it simpler and more legible. These revisions are put off, sometimes for years, in the face of more pressing deadlines. Stopgap fixes may compound the problem by addressing one issue while creating three more.

Zoning codes are full of technical debt. There are provisions that might have made sense at the time they were enacted but have become vestigial and useless in a different context. There are rules that might make sense in isolation but interact with each other to produce unwanted consequences. Somerville's "illegal city" problem was, in part, a function of technical debt. It is easy to make a zoning code more complicated over time. It is very hard to make it simpler.

In the 21st century, as planners have begun to recognize the inadequacy of legacy zoning for delivering a broad range of housing options, they have struggled to untangle the knot of technical debt. Instead, standard practice has been to work around it.

This can be done by adding additional layers of complexity on top of the base zoning. Many cities have implemented optional sets of standards, called overlay districts, to enable things such as mixed residential and commercial development with fewer parking and other requirements.

In other cities, virtually every new development is a planned unit development, or PUD. This is essentially a custom negotiation with a single developer, allowing flexibility from zoning rules. While the PUD process is useful to large-scale developers working at the subdivision scale, it does nothing to help fill in neighborhoods with missing-middle homes.

The hurdles in the way of widespread and meaningful zoning reform remain daunting. Cities that have attempted comprehensive rewrites of their zoning codes have often run aground on the rocks of both the technical and political complexity of this effort. Zoning defines the contours of a real estate market in which trillions of dollars are invested. There is no way to overhaul it without affecting many powerful interests.

And so we kludge along. Perhaps the answer will be that cities simply stop enforcing code provisions that impede the desperate housing needs of their residents and the ad hoc strategies evolved to meet those needs. If this effective decriminalization approach seems unlikely, note that there is precedent for it. Many if not most cities have provisions on their books that prohibit groups of several unrelated adults from living together. Most already ignore these rules.

Another approach is to take bites of the apple. Zoning can be overhauled one neighborhood at a time, exempting an area from large sections of the existing code in favor of simpler rules developed through an intensive public engagement process.

Or one *aspect* of zoning at a time can be targeted for blanket reform. This latter approach has picked up sudden and startling momentum in the second half of the 2010s, in the form of dozens of cities eliminating two specific policies from their code. Those two policies are mandatory parking minimums and blanket apartment bans (i.e. single-family zoning).

We will talk more in Chapter 7 about that unfolding story, part of a growing political movement and the best chance we have had in decades to perhaps, at last, grant clemency to America's illegal cities.

6

Not in My Backyard

Every drama needs a good villain. In the continuous lineup of local dramas created by America's housing crisis, the vocal opponents of building more housing—often labeled NIMBYs, for "not in my backyard," by their critics—could not have done a better job of casting themselves in the villain role.

Organized political opposition to the building of new housing is a standard feature of local politics. Television shows such as *Parks and Recreation* have dramatized the spectacle of the ugly, contentious public hearing, where local officials find themselves ritually berated by a long line of angry citizens exercising their right to comment. These media representations may be exaggerated for laughs, but they are not as exaggerated as one might think. It is not hard to find accounts of such meetings where jeering crowds have shouted down presenters, or where the public comment record includes everything from open bigotry to personal threats to the comparison of local officials to history's great tyrants.

The public hearing is the most visible part of the development approval process, and so it gets top billing in the theater of local politics. But it is not the most important. For every unit of needed housing that is killed in a dramatic flourish by a planning commission or city council in front of an auditorium of spectators, it is likely that at least a dozen more are simply never conceived.

They are never conceived for the reasons discussed in the preceding chapters. Either housing is simply not allowed on a given lot or it is not allowed in a form that would recoup a builder's costs, resulting in a financially viable project. Part of that calculation includes the risks imposed by community opposition. These risks include delays, lawsuits, costly changes to the project's design, or outright denial of the application. Many would-be builders of housing, especially smaller projects with less room for error, will simply not take the risk.

The real locus of NIMBY power is not in the sound and fury of the public meeting. It's in the fact that organized anti-development constituencies are an important factor in local politics. They are the base of support for the zoning and land-use policies, described in Chapter 5, which have resulted in effective no-build zones in a majority of American neighborhoods.

Housing opponents get candidates elected to office and ordinances passed or modified. They write letters, file lawsuits, and organize protest campaigns. They do not always triumph, but often they set the tone for discussions of growth and development in their communities. "The NIMBYs" are a force to be reckoned with, even if many would not want to be counted among their ranks or would protest such a derogatory labeling of their motivations.

Who Are the NIMBYs?

NIMBYism is fundamentally not an ideology. It is a posture. One can be a NIMBY about many things. It is likely many of us have at one time or another been NIMBYs about something.

The term "not in my backyard" seems to have entered the popular lexicon around 1980 to refer to activists who opposed specific land uses near their homes. The target of NIMBY ire could be anything from an airport to a power plant, a homeless shelter to a prison, a public housing tower to high-end condos. But in all cases, the phrase "not in *my* backyard," with emphasis on the "my," connotes a degree of selfishness and hypocrisy. A NIMBY, by definition, is someone who recognizes that a certain activity is needed by society but wishes it would just be placed *somewhere else*.

In the context of today's housing politics, "NIMBY" has come to simply mean anyone who either opposes a specific project to build homes or opposes policies that would enable more home construction.

As a meaningful descriptor of group identity or shared ideology, this is lacking at best. The motivations for such opposition are tremendously varied.

It's nonetheless in vogue to lay a lot at the feet of the NIMBY. "Why doesn't America build things anymore?" lament pundits in elite publications. A significant piece of the diagnosis is always the same: because meddling NIMBYs won't let us.

Perhaps the most prevalent cultural and media narrative about NIMBYism situates it in a long history of haves and have-nots, in which the haves maintain the exclusivity of their comfortable communities by putting up regulatory walls. Opposition to new housing in one's neighborhood, this narrative holds, is rooted in classism and racism, even when it is veiled under more noble-sounding pretexts.

This narrative is incomplete, but it describes something undoubtedly real. There is an enormous historical record of intentional exclusion practiced by people who are often quite clear about their motivations. In Chapter 5, we already saw how residential zoning addressing the physical form of housing could be a back-door route to de facto class and racial segregation. Protest and direct action have often functioned as front-door routes.

In 1917, the US Supreme Court ruled in *Buchanan v. Worley* that explicit racial zoning was unconstitutional. This led many developers to double down on the practice of inserting covenants into property deeds that restricted non-whites from buying homes. When some managed to slip through the paper walls erected by these deed restrictions, they were often met with violence. Mobs threw rocks, vandalized property, and fire-bombed houses. Instances of such racial terrorism continued after the US Supreme Court struck down racial deed restrictions in *Shelley v. Kraemer* in 1948.

Dedicated low-income housing has always been a particular target of strident political opposition, and this opposition has powerfully shaped where such housing is and is not built. In 1969, the Chicago Housing Authority was successfully sued for racial discrimination, in no small part because 99.4% of its public housing apartments—all but 63—were in majority-Black neighborhoods. Records of public

City Council hearings revealed that the racial intent was explicit. More recently, *The Color of Law* by Richard Rothstein cites a 2005 study that found that three-fourths of all units built with the federal Low Income Housing Tax Credit were placed in neighborhoods with poverty rates of at least 20%.

The walls between have and have-not geographies have in many ways only been built higher. From 1970 to 2012, the share of US households living in mixed-income neighborhoods fell from 65% to 40%, while the share living in very poor or very wealthy neighborhoods more than doubled from 15% to 35%. Community opposition to development that might diversify the economic character of the community no doubt continues to play a part in these outcomes.

Research consistently finds that opposition to new housing is strongest among existing homeowners. Those who have crossed the drawbridge into homeownership benefit financially from policies that pull the bridge up behind them, enhancing the scarcity and thus value of their asset. As of 2018, the owner of the median-valued home in San Jose, California, made $100 per hour in appreciation on the value of their home—far more than San Jose's median salary.

The economist Matthew Rognlie (2015) has conducted research showing that virtually all of the increase in wealth inequality in the United States in the past four decades is accounted for by the increase in the share of capital in housing. And home equity is increasingly concentrated among the wealthy. In the 1990s, a household in the highest income quintile had about five times as much housing equity as one in the middle quintile. By 2010, this difference had nearly doubled to nine times as much housing equity.

"The NIMBYs made $6.9 trillion last year," wrote economist Joe Cortright (2022), referring to estimates of the increase in the total value of existing residential real estate in the US. The conflation between homeowner and NIMBY in the headline is deliberate: if you profit from this system, it implies, you are complicit. You are with the NIMBYs.

This is an affirming narrative for a lot of Americans. Who are the "NIMBYs"? They are the beneficiaries and defenders of a regulatory system that is designed to keep housing scarce and unaffordable and thus to heap financial reward upon those who already own it.

This narrative holds elements of truth, but it is incomplete. It flattens a huge, complex range of individual motivations into a sort of grand arc of history.

Ask the NIMBYs what they want, and you won't find many who confess to motivations rooted in prejudice, segregation, or even personal enrichment. And you'll find very few who self-describe as NIMBYs.

In their book *Neighborhood Defenders*, Katherine Einstein, David Glick, and Maxwell Palmer (2019a) characterize the range of attitudes and priorities espoused by those who participated in a local government process to object to the building of housing. This range is extremely broad, including "aesthetics, affordability, density, diversity, environment, flooding, height/shadows, home values/city finances, neighborhood character, noise, noncompliance, parking, pedestrian impact, privacy, safety, schools, septic/water, [and] traffic."

Einstein and coauthors also point out a dissonance with the term "not in *my* backyard," which carries a built-in connotation of selfishness. Most people whose advocacy could be characterized as NIMBY, they observe, speak not in individualistic but in communitarian terms. These people view themselves, most often, as *neighborhood defenders*. They consider themselves the authentic, democratic voice of the community, protecting it against exploitative outsiders (typically a developer).

A civic spirit, a sense of deep obligation to a community rooted in a physical place, is something that the most ardent NIMBYs share with their most ardent critics. That spirit in itself is admirable. And discomfort or dismay at the prospect of change to a beloved place is not unreasonable.

If anything, the desire for continuity and stability in our environment is deeply human. There is almost certainly something, if it were proposed to be built near your home, that could compel you to be a NIMBY. But there is a spectrum from risk aversion to openness when it comes to change or uncertainty in our living environment. We do not all sit at the same point.

If there are more opponents of change today than in the past, or they are more powerful, it is largely because the incentives to occupy one or the other end of that spectrum have shifted. And that has a lot to do with the systemic changes America's development pattern has undergone.

We have already discussed the tremendous financial experiment that North America underwent in housing beginning in the Great Depression. We have also examined the regulatory experiment in zoning and other land-use controls that evolved in tandem.

Those changes have also both responded to, and helped precipitate, an equally momentous cultural and political transformation. The relationship between the average citizen and the development of their community has been profoundly altered.

If you want to understand the NIMBY, a good thing to examine is what the past century has done to the incentives to *not* be a NIMBY.

How the Suburban Experiment Created the NIMBY

Cities are complex adaptive systems. A community that is healthy, which means it is growing and evolving, is naturally going to experience social tension over the speed and the nature of that change. What we need is for this to be a productive tension.

There will always be pressure for a community to alter or modernize itself in response to new social and economic stressors. There will also be people in the community who have a small-c conservative outlook, who are interested in the preservation of tradition and in the character of a place that many residents have invested in. It's natural and healthy for a community to have this range of voices. Yin and yang.

The impulse to control what your neighbors do with their property is not new. There can be no doubt that, as long as humans have lived in proximity to one another, conflicts over land use have occurred. But the solution would most often have been interpersonal. Most governments were limited in either their ability or willingness to get involved.

In the rapidly changing, industrializing cities of the late 19th century, this meant that neighborhoods were often unrecognizable after 20 or 30 years. The pace of change in cities was so rapid and the process so chaotic that even well-to-do neighborhoods were generally not immune from destabilizing transformation.

These transformations were uncomfortable, and the rich often sought to isolate themselves from the effects, buying homes in affluent residential enclaves. But the average citizen also had a direct positive stake in growth and development, because it was linked to their quality of life in ways that are far less direct and obvious today.

In the traditional development pattern, because the city's capacity to take on debt was relatively limited, public, and private investment tended to occur in a tight feedback loop. And private investment would precede public investment. When frontier settlements were platted in the 19th-century United States, it was a speculative gamble paid for with private money, often that of a railroad. The railroad would acquire land along its intended route, build a station, and lay out the basic elements of a town surrounding it.

From there, public services were gradually added as the wealth produced by a growing number of residents came to support them. A fire brigade. Law enforcement. Water and waste management systems. Improved streets and public infrastructure. Later came schools, libraries, parks, and cultural amenities.

This meant that every citizen had at least some direct stake in the community's growth. And they behaved accordingly. When a row of storefronts would arise, all aligned with each other to create a continuous front facade framing a public street, it wasn't because any zoning code mandated this arrangement. It was because the owner of each store understood that by contributing to the ensemble, their own business would benefit. The whole of the place they were building would be greater than the sum of its parts.

In today's cities, growth proceeds very differently. Instead of private wealth leading, it is the collective public investment that leads. Governments frequently invest millions of dollars, or make long-term maintenance commitments, before any taxable private investment has been made.

In the best-case scenario for a local government, a developer will agree to pay for the public infrastructure—all the roads, streets, curbs, sidewalks, pipes, pumps, valves, and meters—and do so completely at their own expense. The developer takes the first life cycle risk; the city then assumes the ongoing maintenance liability.

On the first day that anyone lives in such a neighborhood, the full suite of amenities that the new residents expect is already present. You already have your water and sewer, your police and fire service, your schools, your parks, and your public library. This is, indeed, a central piece of the promise of "planning for permanence" articulated by J.C. Nichols.

What is gained, then, from the addition of new neighbors? The city gains additional tax base to help it sustain those services into the future, but it also incurs additional costs in providing infrastructure and services for new residents. The experience of most communities under the suburban development pattern has been that new development does not cover its costs but in fact worsens the city's financial position over time.

This need not be true; growth can be financially productive. It is *most* likely to be so when new housing is placed in existing neighborhoods already served by municipal infrastructure. But it is no longer obvious to many citizens that this will be the case. The feedback loops between growth and improved public services are far less direct than in the past.

Incentives in the Driving City

Another factor that has increased the incentive to be a NIMBY is that development in the suburban era became mainly automobile oriented. With the rise of Euclidean zoning, cities were increasingly divided into mutually exclusive, single-use zones. No longer are the businesses you patronize for everyday needs likely to be in your building or on your block. The much more typical experience is that you get in your car and drive to them, probably leaving your neighborhood in the process.

You benefit from commercial and recreational amenities in your city. You want efficient mobility so you can access those amenities. You have an interest in residential development, too, because those residents will be customers for businesses that you can then patronize. If enough people move in, your town may finally get that Trader Joe's store you've been hoping for.

But your interests are maximized if all those new people move into neighborhoods other than your own. If you wanted the store to be in your own neighborhood so that you could walk to it, and if its customer base also needed to be in walking distance, you might feel very differently about new neighbors.

In your own neighborhood, new neighbors mean new cars. Cars themselves take up a lot of space, and are capable of making even relatively low-density places feel crowded. They pose safety risks to people who walk. They are loud. As parking economist Donald Shoup (2019) has observed, a primary objective of modern zoning is to limit the density of people in order to limit the density of cars.

An observation by Vince Graham, a developer of new neighborhoods in South Carolina that emulate traditional, walkable forms, perhaps best captures the cultural shift embedded in the rise of autocentric suburbia. "When you sell community and connectedness, every new home enhances that asset. When you sell privacy and exclusivity, every new home is a degradation of that asset" (Herriges 2016). Today, more so than any time in our past, the marketing brochure for most desirable neighborhoods emphasizes their privacy and exclusivity.

In the past, even those temperamentally inclined to dislike change, or crowds, or density, had mixed incentives, because their well-being also depended on the presence of a growing mass of neighbors in obvious ways. The suburban experiment largely does away with these mixed incentives. And when there are few powerful incentives *not* to be a NIMBY, a small number of NIMBYs can exercise outsized influence.

They are aided in this quest by local planning systems that have come to be characterized by an increased number of veto points on development. These systems, by design, amplify the power of well-organized citizen groups to block change.

The Outsized Power of No

The 1960s and 1970s brought a surge of grassroots activism to American cities. For two decades, historic neighborhoods had been ravaged by top-down schemes, from urban renewal redevelopment projects to freeway construction that wiped entire neighborhoods off the map. This era was also the dawn of the environmental movement and saw pitched battles between citizen activists and industrial polluters.

The inevitable and justified backlash against top-down power led to a surge in citizen power. Idealistic young activists fought for, and won, important legal and procedural checks on the powerful forces that menaced their communities. These ranged from public consultation requirements in local planning to laws that empower citizens to sue their government over plans that might cause undisclosed environmental harm. Today, however, these laws, such as the California Environmental Quality Act (CEQA), are frequently used to litigate and delay private-sector housing development, along with local laws that might allow more or denser development.

In the final decades of the 20th century, the overall trend was that cities greatly increased the number of procedural requirements and veto points affecting housing construction. These include things such as long-range planning requirements, traffic studies, and historic preservation and design review panels. Many of these mechanisms can be exploited by small groups of opponents. They need not always win: often, the ability to delay a project's completion is enough to deter a developer or force concessions, usually in the form of a smaller building with fewer homes.

These legal and procedural hurdles were largely developed in a genuine backlash against unaccountable and destructive top-down decisions. They often give a hearing to issues of genuine public concern. But their combined effect is also to create a pronounced asymmetry, in which there are many opportunities for "no" to prevail over "yes" in the planning process.

Relatively few people are committed opponents of development. In fact, in surveys, majorities of Americans typically indicate that they approve of measures to create more housing in their own communities.

A lot more people are, shall we say, NIMBY curious, or NIMBY sympathetic. They don't experience the benefits of additional housing in their community in a direct or obvious way, but they can readily put a finger on the downsides.

In all politics, but certainly in local politics, it is possible for well-organized minorities to wield extremely disproportionate power. Local elections are often decided by dozens, not thousands, of votes. Turnout in these elections can be as low as single-digit percentages. And the vast majority of people are never going to email their council member about housing reforms or set foot in a public hearing.

Public hearings about development are reliably dominated by opponents. An activated and motivated minority can create the impression of overwhelming community consensus where there is no such consensus. This is exacerbated by the nature of development itself.

Development projects, by nature, have diffuse benefits and concentrated harms. The harms fall overwhelmingly on the immediate neighbors, who may experience construction noise and traffic, the loss of greenery or sunlight, and increased competition over parking. The beneficiaries are those who will live in the new housing or who will at least experience less competition for a limited supply of homes. These beneficiaries are farther away, and many are yet hypothetical.

People don't tend to devote time and energy to advocating for things that they modestly support, or support in principle. They devote time and energy when it affects them powerfully. It is the minority of opponents of development, not the majority of passive beneficiaries, who fit this description.

The structure of local governments' public participation process tends to further distort who is seen and heard. Most cities, by some combination of custom and legal requirement, conduct formal hearings to consider new development. These tend to happen on weekday evenings, when people with child care responsibilities or work schedules other than nine-to-five are not easily able to attend.

Studies of who the public is at these meetings find that it is unrepresentative of the actual public in a series of very consistent ways. The people who attend and speak are, on average, older, whiter, and wealthier than the general population. Retirees are greatly overrepresented. But the most important distinction is that the people who participate in public input are overwhelmingly homeowners, not renters.

A team of Boston University researchers compiled a database of 3,327 public comments made at planning and zoning board meetings in 97 Massachusetts cities and towns. They found that 63% of all comments were in opposition to proposed housing development, while only about 14.6% were in support (Einstein, Palmer, and Glick 2019b).

Cities within a larger metropolitan area face a classic collective action problem with regard to housing. Their residents suffer from high prices and scarce options caused by regional housing shortages. But no one city can do much unilaterally to alleviate the shortage. On the contrary, any individual city that zones for additional housing will reap some obvious downsides. There will be more traffic. And residents are expensive where the public purse is concerned, requiring a lot more services, such as schools, than business or industry requires.

On top of all this, local officials face a loud and mobilized constituency that will campaign for their removal if they push for housing policies unpopular with that group, versus a much more diffuse and less mobilized constituency on the other side of things.

It is no wonder that so many local officials, especially in bedroom communities, embrace the policies favored by opponents of new housing.

Homevoters versus the Growth Machine (Spoiler: They Both Win)

It would be too simplistic to suggest there is no countervailing force at work here. There is: it's just that the status quo of growth politics ends up being a compromise largely acceptable to many interest groups—all except those who need housing to be cheaper.

For decades, two theories have dominated the academic study of how local political power operates. One theory, associated with the political scientist William Fischel (2005), is the "homevoter hypothesis." Fischel argues that homeowners whose primary interest is in maintaining their property values are a powerful and often dominant interest group in city politics.

The other theory, associated with sociologist Harvey Molotch, is that of the "growth machine." Molotch wrote in 1988 that "virtually all U.S. cities are dominated by a small, parochial elite whose members have business or professional interests that are linked to local development and growth. These elites use public authority and private power as a means to stimulate economic development and thus enhance their own local business interests" (Molotch 1988).

A coalition resembling Molotch's growth machine wields significant political power in many cities large and small. Real estate developers are often major campaign donors. Money buys influence, but there is also a more basic convergence of interests. City officials want a tax base to fund the services they provide. Developers create that tax base.

Most "neighborhood defender" development opponents identify something like the growth machine as their bête noire. "Citizens versus developers" is the narrative of choice of many, perhaps most, of the NIMBY contingent.

What is not true is that the interests of the growth machine stand in straightforward opposition to the interests of homeowners. These are both powerful constituencies, and the system we have is basically a compromise that works for both of them. If it didn't, it probably wouldn't endure.

To be clear, homevoters and growth advocates have genuine, sincere disagreements and fight bitterly over specific projects. It's just that the system as a whole ends up basically acceptable to both sets of interests.

The big development interests get the ability to build at large scales in specific, limited contexts: suburban subdivisions and large-scale urban infill in the minority of places where it is allowed. They get a land-use regime that, as we discussed in Chapter 5, provides ample opportunity for speculation and windfall gains. They also get an often convoluted regulatory system in which they have an advantage as insiders.

Entrenched developers don't need or necessarily want to maximize housing production region-wide; if anything, the resulting abundance and competition would cut into their profit margins. The developers most likely to be part of a politically connected growth machine occupy a privileged position as insiders in a sector with substantial barriers to entry.

The homevoters get their own neighborhoods mostly insulated from change (though the most ideological opponents of development in general may end up disappointed). They get a substantial amount of input and deference in the political process. And overall housing scarcity means that they get to reap the benefits of home value appreciation, as surely as land speculators in the real estate industry.

What we have is a status quo that allows virtually every politically influential interest group to benefit and profit. This includes homeowners and real estate interests. It includes local governments. It includes essentially everyone except renters (especially aspiring home buyers) and the poor.

The New Battle over "Local Control"

The spread of acute housing unaffordability in the 2010s and early 2020s has brought these power imbalances under great scrutiny. A growing chorus of pundits and policy analysts call for reforming local planning to curb the power of the NIMBY.

The contest over who should get to set the terms of land use in America's cities is often framed as a choice between, on one side, local control and, on the other side, the preemptive use of state (or federal) authority to override local control for the greater good. A 2022 *Atlantic* article by Jerusalem Demsas, titled "Community Input is Bad, Actually," makes the case that a local veto over things such as affordable housing and clean energy infrastructure amounts to giving an unrepresentative minority the ability to hold basic societal needs hostage and that the answer is to move much of this decision-making to the state level (Demsas 2022).

People on the other side of the argument also use the language of "local control": opponents of development will often tell you that is exactly what they are fighting for. Many explicitly believe that groups of local residents or property owners ought to have an effective veto over what is built in their neighborhoods.

Opposition to new housing is typically local and situational. But a natural response to the heightened stakes has been the arrival of an organized, ideological "NIMBYism" on a much larger scale than the individual neighborhood. There are now advocacy groups whose purpose is explicitly to defend single-family zoning, strict development restrictions, and the "planning for permanence" systems of land-use regulation that have been dominant since the 1930s.

If there's an avatar for such groups, it's Livable California. The group's founder, Susan Kirsch, is a 40-year homeowner in Marin County, an affluent suburban region of San Francisco. In a 2022 *New York Times* profile (Dougherty 2022), Kirsch, who likes to quote from E.F. Schumacher's *Small Is Beautiful* (2010), describes the foundations of her advocacy. She uses language such as "self-reliance and self-resiliency" and the importance of "being able to have efficacy in your own life."

"It feels like huge forces conspiring to take away control from people at the lowest level at which they live," Kirsch says of the drive for statewide land-use reforms in California.

The idea of local local control is central to the politics of anti-development activists such as Kirsch. They argue that a community that does not wish to grow in population should be able to choose not to grow, by choosing not to permit new housing. If this is the democratic will of existing residents, then so be it.

Marin County is a poster child for the devastating endgame of this approach. It closed most of its land off to development in the 1960s. Since 1970, the population has grown by only 24%; in the same period of time, the San Francisco Bay Area has grown by 68%. Marin County's median home sale price in May 2022 was $1.65 million. The rental vacancy rate is the lowest in the Bay Area at 1.8%.

Most of the workforce (in Marin's bedroom suburbs this includes many domestic workers, gardeners, and childcare providers) must commute in from elsewhere. Very few children raised in Marin County can afford to live in Marin County as adults. It raises the question of what all of this does for "efficacy in your own life."

Many in Kirsch's generation are sitting atop a mountain of equity in their homes, buoyed by a system of market supports in the form of government-backed mortgages and postwar inducements for suburban homebuilding. Homes that could be bought for $100,000 in the 1970s were worth $2 million by 2022. Thanks to a state law passed in

1978 that caps annual property tax increases, Proposition 13, longtime homeowners are paying taxes on only a fraction of that value.

Ultimately, Kirsch and her ilk are selling a deeply impoverished vision of "efficacy in your own life," one that only applies if the thing you happen to want in your own life is to block change in your neighborhood. What they might characterize as local democracy is better described as "vetocracy": rule by the voices of "no."

Shouldn't a community have the right to say no to unwanted change? Buried in the premise of the question is that refusing change is an option. But that's not the case: change is inevitable. A community that has lost all affordable starter housing already *has* changed irreversibly. It is only the buildings that have not.

Cities must be living, evolving, complex things (Taleb 2014a, 2014b). Preserving the building stock, so that a neighborhood *looks* the same after 20 or 30 or 40 years, is not protective of the community. Too often, preservation, to paraphrase Jane Jacobs, is just taxidermy (Jacobs 1992).

Reclaiming the Banner of Community Empowerment

The Susan Kirsches of the world claim that a local veto over development represents "local control"; their critics claim that we have an excess of local control that is blocking needed housing and must be reined in. Neither group is right.

There may be an excess of veto points in local planning. But the suburban experiment has actually left communities with little meaningful control over the shape of development.

Our communities are fed a standardized set of products, both residential and commercial, that banks know how to finance and developers know how to produce. The form that development takes is largely determined not by local needs or wants but by templates produced for efficient scaling and replicability. The pace at which developers build is influenced as much by macroeconomic cycles as by local housing needs. Local, small-scale developers who might operate according to different priorities are the first to be shut out by veto points, regulatory delay, and NIMBY obstruction.

When residents object to being fed the thin gruel of the development monoculture—chain stores, subdivisions, and 5-over-1s—it does not mean that they retake control over their community. Rather, they surrender that control to the ravages of macroeconomic forces that will sooner or later price out their less affluent neighbors and their own children.

Who is empowered by this system?

Community power can look like voting on things. But it can also look like building things, literally or proverbially.

One current measure of local control is how much the community, through its representatives, can influence or restrict the development process. A different measure concerns a different sort of local agency: How much power do you have to meaningfully alter the place in which you live? Can you build something incremental and innovative in a bid to meet yours and your neighbors' needs?

An affirmative vision of local empowerment would include not just public meetings, comment forms, and consultation but also the freedom to build.

Top-down power may be a useful tool in securing that freedom. The collective action problem faced by local governments is very real: coordination may be required to better align the incentives of multiple cities in a region. This power should be thought of less as a set of mandates than as a set of guardrails. Higher levels of government should always exist in service to local and immediate needs. There is a case that states have a role in saving cities from themselves.

The wrong response is to simply move as much authority over local land use as possible to the state level. This will fail to resolve the basic contradictions that have so empowered NIMBYs in the first place. And the lack of local feedback shaping development choices will sooner or later create its own problems.

The anti-localist crowd of pundits tends to miss this point. Some even argue that NIMBYism was a societally beneficial force a half century ago, when the things the NIMBYs were fighting were freeway expansions through urban neighborhoods. Today, because the NIMBYs are fighting the wrong fights, we must take away the tool kit of citizen power. Unexamined in this line of argument is how we are supposed to feel assured that, going forward, governments will continue to have the right priorities at heart and that we will not need NIMBYism back at some point in the future.

NIMBYism and the problems we can lay at its feet are not the result of an excess of localism. If anything, they are manifestations of an excess of centralization and the disempowering of people to make productive change in their own backyards.

The stewardship of communities by the people who live in them and experience them every day is essential. However, we need to rethink what meaningful local stewardship looks like. Genuinely empowering a community to shape its future ought to mean something far deeper than merely giving its most disgruntled members a protest veto over unwanted change. To the extent that local control is the mantra of the NIMBY, they are waving a banner that does not belong to them, and it is time to take it back.

7

Yes! In My Backyard

The scene: a city council hearing in [your city's name here], circa 2017. On the agenda is a proposal by a private developer to build apartments on the former site of a couple of low-slung office buildings at the edge of a neighborhood of mostly detached houses.

The public comment period begins. One by one, aggrieved neighbors step to the podium to denounce the project in the usual terms. It will exacerbate traffic and parking issues. It will invite crime. It will be ugly, too large, too dense. It is incompatible with the quiet character of the residential neighborhood. These complaints have been heard at thousands of similar public hearings around North America.

What is unusual, though, is that dozens of people also take the podium to speak in favor of the project. Most are young, in their 20s or 30s. Most are locals, but they do not have any connection to the developer or the landowner. Nor do they have any intention of living in the new building. They are simply there because they feel new housing is important to stand up for, and they believe that building more of it will result in greater options and affordability.

As we discussed in the previous chapter, there is a basic asymmetry to the politics of development. The harms are concentrated, felt largely by immediate neighbors, while the benefits are diffuse. As a result, public input around new construction usually consists of overwhelming opposition and tepid, if any, support.

Yet, increasingly, cities in North America are home to well-organized advocacy groups in favor of both individual proposals to develop housing and regulatory changes that will make it easier to build homes. These groups use a variety of labels but generally fall under the umbrella of the "yes in my backyard," or YIMBY, movement. The term is in deliberate contrast to NIMBY.

The YIMBY movement has helped spark a dramatic shift in the politics of housing in the US and Canada. In less than a decade, dozens of cities have rolled back basic land-use restrictions that had gone more or less unchallenged for half a century. This ongoing paradigm shift cannot be laid entirely at the feet of YIMBY activists. But there is no question that YIMBY has helped catapult the issue into the public consciousness.

Two policies in particular, exclusive single-family zoning and mandatory parking minimums, are now on the chopping block in a rapidly growing number of cities and towns. Dozens of major US and Canadian cities have ended one or both policies in the years since 2017. This appears to be the start of the largest era of change in American urban land-use policy in half a century. Hopefully it will not be the end.

The Start of a Movement

It seems obvious in hindsight: YIMBY could only have come from California.

Many parts of the United States have high housing costs. Many cities have strict zoning. Many cities have lengthy and uncertain approval processes before new housing can be built. But it is coastal California where every problem with housing in North America is dialed up to 11.

In some respects, the San Francisco Bay Area was the most economically successful region of the United States in the 2010s. It boasted the highest average wage, the lowest unemployment, and the largest growth industry. Silicon Valley was the economic juggernaut in the 2010s that the Detroit auto industry had been a century prior.

However, one thing was vastly different. In the 1910s, Detroit was a boomtown. It more than doubled its population between 1910 and 1920, as workers flocked to the region to take advantage of the auto manufacturing boom and all the secondary jobs and industries spun off from it. In the 2010s, by contrast, metropolitan San Francisco was merely the 26th fastest growing US region, and adjacent San Jose was 29th.

The metropolitan areas experiencing rapid population growth during the same time frame included places such as Dallas, Phoenix, and Orlando. In all of them, prevailing wages are much lower than San Francisco's—but so are housing costs.

This represents a striking reversal of a historic norm. In the past, workers, on net, migrated from lower-wage areas to higher-wage areas in pursuit of opportunity. Today, the places in America that are growing the fastest are not the places that offer the most opportunity or upward mobility. They are simply places where housing is not exorbitantly expensive.

It is hard to interpret the anemic growth of the San Francisco Bay Area without the context of a severe housing shortage. From 2010 to 2016, San Francisco permitted only one new unit of housing for every 13 new jobs. Suburban San Mateo County added one housing unit per 17 jobs. In Santa Clara County, the heart of Silicon Valley, the ratio was one to eight.

California cities subject new housing to some of the longest delays and the greatest regulatory hurdles in the nation. The median housing-related project in San Francisco in 2022 took 620 days to receive its permits. Building a duplex in Sunnyvale could require $196,000 in fees to support city parks. A rezoning petition in Huntington Beach will cost you $113,000.

Underbuilding, delay, red tape. This combination of factors, on top of a nationwide surge in home prices, has led to truly eye-popping housing costs in California. While the national home price to median household income ratio hovered around 4:1 in the early 2020s, in both San Francisco and Los Angeles it approached 10:1. California has experienced a vast exodus of hundreds of thousands of blue-collar workers who cannot bear the state's cost of living.

In the years that followed the financial crisis of 2008, all the conditions were in place for the emergence of a renters' backlash over housing costs. Mortgage lending rules got tighter, and along with a surge in foreclosures, the US homeownership rate fell from a pre-recession peak of 69% to a low of 63% in 2016. The early 2010s saw a lot of new renters and more high-income renters than ever before. This coincided with historically low rates of housing construction. Virtually no new project could obtain financing in the deepest recession years.

The intense upward pressure on cost of living was felt earliest in America's most expensive cities: coastal hubs of high-tech and other white-collar employment such as San Francisco, Seattle, New York, Boston, and Washington, DC.

Housing affordability had long been a crisis for the poor, but now the pain was being felt by a large segment of the middle class. And this group had excess time and energy to spend on activism. A young, impatient, frustrated group of largely middle-class renters looked at the housing status quo and decided it was time to flip the table.

In San Francisco, high school math teacher Sonja Trauss founded the Bay Area Renters Federation (BARF) in 2014. From the outset, SF BARF attracted attention with the confrontational, irreverent attitude you might expect from a group with the perverse conviction that any publicity is good publicity. (Enough such conviction to name itself BARF, anyway.) SF BARF members shouted over opponents at public meetings. They called people NIMBYs. They called people segregationists. They posted crude memes and started Twitter wars. They pointed out the market value of homes owned by prominent nonprofit and neighborhood leaders who opposed new development. They made enemies, drew publicity, and forced local media to cover their issues.

Affiliated groups in San Francisco and elsewhere were soon using the term "yes in my backyard" to describe their advocacy. Similar groups arose in cities around the US and Canada. Most were not as brash as SF BARF. Some of these groups chose not to use the YIMBY label, in part to distance themselves from the antagonistic San Francisco approach and court more constructive relationships with hesitant allies. A pro-housing group formed in Minneapolis chose the name Neighbors for More Neighbors. A sampling of other groups includes Open New York, East Bay For Everyone, Abundant Housing Los Angeles, and A Better Cambridge. Advocates experimented with rhetoric and framings. What unified them was an insistence that abundant housing was the answer to unaffordability and that the first step to abundant housing was to make more of it legal to build.

Supporting development proposals on a project-by-project basis was never going to be sustainable. By the second half of the 2010s, YIMBY groups were more organized, better funded, and had largely turned their attention to lobbying for legislation at both the local and state levels.

In city after city, advocates drew attention to the ways that zoning erects invisible walls around neighborhoods, preventing the creation of new homes and keeping desirable neighborhoods homogenously affluent and exclusive. Major cities began to revisit the basic assumptions embedded in these codes.

Two basic approaches to upzoning have been pursued by American cities: blanket and targeted. Some cities have done both simultaneously.

The blanket approach takes aim at the apartment bans that are ubiquitous across most neighborhoods. It aims to broadly or universally allow missing-middle housing, often up to a three- or four-plex, on regular home lots.

The targeted approach identifies select areas for significantly denser development than what was previously allowed. This typically means 5-over-1s and similar apartment buildings. These are often around public transit stations or in formerly commercial and industrial districts.

The first large US city to embrace blanket upzoning was Minneapolis. In 2018, the city passed a revised comprehensive plan called Minneapolis 2040. (A comprehensive plan is a document outlining a city's policy and planning priorities. It serves as a road map for local laws and regulations.) The hallmark feature of Minneapolis 2040 was the citywide elimination of single-family zoning, in favor of allowing up to a triplex on nearly every residential lot.

The battle lines of public debate around the Minneapolis 2040 plan were strongly influenced by the YIMBY movement, and in particular by the local organization Neighbors for More Neighbors. The group made yard signs, hosted campaign events, spoke with planners and public officials, and brought a large and diverse contingent of advocates to public hearings to demonstrate broad-based support in the community for zoning changes and additional housing options.

The Minneapolis 2040 plan also implemented targeted upzoning of transit corridors to allow larger apartment buildings, and it abolished mandatory parking requirements citywide. In these things, Minneapolis was not the first, but it was part of a growing wave.

As of this writing in 2023, Minneapolis has been joined in abolishing single-family zoning by cities as diverse as Charlotte, North Carolina, and Arlington, Virginia; and in Canada, Toronto and Edmonton. This is far from an exhaustive list. Parking mandates, arguably the single biggest obstacle to building affordable housing on small urban lots, were first eliminated in Buffalo and Hartford in 2017, followed by Minneapolis, San Francisco, Sacramento, Austin, and dozens more of US and Canadian cities large and small.

YIMBY-sympathetic legislators, with grassroots support, have also pursued and passed statewide legislation. In a legal sense, cities in the US derive their zoning authority from state governments: state law can thus override specific aspects of local zoning. The intent of going to the state level is to overcome the collective action problem discussed in Chapter 6, in which individual cities lack a political incentive to allow more housing unilaterally. These statewide efforts are controversial for their co-optation of a traditionally local domain of policymaking—land-use rules—but the overriding sense of crisis around housing has built popular support for them.

State preemption has been predominantly but not exclusively a West Coast trend thus far. In 2019, Oregon passed a law requiring most cities (with some caveats around population size) to end their single-family zoning and allow two to four units on a lot. California legislators rejected a series of efforts to do something similar, before ultimately passing Senate Bill 9 (SB 9) in 2021, which allows most California homeowners to subdivide their lots and to build up to four units. Washington State joined this club in 2023, and California and Oregon banned parking mandates near public transit lines in the same year. Outside the West Coast, Montana and Maine have also eliminated single-family zoning at the state level.

Particularly in California, YIMBY legislators have also taken aim at the veto points and opportunities for delay built into the permitting process. Senate Bill 35 (SB 35), passed in 2017, created a series of streamlining procedures for housing projects that include a minimum percentage of low-income units. If these projects are otherwise compliant with the objective requirements of local zoning, cities must approve them within 60 days. They cannot require these projects to meet subjective criteria applied at the discretion of elected officials. New legislation promises to expand on these streamlining efforts and apply them to more projects in more places.

One Neat Trick

The YIMBY prescription for housing-starved cities is a simple one, delivered with all the subtlety of a car alarm. As *New York Times* writer Conor Dougherty summarized the YIMBY policy agenda in 2020: "Build build build build build build build build build build build build build build" (Dougherty 2020).

The touchstone phrase for many YIMBY groups is *abundant housing*. Around that limited but insistent vision, it has been possible to build coalitions that are remarkably diverse and bipartisan. When Oregon passed a statewide law in 2019 requiring most cities to allow fourplexes on single-family lots, the Sightline Institute's Michael Andersen described the coalition that supported the law as follows (Andersen 2019):

> *On the other side were AARP of Oregon, which said middle housing makes it easier to age in place; The Street Trust, a transportation group that argued HB 2001 would let more people live near good transit and walkable neighborhoods; 1000 Friends of Oregon, which said the law would advance the state's long fight against exclusionary zoning; Pablo Alvarez of Lane County NAACP, who said the bill would start to undo some of the ways racism has undermined housing affordability for all; Sunrise PDX, which called energy-efficient housing an essential way to fight climate change; and Portland Public Schools, which described the bill as a long-term way to reduce school segregation.*

Oregon's zoning reform law won two-thirds of both the Democratic and Republican caucuses in the House, and passed the Senate by a 17-9 vote, including 14 of 18 Democrats and three of eight Republicans. The bill's sponsor was a Portland Democrat, but a small-town Republican, Jack Zika of Redmond, was one of its chief advocates.

The experience of Montana further belies the notion that zoning reform is either a liberal preoccupation or a West Coast one. In Montana, a bipartisan coalition for statewide abolition of single-family zoning leaned not only on arguments about private property rights and individual autonomy but also on disdain for California, always a winning issue in the interior West. The Frontier Institute, a think tank focused on limited government, ran a campaign in Montana warning that "California-style zoning" would cause the state's cherished rural lands to be gobbled up by subdivisions of single-family tract homes.

These broad and non-partisan coalitions reflect broad agreement that the zoning status quo is broken. Different political actors may reach that conclusion from strikingly different directions and in line with their own priorities.

The key to this boundary-breaking appeal is YIMBY's narrow, "one neat trick" approach to advocacy. The movement invites those who may disagree utterly about a host of political issues to make common cause around the single issue of more housing. *Build build build.*

Does "Build Build Build" Offer an Escape from the Housing Crisis?

The rise of YIMBY has had a seismic effect on the political and legislative landscape surrounding housing in barely a decade. But to what end? The jury is still out on which, if any, of the reforms that have been passed with YIMBY support will lead to a lasting sea change in housing production or, ultimately, in rents.

"Build a lot more housing, and more people will be able to obtain and afford housing that meets their needs." For this vision to bear fruit, multiple things need to be true.

1. A sufficient surge in housing construction will cause rents to fall.
2. YIMBY policies will actually lead to a sufficient surge in housing construction.

The evidence for (1) is currently stronger than the evidence for (2).

We can further break up question (1). Most people have concerns about housing affordability not just in the abstract but in particular: How will this affect a neighborhood or community that I care about? Will the people *I* know who are suffering from housing precarity see relief?

We can thus break up the question as follows:

(1a) A sufficient surge in housing construction will cause rents to fall.
(1b) It will cause rents to fall in a way that is broadly fair and reaches the people who are now in significant hardship or need.

A lot of people's support for YIMBY policy priorities is going to be contingent on (1b), not just (1a).

For many, YIMBY advocacy raises eyebrows because the most immediate and obvious beneficiaries are not charitable institutions but for-profit developers. Homeless shelters, dedicated low-income housing, addiction treatment programs: these things have always had their champions, even if those champions have often been outnumbered and shouted down by angry would-be neighbors. But a campaign for "abundant housing" often means in practice that the most visible result on the ground will be the building of rather expensive new apartments, which those suffering the most from high rents and scarcity are unlikely to live in. This elicits understandable skepticism: *What is carrying water for luxury developers supposed to do for people struggling to make rent?*

It's worth trying to understand the intuitive case for YIMBY, so we shall do so before examining where it may fall short.

Big YIMBY Question #1: (How) Does Supply Matter?

The standard YIMBY answer is that enabling more supply—*any* sort of supply—will have a ripple effect throughout the market that ultimately reduces the upward pressure on rents. Abundance, once things sort out, means more and better choices for everyone seeking housing.

To borrow an analogy first created by Seattle's Sightline Institute, imagine a giant game of musical chairs. This is the children's party game where participants dance in a circle in a room where there are slightly more people than chairs for them to sit in. When the music stops playing, everybody runs to claim a chair. Those who end up chair-less are out of the game.

When you add a chair to a game of musical chairs, in theory, no one is made worse off. Every participant in the game has better prospects than before. Perhaps even more so if the new chair is especially luxurious.

It is of course easy to stretch a metaphor too far. But the basic insight being expressed here is that the housing market is interconnected. Building a new home that I can occupy frees up options for you, and building a new home that you can occupy frees up options for me, in indirect ways that neither of us may perceive. Let's elaborate on what that indirect chain of causation looks like.

Housing as Six Degrees of Separation

Everyone seeking a home has their own unique set of selection criteria, acceptable options, and trade-offs. A family might need three bedrooms, while a single young professional would rather have a studio apartment close to transit. For some people, a detached home is a viable substitute for an apartment or condo; for others, it isn't. Different people will consider different neighborhoods.

It is not intuitive, therefore, that one should care about "supply" in a blanket sense. If you need an apartment in Brooklyn, and your budget is $1,900 per month, a new complex of $2,700 apartments in Jersey City does not appear to do anything to meet your needs.

Consider, though, the person who *does* rent that new apartment in Jersey City. They moved from somewhere: perhaps the Lower East Side of Manhattan, where they had been occupying a $1,800 studio. That studio was soon rented to a divorcée, whose ex-wife sold their house in Queens and moved in with her sister upstate. The house in Queens was purchased by an investor and rented to a group of roommates, one of whom, by coincidence, recently vacated a $1,900 apartment in Bedford-Stuyvesant, Brooklyn.

This thought experiment, reminiscent of the "six degrees of separation" theory (or the party game Six Degrees of Kevin Bacon), illustrates the ways in which others' housing decisions are intertwined with ours in ways we cannot easily map out or predict. This interconnection, indeed, is the hallmark of a complex system.

The succession of hypothetical moves described above is what housing researchers call a "migration chain," and recent studies in the US and Finland have used postal change-of-address data to track and construct such chains of building-to-building moves. What they find is that even when a high-end new apartment is built, within a few "links" of the chain are comparatively inexpensive homes that have been vacated elsewhere in the same city, reducing competition and (at least in aggregate) moderating rents.

The Importance of Vacancy Rates

The relationship between vacancies and falling or stabilizing rents is important to understand. There is, again, an intuitive case for this, as well as empirical support.

Consider when and how the price of a specific home—let's say, again, an apartment in Bedford-Stuyvesant, Brooklyn—is determined. That price is set in a mutual transaction between a seller and a buyer, or a landlord and a tenant.

You're the landlord, and you have an apartment you'd like to fill. For the sake of this thought experiment, let's say you advertise it for $2,200 per month.

You hold an open house and, to your astonishment, more than 50 people show up. The line is out the door and down the street. Prospective tenants are offering to pay more than your asking price, or to offer the first several months' rent immediately in cash, in order to secure the apartment. (This is not a hypothetical but an actual scenario that occurred often in the 2010s in places such as New York City and San Francisco.) If you are profit-motivated, you will end up renting this apartment for considerably more than your initial asking price of $2,200.

What if you held the open house and nobody showed up? What if weeks went by and you couldn't find a tenant? You would face pressure to lower your asking rent in order to fill the vacant unit. Maybe you ultimately settle at $1,900.

This simple thought experiment illustrates how one crucial statistic, the vacancy rate, affects the power dynamic between sellers and buyers, or landlords and tenants. In an environment in which there are many vacant homes or apartments, prospective residents can shop around and be choosy. Because landlords are in competition for tenants, they may be forced to undercut each other on rent or otherwise throw in extra amenities or perks. In a market in which there is a scarcity of vacant homes or apartments, the power dynamic is reversed, and housing costs tend to be bid up over time.

Those who observe the real estate markets pay close attention to trends in the local inventory of homes available for sale or rent for precisely this reason.

When we zoom out to examine housing markets at a coarse, regional scale, the data very clearly back up the importance of vacancy. The regional vacancy rate within a given metropolitan area is consistently correlated with the fluctuation in rents over time. During periods of low vacancy, rents increase rapidly. During periods of high vacancy, they stabilize. As of this writing, recent studies show actual declines in average rent across markets as diverse as Minneapolis, Minnesota; Oakland, California; and Auckland, New Zealand; in all cases, these declines follow several years of substantial apartment construction leading to increased vacant supply.

Try YIMBY™ Today! (*Your Local Experience May Vary)

The musical chairs metaphor is simple and logically compelling. But it is far from the end of the argument. The model deals in a lot of abstraction: we can perhaps agree the market is going to shake out in some fashion, but we aren't able to see quite *how* and *for whom*.

In reality, we are not all playing the same game of musical chairs and competing for the exact same pool of "chairs." Every one of us has a unique list of requirements, preferences, and deal-breakers. And in general, the lowest-income people are participating in the housing market on especially restrictive terms. If you are dependent on public transit, then you need to live somewhere with reliable transportation to the things you need to reach, or to job opportunities, and that's going to represent a much smaller set of options than those faced by a car owner. If you are living with a disability, your options are dramatically constrained. You may be dependent on social networks that are localized. You may rely on people who speak the same language as you, a faith community, or businesses that serve your cultural needs.

Access to community institutions, service providers, support networks of extended family and friends: all of these things can affect or shrink your pool of acceptable housing options. Leaving your neighborhood may result in unacceptable trade-offs to you. In general, it is the wealthier members of our society who are more mobile and have more options with fewer downsides.

To people who experience housing precarity in these specific, contextual terms, to say, "If we just *build build build*, rents will come down across the region" can feel either like cold consolation or like a magical, ideological assertion.

There is strong empirical support for the idea that when vacancy increases at the regional scale, housing prices begin to moderate *at the regional scale*. But in practice, many people are justifiably concerned with what happens in their neighborhood, to their community. And at that hyperlocal scale, the basic observation that supply is good for affordability starts to break down and be replaced by a huge amount of situational complexity.

A large new apartment building might flood a neighborhood with supply, and it might induce other landlords to lower rent as they are forced to compete for tenants with these brand-new apartments.

In a different case, that building might be marketed to a demographic of relative newcomers to the neighborhood who are wealthier than longtime residents. But the experience for the longtime residents is that their landlord in an old fourplex looks at the new building advertising premium rents and concludes that he, too, can charge more than he had been.

Housing scholars refer to the "amenity effects" of new buildings to describe how they may send a signal that a neighborhood is becoming more desirable or affluent. That signal may push rents up, not down, in the immediate vicinity despite the added supply. The academic research on this phenomenon doesn't yield conclusive or comforting conclusions, because it is extremely situational.

This points to something basic about complex systems: they are often legible at very large scales and at the very small scale of individual behavior, but that legibility falls apart at the medium scale, where spillovers and feedback loops are most pronounced.

At very large scales, even systems of dazzling complexity often exhibit a basic mathematical order. Their limits are defined by overarching questions of resource availability. It's why ecologists are able to estimate with some confidence the acreage of forest required to support a given population of wolves.

At the micro level, things are also predictable. The population dynamics of wolves and rabbits might be complex, but if an individual rabbit meets an individual wolf, you can guess what's about to happen.

It's in the middle ranges where chaos reigns. It is easier to mathematically model the wolf population of the Northern Rocky Mountains; it is harder to predict how the wolf packs in the northwestern corner of Yellowstone National Park will fare in a particular winter.

This is how it can simultaneously be true, in a coarse, "zoomed out" sense, that building more housing is crucial to achieving broad affordability and that doing so will tangibly reduce rents. And at the same time, those who are highly skeptical that the YIMBY policy agenda will serve their neighborhood well can have well-founded concerns.

We need to build. A lot. But the analysis cannot stop at *build build build*. The housing revolution we need is not just about abundance in a numerical sense, because housing people is not about putting them into boxes. It's about the ability of people to live in communities where they have agency, security, safety—all the different ways that shelter serves our basic needs at multiple levels of Maslow's hierarchy.

To do this, we will need to build a housing market that is more responsive to local, even hyperlocal needs. One where feedback loops are shorter. One where allowing the evolution of a place in context can once again take precedence over the obsessive demands of Big Zoning and Big Finance for legibility.

The good news: this approach, one which is bottom-up rather than top-down, is also the best bet for actually getting to abundance.

Big YIMBY Question #2: How Do We Get a Housing Revolution?

There is a lot of reason, in principle, to think that a surge in supply would significantly ease housing affordability in the most expensive markets. Faced with intensified competition, many landlords would have no choice but to compete on price or see units sit empty. With bills continuing to come due, they cannot afford the latter for long.

The sellers of owner-occupied housing may have more flexibility—many can and will sit on a property until the market is hot and they can sell for as high a price as possible. But many others are compelled to sell by their personal circumstances and will sell for whatever the market will bear. So a supply surge will also moderate the price of homes for sale.

What it will take to make that supply surge materialize is a different question. A housing revolution will need to happen on multiple fronts: not just what can legally be built but what can practically be built, how it can be financed, and who will do the building.

Many of the celebrated housing policies of recent years appear to have had minimal on-the-ground effects. This is not a reason to declare defeat. Development operates on long time scales and responds gradually, since the actual process of planning, permitting, and building a building is a multiyear affair. But early successes and failures can and should be instructive for housing reform advocates.

The early hero of the national YIMBY narrative was Minneapolis and its 2018 legalization of triplexes citywide. Yet triplexes have been slow to materialize. The number permitted annually ticked up from single digits at first to 63 in 2022, representing fewer than 2% of over 3,600 dwelling units permitted that year in Minneapolis. This is far from a flood, and some regulatory subtleties help explain why.

Under the Minneapolis 2040 Plan, triplexes, though newly legal, were largely confined to the same building envelope as a single-family home: that is, the same restrictions on height and overall size. In practice, this meant that the only way to build one on most lots was to squeeze in three very small units that would be awkwardly configured and difficult to rent.

Zoning reforms elsewhere have met similar pitfalls. Dozens of cities have legalized accessory dwelling units (backyard cottages) only to see a bare trickle of them, if any, built. California's statewide upzoning law, SB 9, was also greeted with crickets in its first year. San Diego, which permitted over 5,000 homes in 2022, processed a grand total of nine applications for SB 9–related housing units.

Far from indicating that there is no market or financial viability for these homes, what these results indicate is that something else is standing in the way. Envision a door locked by a series of deadbolts, which will only open once every deadbolt has been released.

There are success stories of rents apparently stabilizing or falling in the aftermath of zoning reform. One of those stories is actually Minneapolis, where average rents fell in nominal terms from 2017 to 2022. Local experts attribute the difference not to triplexes but to two other policies associated with the Minneapolis 2040 plan: larger and taller apartment buildings on transit corridors, and the abolition of parking mandates. Evidence from other cities, such as Oakland, California, compounds the notion that modest rent declines are attainable in the near term through a surge in large-scale apartment construction.

The open question is whether these gains from large-scale development can be sustained or whether they will halt, whether because market cycles slow the pace of development or because the easy sites with potential for such buildings become claimed.

Research by Eric Kronberg (2021a), a developer and architect in Atlanta, validates the second of those concerns. Kronberg's team conducted an analysis of the potential for infill housing in Atlanta, a city whose planners estimate needs 16,600 new housing units per year to keep up with anticipated population growth. Atlanta currently approves about 5,170 units yearly. Eighty-six percent of new homes built in the city from 2013 to 2019 were in large apartment buildings. Another 14% were single-family homes.

The problem, says Kronberg, is that you could double the production of single-family homes *and* mid-rise and high-rise apartment buildings and still be far short of the gap. The rest, says Kronberg, must come from missing-middle housing forms: accessory units and duplexes through 12-plexes. This means not only legalizing them but also growing a cohort of small-scale developers capable of building them.

"You can't build your way out of it" with a big-developer, big-project-driven model alone, says Kronberg. "You literally can't get there from here. There are only so many towers and multifamily things we can build. There's a limit to the workforce, permitting, the availability of cranes. If we double production of all that stuff *and* single-family homes, we're still 40% to 50% shy of unit needs for the city of Atlanta" (Kronberg 2021b).

When it comes to the depth of the housing shortage in major, expensive cities, big, established developers won't get the job done. They literally couldn't if they wanted to. They would run into capacity limits, permitting delays, and a lack of available and attractive development sites.

They would face labor shortages as well. In the depths of the post-2008 recession, when there was almost no new building occurring, the skilled trades—things such as plumbing, electrical, and HVAC work—lost over one million workers. Many of these jobs have not been replaced. And only a fraction of such contractors work at the scale and complexity that large developers require.

Legalizing housing in more places is not, in itself, guaranteed to radically alter the number of homes the system produces in a year: it may merely reshape the geography of where they are built.

Large-scale developers think in terms of the business cycle and may pull back on new projects in response to sluggish rent growth or higher interest rates. If they don't, their lenders will. In 2023, many US markets saw a steep decline in new proposals for large multifamily buildings in response to interest rate hikes.

If this is true of the companies that build urban 5-over-1s, it is even truer of the production homebuilders that create suburban subdivisions. Their business model will not allow prices to fall substantially. They can and will slow-drip supply if the market appears to be softening.

Put simply, the difference between "increased housing production will drop rents a couple of percentage points" and "increased housing production will crash rents and usher in an era of widespread affordability" is that the latter scenario requires some very powerful market actors to choose to undermine their own profit model. They will not.

Successes That Scale

There are a few success stories in recent years in which a policy change seems to have unleashed an actual surge of building and, perhaps even more importantly, unlocked a new *category* of housing construction that was previously almost nonexistent.

One of these stories predates YIMBY advocacy. In 1999, Houston, which famously does not have conventional zoning, revised its minimum lot sizes from 5,000 square feet to 1,400 square feet for homes within the city's inner beltway. In the two decades since, several Houston neighborhoods, most notably Rice-Military, have seen the explosive growth of townhouse development. The new Houston townhome is optimized for a skinny lot in a car-dependent city: it is a narrow, typically three-story building with a garage on the bottom floor. The mass replication of this incarnation of missing-middle housing has become one significant factor in Houston's relative affordability compared to many cities of its size.

Another success story, fittingly for a discussion of the YIMBY movement, involves homes in literal backyards.

In 1982, California banned localities from explicitly outlawing accessory dwelling units (ADUs). Cities could and did, however, put a lot of hurdles and conditions in the way of building these backyard homes, making them difficult to build and not a viable housing solution at scale.

This changed in 2016, when California passed statewide ADU reform in Senate Bill 1069 (SB 1069). The new law took a sledgehammer to the various barriers that had made ADUs impractical for most homeowners.

Cities must now automatically approve applications to build ADUs on sites where they are allowed. The law waives parking requirements, most setback requirements, and draconian caps on ADU floor space. Cities can no longer require the owner of a backyard cottage to live on site, and they can no longer charge impact fees for those that are under 750 square feet.

The result has been an absolute explosion of ADU permitting in California. Los Angeles led the pack. In 2016, the city approved 257 ADUs. In 2017, ADU permits jumped to 3,818. In 2022, Los Angeles issued 7,160, representing more than a quarter of *all* housing permitted in the city of three million that year. Statewide, 23,000 ADU permits were issued in 2022.

The most exciting thing about California's backyard ADU explosion is that it is activating resources that were on the sidelines: in this case, land owned by thousands of individual California homeowners interested in having an additional home on their property. This is the kind of thing that will be necessary to produce an actual paradigm shift in housing.

This provides us with a tentative road map.

Unlocking massive new supply requires creating flexibility. It's not enough to change the zoning on a property from "one-plex" to "three-plex" and call it a day. A whole host of costs and regulations work in concert to affect whether a given home is actually viable to build or whether a given template can begin to replicate and scale. All the deadbolts must be unlocked.

We must think small, in terms of literal land, as well as in terms of the scale of developer involved and the barriers to entry.

It's not enough to enable existing developers to shift into a slightly higher gear. We must activate a whole new *category* of developer and development—just as the housing innovations of a pre-suburban era, such as the triple-deckers of New England, did in order to rise to the occasion of that century's housing crisis.

It is tempting to take the short-term view, to look at the meager production of triplexes versus the relative success of 5-over-1s in a place like Minneapolis and say, "The missing middle isn't worth the trouble. It won't scale." This instinct is wrong. The conventional approach may yield housing sooner, because all of the institutional arrangements—the zoning, the financing, the politics—are there to support it. But it will also hit diminishing returns.

Unlocking incremental development in *every* neighborhood, on the other hand, represents a bottom-up revolution that can snowball. We'll talk more in ensuing chapters about how to make that happen.

8

Affordable with a Capital "A"

A commonly heard refrain in American cities is some variation of the following: "We don't have a shortage of housing. We have a shortage of *affordable* housing." This is often paired with the assertion that, if we want housing to be affordable, what we need is to build *affordable* housing, not just any old housing.

In these conversations there is almost always a certain rhetorical sleight of hand occurring. This sleight of hand is not obvious to many laypeople, or even to journalists who cover local planning and development decisions. The catch hinges on the definition of the word "affordable."

"Affordable housing" is a term of art in the US referring to housing that is subject to restrictions on its rent and/or the income of its occupants. Such housing is typically subsidized in some fashion.

But "affordable housing" also carries a plain English meaning. It means any housing the occupants can afford without undue burden to their household finances or quality of life.

The former sense of the word is often referred to by those involved in housing policy or development as capital-A Affordable housing.

The latter sense might then be called lowercase-a affordable housing, or by the cringeworthy policy-wonk term, "naturally occurring affordable housing," or NOAH.

The sleight of hand occurs when someone, on one hand, observes that their city has a shortage of affordable housing—that is, in the lowercase "a" sense of housing whose occupants can reasonably afford it—and then proceeds to argue that this necessitates the construction of affordable housing—by which they very often mean subsidized housing, Affordable, with a capital "A."

This definitional switch defines the problem in broad terms and the solution in narrow ones.

Subsidized and non-market housing have a place in the discussion. Reasonable people may disagree on what that place looks like and how large or comprehensive it should be.

Right now, however, the problem is one of scale. There is an enormous gap between the magnitude of housing needs in our communities and the comparatively limited resources available to deliver purpose-built affordable housing. Any serious discussion of housing affordability must reckon with that gap.

Most of the affordable housing in American cities (lowercase "a") is market-rate housing that, for any number of reasons, rents for a relatively modest price. A large majority of low-income Americans live in such market-rate housing. Approximately 4% of all US households receive federal housing assistance.

For those not receiving assistance, affordable housing typically just means "used" housing, just as an affordable car typically means a used car, at least for a buyer who cannot pay the price of a vehicle fresh off the factory floor.

Claims that what is principally needed in American cities is the construction of new capital-A Affordable housing are often advanced by the constellation of nonprofit organizations, government entities, and advocacy groups that directly participate in the creation and regulation of such housing. These claims are supported by statistics from organizations such as the National Low Income Housing Coalition (NLIHC) that indicate that America has a dire shortage of homes affordable to low-income and very low-income households.

For example, NLIHC's "The Gap" report from 2022 asserts that for every 100 extremely low-income households, there are only 36 affordable rental homes available. For 100 merely low-income

households (those earning under 50% of the median income), there are 58 rental homes they can afford. For moderately low incomes, there are 93, and for households at or above median income, there are 101 apartments for every 100 households (NLIHC 2022).

These numbers are based on reported rents, including for private market housing. An "affordable" home is defined as one that costs less than 30% of a household's income in rent. 30% is the standard used by many nonprofits and government agencies to measure housing cost burden.

A fair summary of this data is that there are enough rental units out there that are affordable to the middle and upper classes but not nearly enough that are affordable to the working class or the poor. This *feels* like a damning observation. In terms of the human suffering it points to, it is. But it's also a somewhat obvious, banal observation. Let us return to the musical chairs metaphor from the previous chapter to understand why.

Imagine a game of musical chairs in which there are 100 players and only 95 chairs. Five people will lose this game. This is equally true whether the players are of questionable physical fitness or whether every single one of them is an Olympic sprinter.

It would be possible to make the claim, after observing the outcome of such a game, that the reason the losers lost was that there were not enough chairs for the slowest players. But a simpler statement of the reality is that there were not enough chairs. No one is going to say that there were not enough for the fastest players, because of course the fastest players succeeded in securing chairs.

Applying this analogy to housing statistics, it becomes almost trivially obvious that if there is a housing shortage for anyone in a market system, the first, and worst, affected will be households with the least ability to pay.

The ultimate losers of housing musical chairs are people experiencing homelessness. In the book *Homelessness is a Housing Problem*, Gregg Colburn and Clayton Aldern (2022) examine the wide variation in the rates of homelessness in many different US cities. What they find is that the number one factor correlated with the homelessness rates is not poverty. Nor is it drug addiction or mental health issues.

All of these factors can be *individual* determinants of homelessness: if your personal life is disordered, you are more likely to end up homeless. But at the scale of a city, the *rate* of homelessness is not determined by these factors. It is, however, powerfully correlated with one thing: regional housing costs.

A blunt way of expressing this conclusion is that if you have an addiction problem and you live in Mississippi, you are far more likely to have a roof over your head. If you have the same addiction but you live in New York City, you are far more likely to be on the streets. On some aggregate level, we can understand epidemic homelessness as an outcome of the cruel game of musical chairs that we are all playing.

A step above homelessness, many households experience the constant or repeated threat of eviction, while many others live in unhealthy or overcrowded conditions. It is again an implication of the musical chairs nature of market competition that the worse the overall shortage in a region, the more prevalent and dire such outcomes are likely to be.

Once this is understood, the question then is what policies we should pursue to help the poorest and most vulnerable households obtain housing. There are certainly people whom the market cannot effectively serve: even the cheapest rents available in their community are beyond their ability to pay. Subsidy and government support should thus be in the conversation.

This conversation, however, will look very different in a situation where the market is failing to serve 5% of people with adequate housing versus a situation where the market is failing 20% or 30%. In the latter scenario, choices get harder, resources more strained, and decisions about funding priorities become more painful and zero-sum.

In the 5% scenario, we subsidize housing for the truly poor. In the 30% scenario, we might end up subsidizing housing for schoolteachers and firefighters, while the truly poor become more likely to sleep in cars, in tents, or on sidewalks.

NLIHC's "The Gap" report estimates that the nationwide US shortfall of homes affordable to very low-income households totals 7.3 million. At a very conservative estimate of $200,000 each to construct these, the cost to build our way out of this shortfall one time only would equal $1.46 trillion, roughly the GDP of Spain.

The notion that we can deal with the shortfall of affordable (small-a) housing solely by building Affordable (big-A) housing, with the systems currently in place to do so, is as misguided as telling young adults to skip lattes and avocado toast and thereby save up for retirement. It shows a total misunderstanding of scale.

How Los Angeles "Lost" 111,000 Affordable Housing Units

In October of 2022, *LAist* reported that over the course of a decade, Los Angeles lost eight times more affordable housing units than it gained for its lowest-income residents (Rohrlich 2022). According to city records, from 2010 to 2019, 111,000 houses and apartments affordable to low earners were lost, while only 13,000 were built. (In this case, "affordable" does not mean subsidized or rent-restricted: it means the lowercase sense of costing no more than 30% of such a household's gross income.)

Statistics like this can mislead. The obvious follow-up question to the statement, "Los Angeles lost 111,000 affordable units" is, "Where did they go?" Casual observers of the housing crisis might easily misunderstand the answer or make incorrect assumptions.

Were they demolished? Were they replaced by high-end units? The answer is that, while some were presumably physically demolished, replaced, or renovated, the vast majority were "lost to higher prices." The house or apartment didn't go anywhere; the rent just went up.

The physical differences between "affordable" and unaffordable or "luxury" housing are largely not consistent or meaningful. What determines the cost to live in a given unit is some combination of market dynamics and government policy. Homes can move in or out of various tiers of affordability. Housing economists refer to this as "filtering." In Los Angeles in the 2010s, in the face of a generalized housing shortage, existing homes overwhelmingly filtered up, becoming less affordable over time.

Thirteen thousand subsidized housing units were built in Los Angeles in 10 years. Just to make up for the widening affordability gap caused by higher market rents, Los Angeles would have to increase its production of subsidized, capital-A Affordable housing by a factor of eight. No local proposals to achieve this have been forthcoming.

Herein lies the problem with taking the broad, difficult question of, "How do we make housing affordable?" and conflating it with the narrow, also difficult question of, "How do we build more Affordable housing?" As Stuart Gabriel, director of UCLA's Ziman Center for Real Estate, told *LAist*, building a few subsidized units in the face of overwhelming market forces is like "pouring a glass of water into the Santa Monica Bay and then looking for a change" (Rohrlich 2022).

The "Affordable" System in the US

Non-market housing in the US is currently delivered through a patchy set of policies and programs that are awkward appendages to the much larger private housing market. Many of these policies are fundamentally incoherent: either impossible to scale up or dependent for their operation on the very aspects of the private housing market that make it unaffordable to many.

This incoherence is a direct result of our contradictory societal priorities regarding housing. We want affordable housing to exist. But most interest groups, as we saw in Chapter 1, do not want home prices to broadly fall. The result has been programs that subsidize or reserve a modicum of rent-regulated units, without disrupting the forces pushing market prices skyward.

What follows is an overview of these programs, in rough chronological order of their creation.

Public Housing

Until the 1930s, there was essentially no federal involvement in directly providing affordable housing. There were private charitable efforts, the most prominent of which was the settlement house movement around the turn of the 20th century. These were communal homes in poor urban neighborhoods in which middle-class volunteers helped provide meals, education, and social services to impoverished residents.

In 1937, in response to the Great Depression, the federal government established a public housing program. Local authorities, using federal dollars, would build and operate apartments for very low-income households, who would pay a percentage of their income in rent. This program was saddled with likely insurmountable barriers to success from the very beginning.

Real estate interests immediately balked at the program, which they feared would compete with privately owned housing. To prevent such competition, the Public Housing Act established a policy of "equivalent elimination": one substandard unit of housing must be demolished for every unit of public housing built. In addition, the program set a 20% gap in income eligibility between those who qualified for public housing and what was regarded as the minimum income necessary to find housing in a local housing market. The gap, in theory, would leave room for the private sector to build down to capture that part of the market.

Income guidelines for public housing were so strict that the upwardly mobile were forced to move out. Not all authorities enforced that requirement aggressively. Some did: Chicago's Public Housing Authority would on occasion evict hundreds of families whose incomes had risen.

Public housing thus came to serve an overwhelmingly poor (and in many cities overwhelmingly Black) urban underclass. In the postwar era, "the projects" became intensified microcosms of their surrounding communities' social ills.

It did not help that many of these projects were built according to experimental, modernist theories of design. Rather than emulating a traditional neighborhood with homes and businesses interspersed, public housing authorities would often build a cluster of high-rise buildings disconnected from the fabric of the surrounding neighborhoods. Surrounding these buildings would be poorly maintained communal space that quickly invited criminal activity.

In a vicious cycle, low rental revenue from deepening resident poverty left public housing authorities unable to fund basic maintenance, and living conditions deteriorated. In the 1960s, public housing residents staged high-profile rent strikes in protest of these conditions. Those who could leave did so, only worsening the dysfunction they left behind.

Far from encouraging reinvestment, the abysmal conditions in these complexes further cratered political support for the program. From the 1970s through the 1990s, public housing authorities demolished many of the worst and most notorious existing projects, such as St. Louis's Pruitt-Igoe and Chicago's Cabrini-Green, while almost entirely ceasing new construction.

Despite this, over two million Americans still live in public housing today, 535,000 of them in New York City alone. Many of these complexes now cater to a mix of incomes, with market-rate apartments mixed in. Some have severe budgetary and maintenance issues. Many others are well managed and a far cry from Cabrini-Green. In any case, federal law (the Faircloth Amendment to the Public Housing Act, passed in 1998) now prohibits any net increase in public housing units, and so far there has not been political support for repeal.

All of this has not been the experience of other countries, and the failures of US public housing are not intrinsic to the idea of housing built and operated by the public sector. We'll revisit this idea later.

Housing Vouchers

By the 1970s, policymakers were ready to pivot away from public housing, in light of its disastrous reputation. Since then, almost all subsidized housing in the US has come through one of several programs that attempt to leverage the private market instead of operating a parallel system.

In 1974, Congress established the Housing Choice Voucher program, more commonly known as Section 8. Voucher holders can rent an apartment on the private market, and the federal government will directly pay the landlord the difference between the market rent and 30% of the tenant's income. The program was supported by conservatives in Congress as a way to enable freedom of choice and encourage market competition.

The voucher program has never come close to meeting demand. Most cities have epically long waiting lists, and nationally only one in four households eligible for Housing Choice Vouchers actually receives them. This still adds up to over two million people.

The bigger problem with vouchers is that the program is a demand-side subsidy. As a rule, if you subsidize the supply of something, you will get more of it, and that will tend to push the price down. On the other hand, if you subsidize the *consumption* of something whose supply is constrained and cannot grow, such as rental housing, you may push market prices up. This is similar to the upward effect of down payment assistance programs or low interest rates on home prices.

Inclusionary Zoning

Another innovation of the 1970s was inclusionary zoning. The term sounds like an opposite of "exclusionary zoning," but it isn't. Instead, it is a local policy that mandates that private developers set aside a percentage of the apartments they build for low-income occupants. Because these units almost certainly must be built at a financial loss, they are subsidized by the revenue from the market-rate units.

This immediately creates one of two problems. Either market-rate rents must be set even higher in order to pay for the low-income units, or the developer was already charging the highest rent the market would bear and cannot go higher. Either way, the inclusionary zoning requirement impairs the profitability of new buildings and acts as a deterrent to the development of housing.

This deterrent effect can be witnessed in real time. After Portland, Oregon, passed an inclusionary zoning ordinance that kicked in at a minimum of 20 units, the city saw a curious surge in applications to build 19-unit buildings. Other cities have witnessed similar effects, where developers build just below the threshold to avoid triggering a costly requirement.

There are ways around the deterrent effect, such as offering density bonuses to make the added low-income units effectively free for the developer. But ultimately, inclusionary zoning remains a program that is impossible to scale to make a meaningful dent in the affordable housing shortage. It is hard to calibrate the incentives and costs properly.

The Low-Income Housing Tax Credit

The next big federal policy innovation would not come from the department of Housing and Urban Development. It would come, oddly enough, from the IRS.

The federal low-income housing tax credit (LIHTC, pronounced "LIE-tech") was created in 1986 as part of a comprehensive tax code overhaul. Nonprofit developers can apply for housing tax credits through a competitive grant process overseen by states. The most generous form of LIHTC credits will cover 70% of development costs. The credits themselves are paid for by investors, typically large corporations or investment funds. The investors receive a one-to-one reduction of their federal tax liability.

There are many subtleties we will not go into here. LIHTC, in addition to being the funding mechanism for the vast majority of new subsidized housing units in the United States, might as well be a full-employment program for tax attorneys. Its technical complexity means that it is skewed toward large-scale projects: LITHC primarily subsidizes the creation of city-block-sized apartment buildings with dozens to hundreds of units.

Once a LIHTC building is built, rents must be restricted for at least 15 years. Buildings then "age out" of mandatory affordability. The most common rent restriction is that a unit must be affordable to a household earning 60% of area median income (AMI). This creates a situation in some high-poverty neighborhoods where LIHTC tenants actually have higher incomes than the people in the surrounding market-rate homes, and LIHTC projects are associated with increasing surrounding property values.

LIHTC produces the vast majority of dedicated affordable housing in the US: about 3.5 million units over the program's life from 1987 to 2021. An estimated 25% of *all* apartment construction in the US from 2000 to 2019 used some LIHTC funding, a statement that is more about the dominance of single-family homes in America's housing mix than it is about the expansiveness of the LIHTC program. Recall, again, that the NLIHC estimates the gap for very-low-income households alone at 7.3 million, or about 50 years of LIHTC production. And LIHTC units themselves tend not to serve very-low-income households, whose earnings are well below 60% of the median.

LIHTC is a top-down program difficult to adapt to small sites and granular local needs. It is the affordable-housing component of the 5-over-1 apartment monoculture. The availability of finance for LIHTC units is tied to the overall market cycle, because it is tied to the appetite of giant investors for large tax credits. But the need for affordable housing doesn't go away when the market cools or crashes. In fact, that need gets more acute, because more people are out of work or in precarious situations.

After the 2008 crash, companies experienced heavy losses, and demand for Low-Income Housing Tax Credits cratered. As a result, just as the housing crisis was most dire, and many foreclosed homeowners were beginning to enter the rental market, the nature of this funding mechanism temporarily kneecapped the ability of affordable-housing developers to create more of their product.

Removing Housing from the Speculative Market

A few other options favored by some affordable housing advocates are more bottom-up in nature. These include community land trusts and limited-equity cooperatives. Instead of subsidizing the creation of new non-market housing, the strategy here is to acquire existing housing and remove it from the speculative market, locking in a lower price.

In a community land trust (CLT) arrangement, a nonprofit retains ownership of the land underneath homes or apartments, while selling or renting the homes to qualifying lower-income households. Those households agree to resale price restrictions, often allowing them to capture some limited percentage of the equity gains when they sell. A co-op arrangement is similar: residents own shares in a cooperative rather than owning their home outright, and they agree to a formula which caps the resale price of the share. There is a huge diversity of ways to structure these arrangements to balance different goals, such as maintaining permanent affordability versus allowing households to build some wealth.

These strategies decentralize control of housing, and they introduce long-term tenancy arrangements that fall between the extremes of, at one end, an owner-occupier with the security of a long-term mortgage and full equity in the property once that mortgage is paid off, and at the other end, a tenant with very few legal protections against eviction and no ability to build equity.

There is value in enabling and even encouraging a multitude of local experiments in cooperative housing, and there are many promising overseas models to explore here. One might be Germany's *baugruppen*, which are multifamily housing cooperatives developed by their own residents.

What becomes clear when you examine the workings of these arrangements, though, is that they're still not going to scale up to a mass affordability solution in a world of housing prices that are consistently rising faster than incomes. In a market that is producing housing in abundance across many neighborhoods and price points, it becomes viable for mission-driven nonprofits or community-minded cooperatives to purchase some of that housing and preserve it for access other than by the highest bidder. In a market characterized by scarcity, large no-build zones, and torrents of outside investor money flooding into gentrifying neighborhoods, these strategies will be costly, precarious, and have limited reach.

"How can we shield vulnerable tenants from the market?" and "How can we bring the market price of housing itself down?" are not opposed strategies. They must be complementary.

Social Housing: Public Housing 2.0?

As rents escalate, the idea of a dramatic rebirth of public housing in the US has entered the mainstream in a way not seen in decades. Advocates for this rebirth often use the term "social housing" to distinguish their proposals from past failures. "Social housing" is a deliberately broad term for not-for-profit housing that is built and/or operated by the government.

We mentioned earlier that the dismal experience of the US with public housing has been somewhat of an outlier. Many countries have public housing programs that are structured very differently than ours, and many of these have avoided the American experience of concentrated poverty, crime, disinvestment, and decay.

This includes prosperous cities with robust market economies, such as Vienna, Austria, where 62% of residents live in social housing. The city directly owns and manages over 200,000 housing units and regulates rents in over 200,000 more, and Viennese of all incomes and walks of life live in them. Meanwhile, in Singapore, the government subsidizes the majority of housing construction, and most of these units are offered for sale—again, to residents across the income spectrum.

Places such as Vienna and Singapore treat social housing as a broad social program serving the mainstream of society, the way we might think of public hospitals or community colleges.

Modern social housing proposals all rely on cross-subsidy as their basic funding model. This is the same mechanism employed by inclusionary zoning: the rents paid by market-rate tenants are used to subsidize the rents of low-income tenants. This is intended to avoid the death spiral that befell traditional public housing: a program requiring perpetual top-down subsidy and with no direct constituency other than the very poor to ensure political support.

The difference, versus inclusionary zoning, is that the developer is a public-sector entity, and several resulting advantages allow it to secure deeper affordability for a larger proportion of units than is possible through inclusionary zoning. A public developer enjoys a lower cost of financing, via the government bond market. It does not pay property taxes. Governments might exempt its projects from zoning controls. And it does not require a large return on investment, such as that demanded by equity investors who front the cash for private development projects.

Cross-subsidy is still no free lunch. The premise still requires that market-rate rents be significantly more than high enough to cover overall project expenses. Without additional subsidy, this likely becomes another case in which the policy remedy to a very expensive housing market depends on those very high prices for its viability.

Vienna's social housing program, often held as a global gold standard, supports this observation. It is funded not only through cross-subsidy with a large population of market-rate tenants but also through a broad 1% tax on incomes earned in Vienna, half from wages and half from a matching employer contribution.

Such a tax might be politically viable in some US cities. But another feature of Vienna's model that cannot readily be copy-pasted to the American context is that the municipal government owns very large amounts of land. By strategically releasing this land for development, Vienna is able to moderate land prices and development costs. Any American public developer will need to buy land at market rate from private owners.

A Parallel Option, Not a Panacea

There is a broad, never-ending debate about to what extent basic necessities should be provided by the market or provided by the state. That debate is abstract, it is hugely complex, and it is deeply rooted in competing ideologies and worldviews. We will certainly not attempt to resolve it here. Reasonable people will land in different places. Wherever you land on these larger philosophical questions, it is important to understand the very real constraints faced by existing and proposed affordable housing programs.

The very same problems that bedevil the effort to get abundant, affordable *market-rate* housing to exist are going to make it hard to deliver affordable social housing at any sort of scale. And, conversely, the better the housing market functions and the more responsive it is to local demand, the more effective a complementary social housing program is likely to be.

Our political discourse is rooted in a Cold War binary of capitalism versus socialism. But if aliens landed on Earth to study human society, it is likely that they would not distinguish public-sector from private-sector entities nearly as readily as we do. They would just see a complex array of organizations formed for the purpose of cooperation and collective power.

The history of housing finance described in Chapters 2 through 4 is a perfect example of the blurring of public and private to the point where a meaningful separation cannot be made. The private market in homeownership, after all, is supported by an institution, the 30-year mortgage, that is a creation of the state. This system would not persist without ongoing government intervention.

There has not been a free market in housing in a very long time. Given the state's role in shaping the market for raw land through the provision of public infrastructure such as roads, one could argue there never has been.

More interesting than the public-private distinction is a set of questions about how any organization is set up and to what incentives it responds.

Local governments, like private entities, need to operate in the black. A public agency has certain sources of wiggle room but is not ultimately exempt from this. The difference between for-profit and nonprofit is the difference between the inequalities $x > 0$ and $x \geq 0$.

A key lesson from the death spiral that affected much of American public housing in the 20th century should be that a program on which thousands or millions of people utterly depend for basic shelter must be essentially self-funding. To the extent that any outside funding source is needed, it should be something simple and durable. This implies a large role for cross-subsidy and a mixed-income model.

As in all services we promise to provide to citizens in perpetuity, governments must be highly risk averse and (small-c) conservative about it. An individual, at least, can theoretically choose to walk away from the maintenance of their own home and seek shelter elsewhere. But the government cannot be put in a position to defer or neglect the essential maintenance of someone *else's* home.

Housing reformers interested in social or otherwise non-market housing should also heed the lessons of Jane Jacobs and the pitfalls of J.C. Nichols: that is, successful communities must be subject to an evolutionary process guided by many hands. A successful social housing program at scale will allow for meaningful degrees of resident agency and control, and for bottom-up experimentation and evolution in design and built form. It should not be the public-sector analogue of Lennar, Del Webb, or Greystar: a giant real estate conglomerate in the business of monoculture.

This is one area in which Vienna's success offers valuable lessons for America. Social housing in Vienna is a laboratory for design innovation in terms of building materials, energy efficiency, and public space. Completed projects are often cutting-edge, part of their appeal to market-rate tenants who keep the program solvent and serve as proof of concept for private-sector builders. In Vienna's case, the city facilitates this through design competitions and competitive bidding processes.

Building a social housing portfolio need not mean building new. In many cases, a better use of public subsidy dollars would be to acquire a scattered collection of existing buildings.

One of the great failings of public housing in American cities has been the tendency of large campus-style projects to become pockets of dysfunction, physically disconnected from their surrounding neighborhoods. Just as private-sector development ought to integrate with the fabric of what is around it, so should public-sector (or public-supported) development, even at the cost of sacrificing some economies of scale. This is in keeping with the Strong Towns approach of elevating resilience of result over efficiency of execution.

None of this is intended to convince you to support the expansion of social housing or to convince you not to. It is to lay out the scope of the challenge that deeply affordable housing presents.

We have a cultural consensus today that there can be no return to the pre-Depression status quo, in which housing at the bottom rungs of the ladder was plentiful and cheap but also frequently unsanitary and unsafe. It is also not hard to recognize, though, that the alternative to having some sort of viable bottom rung is that people will sleep in tent encampments and on sidewalks. This is a moral challenge that will not be resolved in one simple, pat way. Nor will it be solved by throwing money at the problem.

Coherent approaches to affordable housing for the poorest are possible, but we largely do not have them today. And they are most likely to succeed against the backdrop of a functioning housing market that delivers abundant housing at a wide range of price points attainable to most, though not all, Americans.

Housing in a Strong Town

9

A System That Produces a Solution

At Strong Towns, we often find ourselves pushing back against the word "solution." Even with this book, our publisher initially wanted "solution to the housing crisis" somewhere in the title. A solution denotes a sense of permanence, something someone like J.C. Nichols would find comfortable to consider. We do not share that comfort.

If we summarize all the challenges we have outlined thus far in this book, they come from an underlying belief that there is an ideal solution that can be successfully imposed on cities. That was the explicit belief of Nichols, who argued that developer-led suburbanization would create permanent prosperity. It was the belief of people who pushed for rigid zoning, building codes, and fire codes. It was the inspiration for those who created the 30-year mortgage, Fannie and Freddie, and mortgage-backed securities. It was as if each reform, each change, brought us close to an ideal that assumed the present reality as the baseline.

All these approaches responded to very real and urgent problems. If we are being generous (and we should be generous), the people who orchestrated these "solutions" thought they were doing good.

151

Maybe they were, for a time. They certainly did not anticipate just how their solutions would give rise to a series of housing price bubbles, a housing shortage, NIMBYs, and the many other struggles of the housing trap.

At Strong Towns, we see cities as complex, not merely complicated. Understanding the difference is essential.

When we understand a city as a complex system, we appreciate that many different people make daily decisions based on an almost infinite number of motivations. They respond to stress and opportunity, react to success and to failure. They come up with novel adaptations to the things happening around them. Those adaptations and responses combine to emerge into a new order. Anyone who has studied ecology can recognize cities for what they are: complex human habitats.

Complexity can be messy. It can be chaotic. When J.C. Nichols negatively described the "fleeting and shifting uses of property" found in cities, he was describing the kind of complex changes, some of them uncomfortable, that emerge in a city as the people within it adapt to their neighborhoods over time.

In contrast, a system that is merely complicated lacks the ability to adapt. For example, an automobile engine is a complicated system. It works by predictable rules, follows a knowable chain of action. Very smart people can work to optimize an engine. If the engine is stressed, it may break and need to be repaired, but it won't adapt. It is incapable of evolving a new form in response to stress or to opportunity. The automobile engine will never become a toaster or a dishwasher, no matter how badly we need it to.

The affluence of post-war America provided Americans with an opportunity to think of cities as merely complicated, as something akin to a machine. We had the money, power, and social cohesion to simplify the complex challenges of the city down to a few discrete problems we could attack. Problem with housing quality? Create codes and regulations. Problem with housing finance? Create national mortgage programs. Banks failing? Orchestrate a bailout. Banks fail again? Organize a larger bailout.

Each one of these actions is, in a sense, defensible, perhaps even logical. Yet each is reductionist, ignoring the complex and nuanced interactions of city building as a whole. When combined, these responses create the conditions where, in the name of solving problems we reduce to merely complicated, we actively suppress our ability to respond in complex and novel ways.

Nichols's concept of a "permanent prosperity" is, at its essence, a rejection of the very need to adapt. We build things all at once, to a finished state, planning and anticipating all details in advance. The notion seems absurd when stated in this way; look around and ask why the myriad of challenges we now face weren't anticipated and addressed. Then, recognize that most of them were, but there was just no way for individuals to respond. We have imposed an artificial stagnation on cities, places that should be responding in complex and novel ways.

At Strong Towns, we push back on the concept of a "solution." There is no solution to the housing trap we find ourselves in. There aren't one or two things we can do that will make housing abundant, affordable, and a solid and stable investment. Even choosing one of those priorities over the others will have destabilizing ramifications.

Strong Towns as a movement has never been about picking a solution; it's always been an approach. Like diet and exercise, it is a mindset. A way of approaching a challenge more than a final step to permanent resolution. People need to be able to try things, to respond to stress or opportunity as it presents to them. Those responses need to be incremental, a discipline that expresses humility, allowing us to be wrong in a way that helps, not hurts.

To escape the housing trap, cities need to replace rigid systems with flexible ones. They need to make room for incremental adaptation. Local housing ecosystems need to be protected and nurtured so they can reconstitute. Our cities must become complex and adaptive once more.

A Paradigm Shift toward Complexity

Housing scarcity and affordability are symptoms of a deeper set of challenges. Those challenges are numerous, overlapping, and rivalrous. Choosing to address one while ignoring the others will undermine the entire effort.

For housing to be affordable, prices must come down relative to income. With those two variables alone—prices and income—there are many ways to get from here to there. Home prices could crash while wages stay flat. Wages could surge while home prices stay flat. A combination of falling prices and rising wages could meet somewhere in the middle, a process that could take months, years, or decades (as it has in Japan since their 1980s housing crash).

If we try and crash home prices, the pain will be everywhere. Banks have begun to experience distress merely from a rise in mortgage rates; a crashing of housing prices will undermine bank balance sheets and force widespread failures. We never experienced the endgame of bank failures in 2008 but, as Hank Paulson on one knee attested to, it's likely it would have been deeply unpleasant. It is hard to imagine experiencing this kind of economic contraction with wages remaining flat. A second Great Depression might give us lower prices, but it is unlikely to give us affordable housing.

A surge in wages seems more doable, but not without another set of deep crises. Wage inflation creates a spiral where higher wages prompt higher prices, which prompt demands for higher wages, and on and on. A policy to increase wages to make housing more affordable seems more likely to enable people to pay more for the same homes. This defeats the entire approach.

This leaves a more blended approach, which feels more moderate but has clear downsides. There are people struggling today, at this very moment, to find housing they can afford. They need shelter. There are other people who, right or wrong, are dependent on their home equity to pay for their retirement. They need their home equity to meet their long-term shelter, food, and medical needs. A blended approach means Americans will experience a decade or two of slow, painful, financial squeezing. This may be the default course of action, but it is not without cost.

This occurs as the long-term liabilities of the suburban experiment overwhelm local governments. All those miles of roads, pipes, and other systems of expansion need maintenance and replacement. These obligations come due without enough tax base to make good on the promises. A reduction in housing prices means a reduction in an already insufficient tax base. This can't happen without devastating consequences for local governments.

The way out of the housing trap must, therefore:

- Rapidly add new housing units at affordable prices;
- Not adversely impact the existing housing market;
- Allow for the flow of capital into the community, but slow the flow of capital out of the community; and
- Grow the city's tax base without adding to the liabilities of local governments.

There is no approach currently on offer that allows these things to happen. In the current paradigm, there is no set of Wall Street investments, federal programs or subsidies, or top-down housing initiatives capable of working even close to these parameters. To escape the housing trap requires a new paradigm.

Calling for a paradigm shift has become an overused trope, but in the spirit of Thomas Kuhn's *The Structure of Scientific Revolutions* (1962), we are at that moment. A paradigm is a set of techniques, understandings, and approaches that have developed out of a common tradition. A revolution, a paradigm shift, occurs when it becomes increasingly obvious that the old paradigm no longer matches observed reality.

As Kuhn states, "Revolutions are inaugurated by a growing sense, often restricted to a segment of the political community, that existing institutions have ceased adequately to meet the problems posed by an environment that they have in part created" (Kuhn 1962).

The institutions and approaches we created to address the housing quality problem of the early 20th century, to solve the financial problems of the Great Depression, and to grow the economy at the end of World War II, no longer work. They have not worked for decades. In fact, it is those very institutions and approaches that have created our current set of crises. They are incapable of solving the problems.

The "sense of malfunction" that we all experience is, as Kuhn states, the "prerequisite to revolution." To address the housing trap, that revolution needs to be led by cities. Local leaders can't wait for the old paradigm to work; they must create a new one. They must do it outside of the current paradigm but while the current system remains intact.

They must do it in the face of powerful NIMBY protests against change by addressing their reasonable concerns and giving them ways to benefit in the new paradigm.

They must do it in the face of powerful YIMBY demands for radical change by committing to rapidly growing the number of housing units in the new paradigm.

They must do it over the concerns of large developers by leaving the current rules largely intact but undermining their privileged business model by introducing competitors to the ecosystem.

They must do it despite the power of a few large banks to control capital by repurposing old tools to leverage local capital and build neighborhood capacity.

They must do it even though the state and federal governments remain locked in the old paradigm.

Kuhn wrote that "to reject one paradigm without simultaneously substituting another is to reject science itself." We can all see that the current paradigm no longer works, but there is no mechanism for people vested in it to fundamentally change it. Local leaders can.

When they do, the new paradigm will become self-evident and eventually replace the old. That is the revolution that will get us out of the housing trap.

The Principles of a New Approach to Housing

We begin to create a new paradigm for housing by focusing on the forgotten cracks in the current paradigm. This starts with the people who aren't well served by today's limited housing offerings. We must rapidly fill the demand for low-cost, affordable units. We need to accomplish this with the resources that are available locally. This means building far cheaper than the current paradigm delivers housing.

This isn't a call to return to the 19th and early 20th centuries. We are not suggesting that we bring back low-quality housing or tenements. Yet we recognize that our ancestors were able to solve, ad hoc, many of their housing problems when they were allowed to do so. We must do the same.

Tolerating a touch of messiness inherent in complex systems will create a more locally responsive market. In the short term, by providing competition at lower price points. In the long run, by creating a local housing market less correlated with the boom and bust of national markets. This isn't a quick fix; it is a shift to a new paradigm.

A new paradigm has new principles that need to become the expected norm. They are as follows.

No Neighborhood Can Be Exempt from Change

For cities to evolve and adapt, we must allow neighborhoods to change. All neighborhoods; no exceptions. As we take radical neighborhood transformation off the table, we need to bring back the expectation that all neighborhoods are works in progress, changing and adapting, on a continuum of improvement.

While we have some sympathy for the NIMBY opposition to radical neighborhood transformation, the NIMBY mindset of opposition to all change is antithetical to a healthy and responsive housing market. In a new paradigm, everyone should expect their neighborhood to change over time.

By necessity, change means adding more housing units. It means the neighborhood thickens up, maturing over time. This change cannot be subordinate to concerns over traffic, parking, or neighborhood character. Accepting that all neighborhoods must mature over time is a conscious decision to substitute the discomfort of working out block-level frictions for the broader pain of a dysfunctional and non-responsive housing market.

The next increment of development intensity needs to be allowed everywhere, by right.

To facilitate neighborhoods that mature over time, all neighborhoods need to be allowed to change. The right to change needs to be embedded in a permitting process that provides rapid, predictable approvals to everyone seeking to incrementally add new units.

We recognize that the "next increment of development intensity" is open to interpretation. Cities won't always get this right. If we start with the idea that no neighborhood can be exempt from change, we know that the next increment always includes adding housing units. This alone will get most of our neighborhoods unstuck.

As a rule of thumb, for a neighborhood of single-family homes, the next increment must include duplexes and backyard cottages. In other words, there should be no regulatory friction for a neighborhood of single-family homes to transform, over time, into a neighborhood of duplexes.

For neighborhoods that are more intensely developed, there is going to be place-specific disagreement over what the next increment of intensity is. Those conversations won't be without tension, but they will begin with a shared principle that there is a next level of intensity. The debate will merely be over how large that leap is. We welcome that healthy discussion.

Our standard for "by right" is straightforward: a property owner seeking to build a new housing unit should be able to show up at city hall with a completed permit application by 9:00 a.m., depart before noon with permission to build, and be legally working on the project after lunch. For many local governments, this might seem impossible.

If we rapidly want to add new units, a new paradigm demands that we change our systems to make it possible.

Some developers might argue that the next increment of development intensity isn't economically feasible, that they need a large leap in the development pattern to finance their projects. We recognize that reality can exist in the current paradigm, but it's not the issue we're trying to solve here. Further, responding to the problem with incentives or subsidies for large leaps in development will only make that imbalance worse.

For cities that are sensitive to this concern, simply retain the current permitting and approval process for large leaps while streamlining the next increment to be by right. Let the large leap developer apply for zoning changes, special use permits, and whatever else is necessary, and then go through the required public hearing process, to receive the scrutiny a large leap in development deserves. Just don't make the incremental developer go through that same process to do something modest and incremental. Approval for the next increment of development intensity should always be quick and simple.

No Neighborhood Should Experience Radical Change

We have become used to a cycle of neighborhood growth, stagnation, and decline. In the current paradigm, we arrest decline with large infusions of capital. The distorting effect of this capital infusion warps the housing markets while creating justified public backlash.

The way the process works is simple. In a distressed neighborhood, multiple lots are assembled into a larger parcel. That process reinforces stagnation and decline as pending redevelopment creates disincentives for landlords to improve properties that will be torn down anyway. Once there is enough land for redevelopment, a developer seeks some type of rezoning or variance from the established rules to build something out of proportion to the existing neighborhood.

For many, this transformation feels like a process to address decline. It feels like progress. For others, it feels like a betrayal. They see special treatment given to a predator that treats their neighborhood like prey. The highest and best use for their home is now understood to be large-scale redevelopment. A cycle of slum living ending in forced dislocation.

The rational goal of residents in the current paradigm is to not allow their neighborhood to become the one chosen for radical change. In chosen neighborhoods, the rational response is to resist all change. This is contrary to everything that needs to happen in a new paradigm.

As a rule of thumb, a person living in a neighborhood today should be able to leave the neighborhood, come back at any point in the next decade, and find it recognizable. Changed, but recognizable, in the same way someone would recognize a friend or family member maturing after a decade apart. We have to say no to radical neighborhood transformation.

There Must Be a Low Bar of Entry to Obtaining Housing

Cities need to invite more people to fully participate in cocreating neighborhoods. Across the board, the standards for obtaining a permit for a home, building a home, and financing a home have increased beyond what many capable people can accomplish. We need to shift our systems to invite those people off the sidelines.

For example, many cities have created regulatory provisions allowing for "tiny homes," houses generally less than 800 square feet. The provisions often require the person seeking to build a tiny house to seek permission from neighbors, attend public hearings, and receive special approval from a planning board. In the current paradigm, there is fear that allowing tiny homes will somehow undermine the integrity and value of the neighborhood. This is not unreasonable when neighborhoods are locked in regulatory amber, unable to change or mature.

In a new paradigm, one that embraces neighborhoods that change and mature over time, there is no such thing as a tiny home. Instead, we can call them what people around the world for thousands of years called them: starter homes.

Low-cost housing units that are designed to be added on to, moved, or torn down and replaced have been the initial building block of neighborhoods throughout time. People start small, building what they can, and expand as resources allow. It is only during the suburban experiment that the starter home became a novelty.

We need to make it really easy to build starter homes. Regulatory reform, training for incremental developers, and creative local finance programs can combine to expand the roster of people invited to do so.

Housing Must Be Part of a Neighborhood-level Economic Ecosystem

Neighborhoods that are evolving and maturing need to be able to respond to stress and opportunity in novel ways. As change occurs, cities need to be able to meet more of the needs of residents within the neighborhood itself. That means introducing neighborhood-scale commercial enterprises, allowing the local market to adapt to meet local needs.

For example, adding more housing to an existing neighborhood frequently raises concerns over parking. If everyone in the neighborhood must undertake an auto trip to perform routine tasks such as getting groceries or medicine, then there will be more demand for parking than the neighborhood can accommodate. The situation quickly becomes zero-sum.

If, however, entrepreneurs can meet the demand for groceries and medicine within the neighborhood, driving trips can be slowly replaced by walking and biking trips. Parking needs can adjust downward over time. Admittedly, there is tension in this transition, but it is stress that has multiple potential responses.

The Covid-19 pandemic created broader acceptance of corner stores, small commercial units tucked into residential lots, neighborhood dining options, and home offices. The scale of these operations needs to be compatible with the neighborhood.

As the ecosystem matures, success looks like businesses that cater to the neighborhood without the need for outside automobile trips. The healthiest economic ecosystem, one with the most positive feedback loops, is one where walking and biking is so pleasant and convenient that these become the preferred alternatives for most trips.

Public Infrastructure Investments Must Focus on Where People Struggle to Use the City as It Has Been Built

The developer-led suburbanization model builds a lot of housing on the edge of the city. This is enabled through massive infrastructure expansions. A new paradigm for housing will incrementally thicken up existing neighborhoods with housing units. There must be a corresponding pivot in infrastructure investment, away from building out new roads and pipes for greenfield development and toward serving the evolving needs of existing neighborhoods as their populations grow.

Those needs won't be identified through a top-down process: they must be identified from the bottom up. Fortunately, the scale of the activity means that it's the kind of thing any community can undertake, regardless of size, regardless of budget. It begins with the recognition that the best investments, the ones with the highest financial rates of return, address an urgent need experienced by a real person.

At Strong Towns, we've developed a simple, four-step process for identifying this kind of opportunity and making it happen:

1. Humbly observe where people in the community struggle.
2. Ask the question: What is the next smallest thing we can do right now to address that struggle?
3. Do that thing. Do it right now.
4. Repeat.

The key to the first step is humility. Emptying our minds of as many preconceived notions about the problems and solutions in a place as possible, we humble ourselves to observe as a proxy for lived experience. We are trying to understand, from the perspective of those who use the city, where the struggles are. A great way to observe is to walk with someone, literally treading the path with them, to understand how they struggle.

Observation is so much more powerful than asking. When cities do surveys, focus groups, or public hearings, they are engaging in a process for receiving input that is orderly and comfortable. To identify the best investments, technical staff need to venture outside their comfort zones.

Where the first step requires humility, the second requires self-discipline. Instead of seeking a comprehensive solution, instead of trying to fix everything once and for all, take the humble observations and simply try to make that struggle a little bit easier. What can be done, immediately, with the materials and capacity we have available right now?

Local leaders interested in maturing neighborhoods need to discipline themselves to work in this manner. As Jane Jacobs suggests, neighborhoods must be a cocreation. By disciplining ourselves to act incrementally, we allow the people living in the neighborhood to react to the change. Their actions then demonstrate to us where the next struggle is.

This is why, in the third step, don't form a formal committee. Don't hire a consultant. Don't pause eighteen months while a grant application is processed. Once a struggle has been humbly observed and the next smallest thing to be done identified, go out and do that thing. Make things better right now.

Obviously, this is not a comprehensive solution. This small step will not eradicate struggles from the neighborhood. That is why the fourth step is to repeat the process over and over and over. This is the process of cocreating, the way neighborhoods are made by everyone, for everyone. It's the way neighborhoods mature to provide more housing while becoming financially productive.

This approach may sound baffling to local government officials comfortable with the current paradigm. What we are describing is a new paradigm, a radically different way to deliver local government. Cities can start building new muscle memory within a shifting paradigm by establishing rapid reaction teams tasked with implementing the four-step approach.

Maintaining a Sense of Urgency

A response that doesn't immediately address people's need for shelter can rightly be accused of being callous, even if it establishes a system that, in the long run, turns out to be beneficial to those struggling in the current paradigm.

People who are homeless, having extreme difficulty finding shelter, struggling with excessive rent increases, or saddled with an unaffordable mortgage are likely to be uninspired by an approach that does not provide immediate relief.

These are reasonable critiques, and we acknowledge them. We are not proposing a solution that eliminates all struggle. To the contrary, a paradigm that embraces complexity and bottom-up responses to stress depends on there being stress to respond to. We are not providing a solution but a mechanism for solutions to emerge from within complexity.

That provides little solace for those who don't know whether they will have a roof over their heads next month. The strategies we outline in the following chapters have a sense of urgency behind them, but they will take time to put in place. Any worthwhile change will.

That means there remains an immediate need for housing that advocates and local leaders will have to address. How does this immediate work align with a new paradigm for housing?

When it comes to temporary measures, we find ourselves open to an expansive toolbox, even though we may favor some tools over others. For example, we tend to be suspicious of rent control as it reinforces a cycle of stagnation on systems that need to be adaptive. A temporary rent stabilization measure, however, can address displacement concerns in a surging market.

In the short term, there are very few policies or projects that add more housing units that we would aggressively say no to. However, that list starts to grow as time horizons lengthen. Where to draw the line is always open for debate; reasonable people can disagree.

As a guideline, we should pause when an approach to address immediate needs breaks a critical feedback loop, such as rent control locking in an artificial price. We should also avoid approaches that entrench the dysfunction of the current paradigm, such as building new single-family homes on greenfield sites or 5-over-1 apartments in a poor neighborhood subject to gentrification.

The more we can expand the ecosystem of those working bottom-up on housing issues, the quicker we will make that transition to a new paradigm.

10

Releasing the Swarm

To break out of the housing trap, we need a housing revolution. We must rapidly add new homes in abundance, broadly distributed across many existing neighborhoods. Many of them must be at a lower price point than what is typical of new construction today. Who will build them?

The large players that dominate the homebuilding industry today will not. Their business model relies on economies of scale, standardization of design elements, and streamlined finance. The kinds of opportunities that exist to incrementally thicken up existing neighborhoods offer none of those advantages.

In many local housing markets, these large players constitute an effective oligopoly: a small number of producers who collectively enjoy price-setting power due to limited competition. Think of airlines or broadband Internet companies as classic examples of how oligopolies lead to high prices and poor service.

These companies all respond to similar incentives, and largely pull back on new buildings when the market cannot guarantee their required profit margins. This implicit collusion strategy practiced by the oligopoly will limit any correction in housing costs. Unless, that is, it can be undermined by upstart competition.

A new paradigm will need to come from outside and from below. Many of those who develop housing now will continue to do so. But it will be new entrants to the game, not the existing players, who upend business as usual.

These new entrants will be incremental developers.

A good working definition of incremental development is that which builds on the fabric of a neighborhood that already exists, iterating on what's there. This can be contrasted to development that introduces a total transformation or a radical leap in the development pattern of a place.

We know that incremental development can produce rapid growth in housing because it has done so before. It is the model that built virtually every American city before the Great Depression. What we today call missing-middle housing was the principal building block of those cities.

American cities experienced rapid growth in the late 19th century, often staggeringly rapid by today's standards. The fastest-growing major metropolitan area in the US in the 2010s was Austin, Texas, which grew at about 3% per year over that period. In contrast, Chicago in the 19th century experienced population growth of over 9% per year.

This was possible because of the decentralized nature of that growth. A multitude of small developers bought lots and built housing, following basic patterns that had been shown to work. The two-flats of Chicago, the row houses of Philadelphia and Baltimore, the brownstones of Brooklyn, the triple-deckers of Boston: all were produced in great quantities by a largely decentralized swarm of incremental developers and builders.

Ad hoc adaptation shaped these patterns. Where a design choice was widely replicated, it was because something worked and was copied and became part of a development vernacular. People talked to each other; people shared know-how. There was an ecosystem: decentralized networks of tradespeople, laborers, lenders, and small-scale developers you could plug into and learn how to do the work.

This doesn't mean development wasn't ever big business. It was. Land speculators carved up subdivisions at the edges of cities and faced criticisms that would sound quite familiar today. But even the big developers of the time were working on the scale of a few blocks, not a few square miles, and almost always contiguous with the urban fabric around them.

This meant that smaller-scale operators could play in the same league. You could subdivide a few blocks, but you could also buy a single lot and build on it. And cities under tremendous demographic and social stress were able to accommodate dramatic change because of that.

This was possible because there was an economic ecosystem that supported this activity. Today, much of that ecosystem has been lost. If incremental development is to achieve the kind of scale our cities need, we must rebuild communities of practice and expertise. One of the most compelling experiments in doing just that is unfolding in South Bend, Indiana.

Building an Incremental Development Culture: The South Bend Experiment

Picture a lively open house taking place in a spacious living room on a cool evening. It's a networking event of sorts. There are over 50 people there, including the mayor and members of the city council. Everybody is talking about their latest business venture and exchanging ideas on how they can collaborate.

Now imagine almost everyone in that room, aside from the public officials, is some kind of small-scale developer. More than half of them are women and people of color. Most are working in low-income neighborhoods pockmarked with vacancies, the kind where conventional wisdom says it's impossible to build *anything* profitably, let alone obtain financing to do so. And many of those people live in, and grew up in, those neighborhoods themselves.

It's possible to attend just such a gathering in South Bend.

Belying the idea that incremental development is a sideshow or "doesn't scale," in South Bend a cohort of small developers representing over 100 properties in poor, disinvested neighborhoods are, if taken collectively, the largest developer in the city. And they didn't get there by competing with each other for opportunities but by creating opportunities for each other.

Furthermore, they've done it essentially without subsidy. In the process, they've often provided below-market residential and commercial rents, and space for community-serving activities.

The most important thing to underline is *who* is doing it. Real estate development tends to be an exclusive club. The easiest way to get started is to be independently wealthy or partner with someone who is.

But South Bend's upstart developers are a group that is representative of the city's diversity, and many have come to development without wealth, connections, or formal training.

Building an incremental development ecosystem and support network is like getting a snowball rolling: It takes a long time to acquire momentum, but once you do, the heaviest lifting is behind you. At that point, a whole different story is possible.

A post-industrial city once known for being the headquarters of the Studebaker car company, South Bend's population stagnated in the late 20th century as wealth drained to the suburbs. But it was not until the early 2000s that the city suffered what local planner and demographic historian Joseph Molnar calls "the worst decade in South Bend's history." The city lost 7.5% of its households, or a total of over 3,000. Neighborhoods in economic freefall saw homes and storefronts abandoned or demolished.

It wasn't long before the good news stories began—if you were in the right parts of South Bend. During the 2010s, the city's downtown underwent a tremendous revitalization, with $160 million of new private investment. Massive new developments have also transformed the area immediately south of the campus of Notre Dame University, where the town-gown wall used to be stark.

But on South Bend's west side, the story was different. There, predominantly Black and Latino residents bear long-simmering resentments over disinvestment and neglect of their neighborhoods. In the Near Northwest neighborhood, the neighborhood school was demolished and not replaced after a ceiling collapsed in 1966. There is no full-service grocery store. Older residents remember long-gone professional offices where vacant buildings stand today.

Development that serves these neighborhoods and their existing residents isn't going to look like the slick mid-rise apartments and chain restaurants popping up near the University of Notre Dame. If it is to happen, it must follow a different model: an incremental one.

"Find Your Farm"

This is not one person's story, but Mike Keen is as good a person to start this story with as anyone. Until recently, Keen was a professor of urban studies and sustainability who founded the Center for a Sustainable Future at Indiana University South Bend. In 2016, he decided to walk his talk and, with business partners Dwayne and Corbin Borkholder, become a developer of net zero energy-efficient homes. They launched a small development company called Thrive Michiana.

Keen and his partners envisioned their project filling a need in South Bend's Near Northwest neighborhood, which had not seen a new residential development in over 40 years. But they struggled to obtain financing because of a typical catch-22 in a neighborhood that's been through decades of decline: an appraisal gap. Absent any comparable properties nearby, they could not convince appraisers that their homes would sell for enough to cover their construction costs.

They could wait a generation for the market to catch up. Or they could "work on the neighborhood" themselves. Keen and his partners bought and renovated nearby properties and acquired some 20 vacant lots. Soon, they found themselves with an area of several blocks they were systematically working to cultivate. "What started out intended to be one house became a sustainable neighborhood demonstration project" dubbed Portage Midtown.

And the market is turning a corner. Rising property values mean that appraisers now have comparable sales to point to, which will help more aspiring small developers obtain the loans they need, in a virtuous cycle.

Keen and his collaborators' approach to development can be summarized as "find your farm." This means to pick an area—smaller than a neighborhood, maybe just a few blocks—where you intend to commit for the long haul, and then come to know that area intimately. Live there if you can. Frequent its businesses. Get to know every neighbor, every property. Do multiple projects there: You'll find opportunities once you're a known, trusted resource to your neighbors, and you'll bring them along with you. Keen has helped other developers acquire property and do projects in the vicinity of his own, to the mutual benefit of everyone involved.

The Portage Midtown "farm" now includes about 100 properties. About 50 are homes that have been renovated; about 45 are vacant lots picked up in tax delinquency sales. Estimates are that by 2031, redevelopment in Portage Midtown alone will total $15.2 million in private investment and deliver about $300,000 in taxes to the city per year—a staggering 2,334% increase from before Keen started.

Growing an Intentionally Inclusive Developer Community

South Bend would not have the community of citizen developers it does today without the involvement of Monte Anderson. Anderson, a Dallas-area developer, has long worked to teach aspiring developers the basics of the work: how to find a farm, identify a project, raise capital, plan, design, build, and manage. Anderson cofounded the Incremental Development Alliance, an organization that seeks to encourage small-scale and incremental development efforts nationwide by training both aspiring developers and municipal officials on how to make these projects work.

Keen met Anderson in 2016 and began attending the group's programs. In late 2017, he helped get the City of South Bend to bring the Incremental Development Alliance team in for a workshop and a stress test of their zoning code, identifying obstacles to infill development. The city kicked in $4,000, while Keen raised the other $16,000.

Keen believed incremental development had the potential to transform Near Northwest and other South Bend neighborhoods. It was important to him to engage those neighborhoods from the beginning in an intentionally inclusive way. Keen reached out to community organizations and offered to have them be cosponsors of the IDA events at no charge if they would send the information out to all their contacts. The result was a diverse group of interested attendees at the first lecture and workshop. Keen also worked to arrange scholarships for participation in the developer workshop.

The goal is real estate development as a form of community organizing. To do this well, deliberate discomfort is a must. "Take a look at what you look like, and whatever you look like, try to find some folks that look different than you and really connect with them," says Keen.

Keen began to host regular small-developer receptions at his house, as a community formed around the group. "We call it, informally, the Michiana Incremental Development Alliance Ecosystem. But all that is, is a spreadsheet where I've got a bunch of phone numbers. There are 15–20 people actually doing development. But we've got city officials, financial people, contractors, architects, engineers, community members, nonprofits; we've got about 180 people on that list."

Paraphrasing Anderson, Keen says, "We don't want to have any secret handshakes. We don't want a situation where you've got to be invited to the Christmas Party of a law firm on the 20th floor of a building to know how to make things happen in the city."

The incremental developer cohort in South Bend has a culture of generosity. They share knowledge and connections, with no proprietary hoarding of trade secrets. Keen explains: "You know a contractor? Cool, now I know a contractor. You know a banker who understands mixed-use buildings and is open to issuing a loan for one? Hey, I want to know that person too. You know the mayor? Now I know the mayor."

Connections open doors, especially in small-scale development, where knowing the right lender or the right affordable but also highly competent contractor is worth its weight in gold.

The result is that a remarkable cross section of South Bend residents have become small-scale developers in the past few years. Many are graduates of local entrepreneurship programs, including the SPARK program through St. Mary's College for women and minority entrepreneurs, and the Entrepreneurship and Adversity Program at Notre Dame. Most are South Bend natives, and many speak of being motivated primarily by a desire to see their neighborhoods revitalized.

Barbara Turner, the daughter of Mississippi sharecroppers, now renovates homes in South Bend. Sarah Hill, a public library administrator, does the same. Consuella Hopkins has turned a home base for her tax preparation business into a shared workspace with 15 rentable business suites, and has long-term dreams of a residential "village" alongside the project. When asked, Keen is quick to offer up more such names and stories. South Bend's incremental development ecosystem now offers a viable pathway into development for people who do not come with prior connections or fit the conventional profile of a real estate developer.

Cities Built by Many Hands

The underlying question raised by efforts such as South Bend's is, "Who gets to be a developer?"

For most of human history, much of the work of city building was done by people who were not professional developers in the sense we recognize today. Barn raisings were big events in farm communities.

Homeowners put a second story on their own home when they had kids and needed more space. The most common housing configurations in the pre-suburban era were essentially home-cooked solutions.

In the modern world, development, like so many other areas of traditional life, has been professionalized and siloed. It is understood as a specialized industry and a particular skill set that most of us no longer involve ourselves with—with the notable exception of home remodeling projects.

There are good reasons to have a class of professionals who know the ins and outs of building, of course. Most of us find it good that we don't have to be expert car mechanics but can simply take our car to one for repairs as needed. Buildings have higher safety and quality standards than they once did, and specialization frees up what wasn't necessarily time people of the past chose to spend.

But we have overcorrected. The bar of entry to participate in creating housing is now too high, and the number of participants too few.

We need a class of semi-amateur citizen developers many times larger than exists today. This will involve a range of levels of financial commitment and expertise.

On one end of that range are house hackers. These are individual homeowners modifying their own property in ways that create a new housing unit, by carving out a basement or attic apartment or adding a backyard cottage. These projects should be attainable to the same sorts of people who would undertake a home remodeling project, and they can be made so with regulatory and financing changes.

At the other end of the range will be those who do make development their day job, and who acquire properties for the purpose, but who generally do so in or near the neighborhood in which they live and at the incremental scale of individual lots within an existing built fabric.

That would still mean that most people aren't doing development themselves. But it would mean the potential for 10 to 100 times more small projects that are neighborhood-enriching and fill gaps. The vacant-lot infill building, the historic building renovation, the duplex or fourplex conversion, the corner store or accessory retail space (non-housing uses that nonetheless support local housing options), and other such things are ideal projects for the small-scale developer.

How many people do you know who have considered doing a development project in their neighborhood? These are people who have asked, "What if I were the one who bought that vacant lot?" Most will not go through with such a daunting prospect. What would it mean for our neighborhoods if more of them felt equipped and empowered to pursue those dreams?

The Incremental Developer's Business Model

One thing that it would almost certainly mean if more ordinary visionaries pursued incremental development projects is that we would see a greater variety of housing types, sizes, and price points.

Already in this book, we have seen that the development industry is configured to deliver housing monocultures. A handful of ubiquitous products are replicated in city after city because they are easy to finance and build in a way that exploits economies of scale. The creation of secondary financial markets for certain common loan products has strengthened the tendency toward monoculture. So have zoning codes and permitting processes that are optimized for the familiar and legible.

These monocultures do not serve the needs of many Americans. Whole neighborhoods in need of housing and reinvestment experience no development activity whatsoever. Others see housing built that is mismatched to local demand, in size, configuration, or price point. An illustrative example is that while two-thirds of American households have one or two members, a full 88% of new homes built have three bedrooms or more. This is a function of a broken market that is more responsive to capital flow than to local demand.

The business model of the incremental developer is based not on financial economies of scale but on hyperlocal knowledge. Deep knowledge of a neighborhood makes it possible to identify opportunities that are invisible or inaccessible to a larger developer operating at a greater remove. Many incremental developers do not merely live in the neighborhood in which they do all their development work: a common strategy, especially for getting started, is to live in your own project. This allows your own rent to cover construction, in much the same way that the builder-owners of New England triple-deckers once did.

Developers working at such a hyperlocal scale will recognize and fill in the gaps in existing neighborhoods. This means working with constraints: small and irregular pieces of land and unusual contexts. The result is more experimentation and a greater diversity of housing configurations.

If the city is akin to a complex ecosystem, then the work of incremental developers is capable of filling ecological niches, like weeds that grow in sidewalk cracks, or shrubs that fill in the forest understory, adapted to live in the shade of larger trees.

Incremental Development as "Gentlefication"

The work of community-minded incremental developers can also help stabilize low-income neighborhoods and communities that might otherwise fear a lose-lose choice between stagnation and decline, on the one hand, and transformative change and displacement on the other.

This has been Monte Anderson's goal across a series of development projects in his own hometown of Duncanville, Texas, a working-class suburb of Dallas. Anderson calls his approach "gentlefication," as opposed to gentrification. What distinguishes it is that it is focused on people as much as buildings.

Anderson's strategy in Duncanville was to rehabilitate the town's small downtown, one mixed-use commercial building at a time. Because he knew the community closely, he could have a tenant in mind who wanted a long-term presence in the neighborhood, and he would work with them to design a space that they could not only occupy but eventually buy from him. Often this meant creating a small storefront with a studio apartment or two behind or on top, allowing a local entrepreneur to have a small space for their business and a modest rental income, or a home for themselves attached to their shop.

Over time, the roster grew. A donut shop owner. A photographer. An insurance agent. A tamale shop, a music store. A cluster of buildings are now owned by local businesses with a long-term commitment to the neighborhood, which acts as a stabilizing force against the prospect of gentrification.

Anderson incorporates housing into many of his projects. This is possible in part because FHA mortgage financing is now available for residential projects that contain up to 49% nonresidential space, following a 2016 rule change.

The housing units associated with Anderson's projects are a flexible and low-cost option that can serve neighbors who might not be served well by conventional housing options. "If I've got two apartments in the back of my business," he says, "I can rent to the bus boy down the street, who I like because he mows my yard. The lady's daughter, my friend down the street, who's come back to her hometown and is a single mom. I can rent it to the kid down the street with schizophrenia who drinks too much, but he's not dangerous. The adult with Down syndrome."

If this has echoes of the way working-class Americans a century ago made housing work for themselves by such strategies as living above the shop, or renting out a floor in a triple-decker, it should. This is the inherent wisdom of the traditional pattern of development, one that rewards small and improvisational bets.

Incremental development based on a "farm" model has the potential to build social capital and strengthen community support networks in a way that is far less likely with conventional real estate development. This is not to paint with a broad brush or to romanticize the landlord-tenant relationship. And it is not to suggest that real estate development is even remotely a comprehensive community development or anti-poverty strategy. But in places where needs are acute and immediate, a developer who is deeply embedded in the community in which they work can be a different sort of presence.

Bernice Radle, an incremental developer from Buffalo, New York, and a collaborator in a new consulting and coaching venture with Anderson and Keen, tells of an experience that reaffirmed the value of this approach for her. When Buffalo was hit by a crippling snowstorm the week of Christmas 2022, the occupants of Radle's 27 properties were beset with problems: freezing pipes, cats that needed feeding, owners who couldn't get back into town. Because Radle's "farm" is geographically small, she knows all of her tenants, and they quickly banded together to help each other out with these needs at a time when formal institutions were overwhelmed.

It Takes a "Swarm"

The hyperlocal context that makes incremental development successful means that it cannot be scaled in the way that the suburban experiment scales: by the top-down deployment of massive capital. An incremental development revolution will not be built. It will grow.

If you want to grow good things that will propagate at scale, you need to set in motion processes that take care of themselves without micromanagement. When we refer to incremental developers and builders as a "swarm" (a term borrowed from urban designer and planner Kevin Klinkenberg [2021]) it's for a reason—and not the menacing one you might associate with a word such as "swarm."

What we need are ecosystem builders. We need pollinators. People who will share and transport the seeds of good ideas and help them take root in more places. It's not just about who does the work of pouring cement or hammering nails or placing a pipe in the ground. It's about who is working to grow, share, and keep alive a culture of building needed homes. A "swarm" of neighborhood-scale builders does this work separately but together, in harmony but without one guiding hand.

How Cities Can Support the Growth of Incremental Development

If there's a simple answer to the question "Where did all the incremental developers go?" it's that incremental development is no longer any sort of path of least resistance to making money in real estate. It requires overcoming unusual, intersecting, and overlapping obstacles to make it work.

Cities serious about growing an incremental development ecosystem must bring their existing small builders to the table and seek to acquire a deep understanding of where, and why, local regulations stand in the way of housing opportunities.

If there were only one or two pervasive policies or practices standing in the way of good development projects, the call to action would be easy: repeal them. Eliminate them. But often, there are dozens of regulatory barriers—and they interact to cause problems in ways that aren't obvious. Individually straightforward rules—for example, parking mandates and height limits—can interact with each other with a sort of Rube Goldberg complexity.

Every small developer has "war stories" in which an unseen complexity derailed a project. Parking mandates require a 16-unit apartment project to be scaled down to four units. Commercial stormwater requirements applied to a residential fourplex impose $60,000 in unanticipated costs. These are just two of many examples we have collected at Strong Towns from the incremental developers we know.

To make their work viable in more contexts, small developers need simplicity and flexibility. The elimination of single-family zoning and parking mandates are near prerequisites for incremental development to have a meaningful impact in any neighborhood. But they are not the end of the story.

Cutting the Gordian knot of regulatory complexity should also mean broadly legalizing the next increment of development on small lots, unusually configured lots, and unusual arrangements of homes on a property—for example, cottage courts, in which a handful of small homes surround a central courtyard. The norm in pre-suburban cities was that developers experimented and arrived at replicable, successful forms. The same idiosyncratic process must be allowed to unfold again.

If you are a local leader who wants more small-scale development in your city, you need to make it attractive. Not all scale economies can be overcome, but cities can compensate by streamlining the regulatory process for small-scale development in a way that they do not for large projects, whose neighborhood impacts deserve more scrutiny. A 5-over-1 developer can afford to go through a public hearing and a city council vote. A triplex developer should be able to walk into City Hall and walk out with a permit.

In South Bend, the local government has been deeply involved in supporting and sustaining incremental development through policy changes. The planning department has worked to simplify regulations and eliminate barriers to filling in neighborhood gaps. This has resulted in an award-winning zoning code that Planning Director Tim Corcoran says is intended to require only "a high school education and an hour of your time" to understand and use.

The city abolished its parking mandates in 2021. In 2022, South Bend introduced pre-approved building templates for housing and commercial structures that would fit into its existing neighborhoods and meet its zoning requirements.

The establishment of preapproved templates is a policy many cities might consider. It costs the public only a modest amount up front, and it can pay dividends for years. It is a policy that deliberately seeks to recapture a key element of the pre-suburban building culture: tested, resilient patterns that small builders can effectively "plug and play."

Just as important as all those policy changes, though, is South Bend's embrace of its small developer community. The city has worked as a convener for this community, taking over the sponsorship of the regular small-developer meetups and seminars that Keen helped launch.

City Hall's enthusiasm reflects a commitment to community development and a willingness to try unorthodox things. As Alkeyna Aldridge, who served as the first director of engagement and economic empowerment at the city, puts it, that willingness is rooted in the recognition that "our system is so broken, the need is so big, and the cavalry's not coming."

The whole concept of a Department of Economic Empowerment is unusual. It was established in early 2019 in response to residents' concern about the huge disparity between redeveloping areas of South Bend and the continuing problems west and south of downtown. Then-mayor Pete Buttigieg greenlit the concept of a department that would facilitate neighborhood-level economic development.

The city assists its small-developer cohort in two principal ways.

1. **Technical assistance.** The department holds Build South Bend workshops in which participants can hone their understanding of the basic steps in development—"How do I stabilize my building, develop a rent roll, talk to a contractor or an architect?" They can also share what their "farm" is and connect to neighbors who might be touching it. "Hopefully the technical assistance process helps them get some numbers that they can take to the bank," says Aldridge.

2. **Facilitating networking and peer support.** "This is for the people who say, 'I've never worked with an attorney before, and I find attorneys to be really scary and intimidating and expensive,'" says economic development specialist Marty Mechtenberg. The city can help facilitate introductions to bookkeepers, CPAs, contractors, and architects "who we know get how to work with the little guy. We're giving folks access to that ecosystem, peer-to-peer, and peer-to-broader-network. And also to the city itself. People don't know how to work with the city, who to ask questions about zoning, building codes, et cetera. People buy properties because they have an idea, and we don't want them to later find out 'You can't do that.'"

Not "Does It Scale?" but "Does It Replicate?"

Is South Bend unique? Does its experience hold lessons for other places?

South Bend is illustrative of a crucial point about incremental development. The historically depressed economy in South Bend is part of what creates opportunities to do this work. This model would not port in the same way to an affluent place with extremely high property values, or a market already dominated by deep-pocketed investors. Such places may need to wait for incremental development in cheaper locations to bring prices down organically, before certain incremental opportunities become viable.

Incremental developers, because of their deep connection to a place, are able to identify underappreciated opportunities and undervalued property. They can prove the market where the conventional wisdom is that there isn't one. And the model of development is fundamentally rooted in long-term cultivation as opposed to short-term extraction. You're creating value through patience and commitment to a place.

This can happen anywhere there's a community and work to be done. But the energy can only come from within. For this reason, Keen says, the right question is, "Not how does it scale, but how does it replicate?"

"I see this as a form of biomimicry, because I come at it from a sustainability perspective," says Keen. "I see the small-scale development approach as a form of DNA. It's a pattern; it's a method. It's going to adapt differently in different contexts. But if you have a dandelion seed, a bird can drop it anywhere, and it's going to create dandelions. Unless something is really wrong with that place, something will grow."

11

Financing a Housing Revolution

At Strong Towns, we constantly challenge ourselves to not get lost in "after the revolution" thinking. *After the corporate financial system is overthrown, then we will . . . After the market crashes, then we will . . . After this or that political party wins a supermajority, then we will. . . .*

"After the revolution" thinking is the stuff of Reddit threads and graduate school parties. The reality is that the financial system seems unstable, but it has been that way for decades now. Things may change rapidly in the coming months, or it may take additional decades to reach a new equilibrium. We don't pretend to know, but we also can't wait around for something to happen.

Local leaders who want to address the housing trap, who want to ensure there is adequate shelter at prices people can afford, need to accept that the injustices of the American financial system are a separate problem. People called to work on that problem should do so, but the rest of us can't wait around for a resolution. We need to do what we can to address the housing trap using the tools we have on hand locally. We need to do it now.

This doesn't mean we are powerless, but there are trade-offs. Developing nations use capital controls to regulate the flow of what is called "hot money" into and out of their countries. Without capital controls, a small country in a globalized market can be overwhelmed with a sudden flow of money coming in. This rising tide will raise all boats, providing cash for investment and consumption and often broadly raising standards of living. It all feels good, until the tide goes rapidly back out. At that point, crushing debts and revealed malinvestment lead to economic stagnation, even depression.

Capital controls are designed to buffer a smaller nation from these rapid and distorting money flows. The goal is to have local markets that are responsive to local supply and demand, not the mania of much larger outside capital markets. The trade-off of a system of capital controls is that the small country gives up the boom to avoid the bust. They are giving up rapid growth to gain stability.

American cities cannot enact capital controls. However, there are ways to buffer the inflow of capital and reduce the boom-and-bust distortion it has on local housing markets. There are two reasons this is difficult to do.

First, as discussed in Chapter 1, seemingly everyone likes the boom. When housing prices go up, lots of people benefit. Lots of businesses benefit. Government benefits. A policy to reduce the boom, to keep housing prices responsive to the local ability to pay, requires a lot of intention. How many homeowners, if given the choice, would give up 7% annual appreciation of their home? We all want affordability, but what will we forego?

Pretend that, a decade from now, your personal home can (a) double in value, but housing in your community will be even less affordable than today, or (b) not change, but housing in your community will be far more affordable for more people. Regardless of your answer, acknowledge that it is challenging for any individual to forego large personal gains and choose (b) in that scenario.

We have no idea what housing appreciation rates will be over the next decade. We can't present this trade-off to voters. We can, however, choose a path that trends closer to the stable and affordable scenario in (b) than the boom and unaffordability scenario of (a). That is the difficult path, one far less traveled.

The second reason why tempering the boom-and-bust cycle is so difficult is that we have an urgent need to build a lot of housing. We actually need a boom in housing construction. It is counterintuitive to suggest that reducing our enthusiasm for some forms of new home construction will lead to a net increase in new homes. Yet this is what is needed to break out of the housing trap.

Our goal is clear. We need rapid growth in new housing units. We need it without the flow of distorting levels of capital and subsequent rapid price appreciation. This will only happen with a housing market that is more responsive to local supply and demand dynamics and less sensitive to Wall Street–derived capital flows.

Take the edge off the distorting boom while rapidly growing the number of new units, particularly those that anchor the local market to a lower price point.

Buffer from the Distorting Boom

The financial system pours capital into standardized products that can be easily securitized. Single family homes on greenfield sites. Multistory condos or apartment buildings in gentrifying neighborhoods. This is the core of the North American housing strategy.

We need to aggressively pursue other housing options. Simultaneously, we need to dampen our enthusiasm for housing products that keep us locked in the housing trap.

Many local governments subsidize new home construction. They assume the infrastructure service and replacement liability at a financial loss. Sometimes they give a developer free infrastructure or reduced connection fees. Sometimes they serve as the developer and then sell lots to individual home builders.

There are many other variations on this theme. In all of them, the local government is willing to lose money to have more single-family or duplex homes built. Some lose money up front. Nearly all lose money long-term when they assume the ongoing service and maintenance responsibility. In *Strong Towns: A Bottom-Up Revolution to Rebuild American Prosperity* (Marohn 2019), we show how this trade-off has made many American cities insolvent. The result is rising taxes and debt along with declining local service capacity.

Building more homes increases supply. In theory, an increase in supply should lower prices. In reality, a meaningful surge of new homes in new neighborhoods on the edge of the community will ultimately overwhelm a local government with unpayable service and maintenance liabilities. It will also create massive traffic congestion problems. These two constraints alone will impair a local government's ability to pursue this approach to an outcome that affects home prices.

New single-family and duplex homes can be part of a response to housing affordability, but there is nothing gained in subsidizing them. This is particularly true for greenfield development.

Cities such as Fate, Texas, have implemented standards requiring new greenfield developments to have enough tax base to sustain their services. This is a minimum requirement for responsible local governance.

There is no reason for a local government to ban single-family homes. The same with duplexes. Most cities have sites where a single-family home or a duplex is the next increment of development intensity. In those places, we should welcome that construction and make it as easy as possible. Cities simply need to stop subsidizing them. It is a distraction that does nothing for affordability.

The multistory condo or apartment building can be similarly problematic. There is more nuance with this type of construction. In the right location, these buildings provide housing units that meet an urgent need. In the wrong location, they distort the underlying economics of the neighborhood. Neighborhood stagnation and dislocation is the result.

In Chapter 9, we put forth the notion that no neighborhood should experience radical change, but no neighborhood can be exempt from change. Neighborhoods are ecosystems that need to adapt and evolve over time. A neighborhood starved of resources stagnates and does not evolve. Likewise, a neighborhood flooded with resources also broadly stagnates and stops evolving, except for the handful of places chosen for radical transformation. The extremes of too little or too much capital are what we need to avoid.

There is no simple answer, but consider three scenarios. In the first, the public made a multimillion-dollar investment in a transit stop. And yet the neighborhood surrounding the transit stop is filled with parking lots and single-family homes. The immense value of the public investment is misaligned with the small value of the neighborhood. Maybe the transit investment was premature, but it is there. To have any chance at financial viability, the large leap in public investment needs to correspond with a large leap in private investment. This is a place where a multistory, multifamily building should go. In fact, many such buildings are now urgently needed.

In a second scenario, a developer has amassed a handful of single-family homes in a poor and struggling neighborhood. The neighborhood is mostly one- and two-story buildings in marginal condition. The developer is seeking permission to replace the homes with a four-story apartment building.

This feels like progress in many ways. The proposal replaces declining housing with new housing. There is a net increase in units. These are desirable outcomes. However, the proposal is a large leap in the development pattern. As such, it won't stop the decline in the surrounding neighborhood; it will only reinforce it by increasing land values, which makes modest evolution of the neighborhood financially improbable.

Once large leaps are the expected outcome, there is very little incentive to reverse decline. The highest sale price for homes in the neighborhood will come from selling to speculators or developers. In such a place, speculators become slumlords, and developers end up as gentrifiers. Each transaction extracts wealth and capacity from the neighborhood. The large leap in development intensity makes the apartment a less desirable outcome than other approaches.

The third scenario is a proposal to build a 12-story condo building a couple of blocks from the edge of the downtown in a midsized city. The downtown is one- to three-story buildings. The first floors of the downtown buildings have a healthy mix of restaurants and retail. The second and third stories are vacant, largely in a state of disrepair.

The condo building will place more people next to the downtown. This is good for restaurants and retail establishments. Yet this is a large leap in the development pattern. There needs to be caution about the distorting effect on property values and the stagnating effects on the neighborhood.

The scale of the condo building means it is not an organic extension of the neighborhood. Residents will need to leave the neighborhood for employment, groceries, and other daily needs. Extensive investment in parking facilities will enshrine auto dependency. This will slow, maybe even stall, the evolution needed to strengthen the downtown.

These three scenarios are extreme simplifications; the real world is much messier. However, there are some unifying themes.

The proposed multifamily building in each of these scenarios can be financed fairly easily. There is secondary market demand for such a financial product. It can be bundled with other, similar, products and securitized. There is a large and liquid investment market for such securities.

This means that Wall Street capital is easily accessible for the kind of builder ready to deliver. As such, there is no need to subsidize this type of construction. If the project makes financial sense, it will go ahead. Promises to make units affordable in exchange for subsidies have a low return on the public investment. There are far more productive ways to use public resources in pursuit of affordability.

A large leap in the development pattern distorts financial gravity in the neighborhood around it. The greater the leap, the greater the distortion. In mature neighborhoods where there are many large buildings, any distortion is likely to be minimal. In less mature neighborhoods, the distortion effect is much greater. There it will tend to accelerate prices overall, arrest tendencies for organic neighborhood evolution, and drive smaller competitors out of the market.

A final unifying theme is that these types of buildings are almost always controversial. In communities desperate for more housing, they create high stakes, all-or-nothing decisions. Frequently, we see Strong Towns invoked by those who support and by those who oppose these kinds of investments, often in the same meeting. It is possible that both sides are acting in good faith.

Buildings that constitute a large leap in the development pattern stagnate the local market, but it is a stagnant and constrained local market that makes these proposals financially viable in the first place.

The way to eliminate the worst multifamily proposals and to reduce the number of questionable proposals is to have a robust market for affordable units. Large-scale multifamily buildings are easy to finance, but they are costly to build, and thus they require high rents to be a viable product. Their proliferation is, to a large extent, the *result* of a market where other forms of supply are artificially constrained. An abundance of units at lower price points will undermine the profit strategy of the large, entrenched developers and make most of these large multifamily projects financially impractical.

There are valid reasons to oppose some multifamily projects. Even so, anyone who claims to support a Strong Towns approach must be committed to rapidly adding new housing units. That commitment must extend to every neighborhood of their city.

Don't spend energy opposing multifamily construction unless you spend 10 times as much effort supporting the bottom-up approaches outlined in the rest of this chapter.

Repurposing Empty Bedrooms

Since the end of World War II, the size of American homes has grown while the size of American families has shrunk. The result is that there are millions of homes with empty and underutilized bedrooms, some in every city in the country. These bedrooms represent the fastest and cheapest way for any city to rapidly expand their housing supply.

Imagine an elderly widow living alone in a suburban single-family home. She is on a fixed income; money is tight, and the expense of maintaining such a large home is a growing burden. Yet, she does not want to move. She has friends in the neighborhood, attends religious services nearby, and has nostalgia for a place she is not ready to let go of.

What if this elderly widow were allowed to convert one of her spare bedrooms into a studio apartment, which she could then rent? In many instances, it is not an expensive undertaking to install an egress door, put in a kitchenette, and perform upgrades to meet the building code. The only real obstacles are zoning and financing.

Remove the zoning obstacle (see Chapter 9). She could go to the bank and get an equity loan. That will mean taking on debt, making payments, and having ongoing tension over keeping the unit rented. These are barriers enough to stop the project, but they can be easily overcome.

For a local government committed to rapidly adding new housing units, a program to finance the widow's project is relatively simple. The city fronts the cash for the renovations in the form of a loan. Since the city can borrow money at favorable rates, those savings can be passed on. The loan is then repaid through the added tax receipts from the second unit, a micro form of a Tax Increment Financing (TIF) project. A lump sum payment for any remaining balance can be due upon the sale of the home.

To reduce costs, the city can fund a fixed number of these projects each year and bid that work competitively to local contractors. This will save the widow, and any others who wish to do something similar, the burden of having to find contractors or even oversee the project.

There is no need for the elderly widow to front any cash. The local government has patient capital; it can wait a decade or even two to get its money back. But it will get its money back. This kind of approach will rapidly create a new housing unit without any net cost to the taxpayer.

And that's not all. The widow now has additional income, which is quite helpful for obvious reasons. She also has someone nearby who can help with yard maintenance, maybe drive her to the grocery store, maybe even grow to be a cherished friend. It won't always work out beautifully, but adding more housing units in this way supports the community. It is far more valuable than a rent payment to a distant holding company or a mortgage payment to owners of an MBS.

This approach won't be for everybody. Even so, it will benefit people in a position to trade underutilized space for extra monthly income. And since it won't involve expansion of the home, there is no need to expand sewer and water systems. For utility systems, the space is already accounted for. There is no additional stormwater runoff. No traffic study or additional parking spaces are necessary. This is about as simple as adding new housing units can be.

Simple, however, is unlikely to mean easy. Local governments don't work in this way. It's not that they can't; they just rarely do. Local governments today are structured to implement the post-WWII development pattern. What is needed to make this work is a bit of expertise in a bunch of different areas. Construction, finance, contracts, human relations, and a handful of other skills of the small developer.

Many local governments have these skills. They are spread among different individuals working in different departments. Internal restructuring and reframing is necessary to pull this off at scale.

Many cities are up to this challenge. For those that aren't, philanthropy can step in and play a similar role. Community-based nonprofits can bring together homeowners, contractors, and local banks to make these simple housing units happen. A bit of coordination and education lubricated with some modest financial guarantees can get many units built with only a modest commitment of resources.

Financing Backyard Cottages

Slightly more challenging than financing the conversion of the spare bedroom to a studio apartment is financing the accessory dwelling unit (ADU). These are sometimes called "granny flats" or "mother-in-law" suites." For most people, those terms are off-putting jargon. Always communicate to build consensus; it is a cottage.

The great thing about a cottage is the myriad of affordable ways to construct one. The most straightforward is to have it manufactured off-site and then delivered. Manufactured housing is safe and, at the scale of a cottage, can be quite attractive. The manufacturers are experts in permitting, site preparation, and installation. In the right regulatory environment, purchasing a cottage and having it installed is almost as simple as purchasing a car.

This simplicity allows financing to be almost as easy as buying a new car. In Chapter 7, we discussed the explosive growth in backyard cottages in California following a 2017 change to state law. Since then, the market has responded to overwhelming demand with new products that streamline the process. There are many California companies now offering turnkey cottages. They can deliver and install a new cottage, sometimes within 45 days of ordering. They even offer financing from local banks like a car dealership might offer on a car.

Like the studio apartment, a city government can be the patient capital that finances these projects. This can be done at no cost to the taxpayer. The increase in property value will increase tax revenue. That revenue can retire the loan, with full payment coming due upon sale of the property. This is another example of a micro TIF project.

Some states hamper their cities from doing this kind of financing. Local banks can fill that need with the local government providing payment guarantees. This is reminiscent of the role the federal government filled in the Great Depression. Philanthropy can fill the guarantor role as well.

A home with a backyard cottage builds wealth that stays in the neighborhood. The homeowner collects the rent and experiences the increase in property value. There is more housing but no displacement. A modest increase in the use of public utilities won't stress existing infrastructure. The increased monthly utility fees will help with future maintenance costs.

We should place a backyard cottage on any lot where the property owner wants it.

Getting Capital off the Sidelines

There are many neighborhoods where studio apartments and backyard cottages could be built, but the trajectory of the neighborhood prevents it. They are stuck in a cycle of stagnation and decline.

These neighborhoods are often written off as needing an outside savior, some kind of large intervention that shocks things onto a new path. The people there are discounted as helpless victims of this or that social malady.

Many such places can be turned around. It can be done without a flood of capital. And it can be done in a way that primarily benefits the people who are there, the ones doing the transforming.

The first step is recognizing that there is a lot of capacity there, ordinary people who are ready to do helpful things. The primary obstacle is a lack of confidence in the trajectory of the neighborhood. Why invest the time, energy, and resources in a project if the neighborhood is going bad regardless? This is not an unreasonable conclusion.

Paul Stewart of the Oswego Renaissance Association, a private neighborhood-based organization in Oswego, New York, calls this a "bank run on confidence." People have the capacity to do more than what they are doing. They also have the motivation. What they lack is confidence that it will make a difference.

Stewart and a handful of neighbors started the Oswego Renaissance Association to stop the run on confidence. Their group provides modest matching grants to homeowners who are prepared to do something to improve their property. There are two catches.

First, the change must be visible from the street. Whatever is done needs to signal to everyone else that there are people pushing back against decline. It might be a new coat of paint, replacing old windows, or planting some flowers. It doesn't matter how big or small, so long as it is visible to others.

Second, no individual can apply on their own. Applications are only accepted when they come from groups of at least five homeowners on a single block or, in some cases, a target street. Part of the strategy to stop the bank run on confidence is to get people talking to each other about their positive vision for their property. When people discover that their neighbors are also motivated to make things better, barriers to action go away.

A side benefit of having homeowners apply in groups is that entire blocks transform all at once. These blocks are a beacon of hope, and a positive example, to a struggling neighborhood.

The grants are small amounts of money; a neighborhood pride grant is up to $3,000, but awards are often much smaller. The results, however, are transformative. The group was founded in 2013. By the end of 2022, they had awarded $560,000 worth of grants, an average of just over $50,000 per year, money they raised from foundations and businesses in the community. This modest amount leveraged over $5.1 million in private investment throughout the neighborhood.

That is millions of dollars of private wealth taken off the sidelines in what once was a struggling neighborhood. That wealth didn't end up in the pockets of outsiders. It built the capacity of the people in the neighborhood, magnifying their own investment by joining it with the incremental investments of their neighbors (Oswego n.d.).

Financing Small Developers

There is no need to subsidize single-family homes or duplexes being built on greenfield sites. Likewise, there is no need to subsidize the construction of multistory, multifamily housing, such as the 5-over-1. These products already receive massive subsidies from the financial system. They will not become affordable through subsidies but only through a locally responsive market that provides alternative products at competitive price points.

Converting underutilized rooms to studio apartments, installing backyard cottages, and creating an environment where neighborhoods invest in themselves is a great start. The next step to making the market locally responsive is to release the swarm of incremental developers to provide missing-middle housing.

For this, the tools that were used to help homeowners stay in their homes during the Great Depression can also help facilitate the construction of the missing middle. Construction loan guarantees can be provided by the municipality or by philanthropy. Payment guarantees can also be provided to the buyer for the down payment which can be financed locally and help the purchaser avoid having to pay for mortgage insurance.

Guarantees are not without some downside risk, but even factoring that into account, there is no cheaper way to leverage resources to get new units built. Spreading these out over multiple small developers, allowing no more than one or two projects per developer at any one time, will hedge a lot of that risk. Without any defaults, the public's direct cost for a loan guarantee is nothing.

For missing-middle housing, the municipality can also finance connection fees and any infrastructure costs. As patient capital, the city can delay repayment, collect interest only, or phase in principal payments. These can be run through the assessment process allowing the city to receive payment in full upon transfer of the title. Long-term, there is no reason for the local government to lose money financing infrastructure.

Waiving utility connection fees or rebating permit fees sounds enticing, but the economics are generally bad for the municipality. The people who ultimately live in these new homes need the city to properly maintain sewer, water, electricity, drainage, and other systems. They need building and safety inspections. Any housing strategy that doesn't improve the financial health of the city's utilities and ensure a quality housing stock is hurting the community.

Transforming Entire Neighborhoods

There are entire neighborhoods that are starved of capital. They are in need of transformation, but a flood of money will do little except displace and impoverish the people who are there. Many of these neighborhoods are places that went through redlining. The residual impact of discriminatory policies is still evident today.

For example, in Kansas City, Missouri, the core downtown was one of the areas given a top-tier rating when the federal Home Owner's Loan Corporation (HOLC) assembled the city's residential security map. Property owners in this tier were given access to federal financing support during the Great Depression and favorable treatment for decades after. The result is wealth created at a rate just short of $1.9 million per acre (Marohn 2020).

An area directly adjacent to the downtown was designated fourth tier, the lowest rating. It was colored red on the map. These redlined neighborhoods were denied federal support. When others received a boost, these neighborhoods were intentionally marginalized. The result is a wealth creation rate of just $0.2 million per acre, a mere 9% of that of the privileged area (Marohn 2020).

In Kansas City, there has been a lot of community discussion about reparations. Redlined neighborhoods are an obvious cause of lingering disparity. A high percentage of redlined properties were owned by Black property owners in the 1930s. Today, descendants of those families are overrepresented in these struggling neighborhoods.

Nationally, the discussion on reparations is complicated. There exists no consensus course of action. Yet for cities like Kansas City, there are ways for the community to make investments in redlined neighborhoods that begin to address disparities. In fact, all these investments make financial sense on their own. There is no barrier to making them happen.

The redlined neighborhoods in Kansas City have hundreds of vacant lots. These lots are served by municipal infrastructure. This represents a public investment of tens of thousands of dollars in streets and pipes per lot. The infrastructure is already in the ground, not being utilized. The average tax value per lot is $400. The market value is surely higher, but not by much.

The city should give these lots away to anyone ready to build a home. Start with the lots in tax foreclosure. Instead of auctioning them off, make them available to anyone ready to pull a permit and start building. Include stipulations allowing the local government to reacquire the property if construction doesn't happen in a reasonable timeframe. Allow a single person to own no more than two at a time. Get people building.

If the city runs out of tax foreclosed lots, buy up remaining vacant lots at market prices and give them away. Developed lots in redlined neighborhoods have an assessed land value of $17,000 per lot, a 42,500% increase in value over the vacant lots. The mere act of getting a home built on a vacant lot will give the city a couple of hundred dollars per year in additional tax revenue *just for the land*.

As stated in the prior section, waiving utility connection fees for greenfield construction or for construction of multistory, multifamily buildings is a gimmick. It undermines the financial solvency of the public utility. Private utilities, such as electric or natural gas companies, don't do this. It's a sure path to insolvency. Even for infill lots where missing-middle housing is being constructed by incremental developers, the practice is a bad one.

In the case of a place like Kansas City and its redlined neighborhoods, a policy of neighborhood transformation should go ahead and waive the utility connection fees. The pipe is in the ground. It's not being used. Unlike the infill lots, there is no momentum toward making use of this infrastructure. Waive the fees, get a house built, and the property owner will start paying a utility bill. This will be a tremendous benefit to the utility.

As with missing-middle infill projects, the city should provide construction loan guarantees, especially to incremental developers from the neighborhood. Philanthropy can also provide this type of assistance. Philanthropic organizations have a role to play as well in training and supporting incremental developers living in the neighborhood. There is a positive feedback loop with having developers from the neighborhood be the guides of the neighborhood's revival.

The city should also assist the purchaser of a new home with money for a down payment. This can be done using a direct tax subsidy. Such an approach may seem unorthodox. Tax subsidies like this are rarely used for projects as small as a starter home, but there is no reason why they can't be. There are some transaction costs that scale better with larger projects, but most of that comes down to staff time.

A city committed to rapidly adding housing units will naturally redirect their staff. No more time spent on greenfield developments and large commercial projects. Instead, shift their time to working on incremental development projects. The results will be far more profitable for everyone.

Eligibility provisions should be used to restrict down payment subsidies to people from the neighborhood. At least, they should only go to people who will live in the home. Vesting and claw back provisions are common in tax subsidy agreements. They can ensure the program doesn't attract speculators or property flippers.

Cities frequently provide this kind of subsidy on large commercial properties. Kansas City has a history of providing questionable tax increment subsidies on a variety of commercial projects. Many of those projects have lost the taxpayers money (Tuohey and Rathbone 2014). A down payment subsidy in a distressed neighborhood need not.

Home buyers in these neighborhoods also need new mortgage financing tools. Heading into the Great Depression, homes were financed locally, through local banks. The loans were short-term, no more than five years, with a balloon payment at the end. This is because local banks can't assume long-term interest rate risk; they are borrowing short from depositors and can only lend so long.

With federal interventions in the mortgage market, this localized, short-term mortgage product has disappeared. At the same time, it is difficult for local banks to originate small mortgages; the fees they collect as a percentage of the loan amount don't cover their costs when the loan is too small. The secondary market for small loans is, likewise, practically nonexistent. A competitive local product is needed, especially for smaller loans.

This is another instance where local government and philanthropy can intervene to expand the number of options in the marketplace. Simple loan guarantees will allow local banks to resurrect these old, but needed, mortgage types and use them for start-up homes. Done responsibly, there is no cost to the taxpayer. The city is, essentially, cosigning a loan in a neighborhood they are working to see improved. There is no easier way to direct significant resources to the cause of neighborhood transformation.

To transform a neighborhood, it is not enough to have capital available. The people living there need to believe in a better future. They must see their neighborhood as one worth investing in. When the city neglects basic maintenance, it signals that the neighborhood has no future. That is a tragic signal to send to a neighborhood in need of investment.

The infrastructure in affluent neighborhoods tends to be maintained. Enfranchised people complain when it is not. Cities find it easier to neglect neighborhoods with less access to power. Overall, local governments must prioritize basic maintenance of existing infrastructure over system expansion. Within that shift, low status neighborhoods must get a disproportionate share of attention.

Finally, for this effort to transform the neighborhood, the people there need to accumulate wealth. An increasing percentage of the capital that flows into the neighborhood needs to stay in the neighborhood. People not only need an opportunity to own their own homes. They need to own and operate the businesses that serve the neighborhood.

Public investments and subsidies need to be accompanied by zoning code reforms. There should be no regulatory friction to establishing corner stores, accessory commercial buildings, and small start-up spaces throughout the neighborhood. Size limitations for commercial buildings, as well as limitations on parking, are also critical to limit the pressure from dollar stores and other franchises, giving room for a local economic ecosystem to grow.

Reinforce that ecosystem by helping the neighborhood become more walkable. It frees up significant capital when a family can meet its daily needs without having to get in a car and travel to a different neighborhood. Reinforce success with transit investments that connect walkable neighborhoods to each other.

Transforming a neighborhood is an all-in effort. Local governments ready to pursue this strategy need to shift their systems to be bottom-up. In the context of a discussion on reparations, it is a place for any community to start. Yet a bottom-up orientation will benefit all neighborhoods. In this way, the best housing strategies are also the best economic development approaches.

Aligning Local Tax Policy

Research performed by Asheville-based consultancy Urban3 reveals consistent discrepancies in property assessments. In states with property or land-based taxes, there is a process used to determine the value of properties within a jurisdiction. That value, called the "assessed value," is the basis for much local taxation.

The assessed value is supposed to reflect the market value of the property. Obviously, values fluctuate for a variety of reasons. Determining the correct value is an imperfect process. Urban3 studied hundreds of communities, tens of thousands of properties, and identified a troubling trend.

The higher the value of the property, the larger the gap between the assessed value and the market value. Assessed value was consistently under reported, resulting in a lower tax bill for owners of more valuable properties. This is true in absolute and in percentage terms. The pattern held across all communities.

Assessors tend to be closest to the market value for lower-valued properties. There they are generally within a few percentage points. The sale of a lower-valued property consistently prompted an adjustment in assessment to reflect the sale price.

When evaluating expensive properties, assessors underestimate the market value by wide margins. Some properties were assessed at only 20% of their real market value. When expensive homes sell, adjustments are sometimes made but rarely to the sale price. Wide margins persist.

A tax levy is applied proportionately across the tax base. The net result of these errors is that a disproportionate amount of the tax levy is paid by the owners of lower-valued properties. This is a subsidy for owners of expensive properties and an added burden for those owning cheaper properties.

"What you have here are poor neighborhoods subsidizing rich neighborhoods," said Joe Minicozzi, principal at Urban3. "We see this everywhere. It's not only unfair, the laws say this is not supposed to happen."

There are many potential reasons for this discrepancy, but the most obvious one is the appeals process. All property tax systems have a hearing for protesting an assessment amount. Owners of expensive properties have more incentive, and typically more resources, to challenge their assessments. Assessors save themselves a lot of grief by staying well below market value for higher-end properties. There is no similar fear for cheaper properties.

This is another challenge for cities trying to increase housing affordability. The tax process is required to assess homes at market value. With modern database technology and analytical tools, there is no reason it can't. Local leaders need to insist that it does.

The local tax system itself often works against the goal of creating a healthy and responsive housing market. Cities that rely on the sales tax have an incentive structure that devalues all housing. While there are sales taxes paid on construction materials, that ends once the house is finished and occupied. From that point on, the property provides no revenue to the local government. Only in the occupant's role as consumers does a home create local tax revenue.

That creates an overwhelming incentive for a sales tax community to add more commercial development. This is especially true when it caters to people outside the city limits. States where cities are funded by sales tax evolve a unique land-use pattern. Boom-and-bust tracts of commercial buildings cluster on the landscape. Often they migrate near the edge of the city or along a major thoroughfare, far away from anything else. The goal is to capture the most sales tax with the least amount of immediate public investment.

Such places also develop an aversion to adding new housing. That aversion might not dominate, but it will be there as part of the decision-making process. New homes bring additional expenses for roads, pipes, parks, drainage, police protection, fire service, garbage collection, and more. For people already living in the community, why add the expense of more neighbors? This disincentive creates resistance to welcoming new housing.

The sales tax is the most adversarial of local government funding mechanisms. It places the incentives of the local government in opposition to the incentives of its residents. These interests are more aligned with a property tax. Yet, the property tax also creates tension with perverse incentives.

A property tax is applied to the total value of the property (land plus buildings). As property values go up, the city's tax base increases. The local government will then gain more revenue or they can maintain the same revenue while lowering the overall tax rate. On the surface, this seems to align everyone's interests around having property values climb.

From a homeowner's perspective, rising property values mean rising taxes. In fact, someone who adds a studio apartment or a backyard cottage to their property will see their local taxes immediately go up. This creates another disincentive for adding more housing. It punishes those who do with higher taxes.

The disincentives of the property tax could be overcome in the post-war boom as cities expanded horizontally. New homes created new expenses but also new revenues for local government. Today, in contrast, horizontal expansion has slowed, and cities are experiencing widespread fiscal distress. The disincentive to thicken up an existing property by adding more housing is deeply harmful.

While it remains a fringe idea, the land value tax has growing support. It is perhaps the best mechanism to overcome neighborhood stagnation and decline. A land value tax is applied only to a property owner's land, not to any buildings on that land. The local government may have the same tax levy, but that levy is now divided among all the properties in the city based only on land values, not overall property values.

This eliminates the disincentive to building more housing. In fact, there is a tremendous incentive to build more. A property owner can build more housing units and improve the overall value of their property, yet it won't directly increase their local taxes.

Where a property tax punishes those who improve their property, a land tax punishes property that is left idle. Much of the reason cities struggle to get missing-middle housing built on underutilized lots is that the cost of holding onto those parcels is so low. This despite the massive public expenditure in providing municipal infrastructure.

An underused parking lot might seem like a logical place for more housing, but the financial incentives keep it a parking lot. With a sales tax or a property tax, that parking lot is very lightly taxed, even as it rises in value. A speculator can hold onto it, waiting for their target payout, without feeling any tension to sell. Whole neighborhoods can get stuck, trapped in financial amber while the market matures.

With a land value tax, that same parking lot will be taxed at a rate closer to the cost of providing services. There is no subsidy for idleness and there is no punishment for improving the lot. A speculator will have an incentive to make some use of the property, if only to cover their holding costs.

Switching to a land value tax will thaw frozen property markets and create incentives aligned with the building of more housing. In states such as Pennsylvania, where cities have the option to adopt a land value tax, local leaders should transition their cities away from the property tax. In other states, city officials should ask their statewide leaders to give them the authority to use a land value tax system.

12

Building a Strong Town

Strong Towns is an international movement to strengthen cities, towns, and neighborhoods through bottom-up action and local reform.

We recognize that the post-war pattern of development, what we call the suburban experiment, is a radical departure from the norm. Wisdom accumulated over thousands of years of humans building their habitat was cast aside. It was replaced with a top-down, central-ized, technocratic, continent-wide experiment in building cities. We are all lab rats in this experiment. It's not going well.

Our mission is to replace the suburban experiment with a pattern of development that is financially strong and resilient. We don't seek a restoration of the past; we must live in the world we have inherited and make the most of it. Yet we recognize that traditional approaches to building cities harmonized many human priorities. We can learn from practices of the past. Humility in the face of the unknown is core to a Strong Towns approach.

Through dialogue, study, and experience, we have come to believe that:

- Strong cities, towns, and neighborhoods need strong citizens working together to improve the community.
- Local government is not the lowest level of government but the highest level of collaboration for strong citizens working to build a prosperous place.
- For local government, financial solvency is a prerequisite for long-term prosperity.
- Land is the base resource from which community prosperity is built and sustained. It must not be squandered.
- A transportation system is one of many means of creating prosperity in a community but never an end unto itself.
- Job creation and economic growth are the results of a healthy local economy, not substitutes for one.

The Strong Towns approach is a way of rationally responding to the many challenges we face. While there are few insights that are universal, we have found that a strong city, town, or neighborhood:

- Relies on incremental investments ("little bets") instead of large, transformative projects;
- Favors resiliency of result over efficiency of execution;
- Is designed to adapt to feedback, to evolve over time to meet the changing needs of the community;
- Is inspired by bottom-up action ("chaotic but smart") and not top-down systems ("orderly but dumb");
- Seeks to conduct as much of life as possible at a human scale;
- Is obsessive about accounting for its revenues, expenses, assets, and long-term liabilities ("do the math").

Strong Towns, the organization, was founded as a 501(c)(3) non-profit organization in 2009. We set out to build a movement centered on these principles and approaches. Millions of people now read our articles each year. Many more listen to our podcasts, watch our videos, and follow our social media feeds. Thousands of individuals have chosen to support the movement financially by becoming members. Strong Towns has grown into one of today's most influential reform movements.

This book is the third in a series. The first, *Strong Towns: A Bottom-Up Revolution to Rebuild American Prosperity*, examined the financial implications of the post-war development pattern. We have created an economy that can grow very quickly through top-down investments in transportation, infrastructure, and housing. Local governments benefit financially from this growth in the short term and typically position themselves to aggressively participate.

Yet each of these transactions creates a long-term liability for ongoing service, maintenance, and replacement, an obligation that far exceeds the capacity of the community to meet. Our cities have grown themselves into insolvency, a condition that results in cuts in services, deferral of critical maintenance, increases in taxes, and accelerating levels of debt. The Strong Towns approach can arrest this decline and help us rebuild broadly shared prosperity from the bottom up.

The second book in the series is *Confessions of a Recovering Engineer: Transportation for a Strong Town*. Transportation investments are the primary top-down mechanism used to spur local economic growth. Highways are expanded, interchanges built, and frontage roads put in to facilitate yet another iteration of the post-war development pattern. Transit, where it is maintained, is a largely dysfunctional appendage to this auto-based system.

There is a cultural consensus across North America that transportation investments create prosperity. Yet, once again, the long-term trade-offs at the local level have become too overwhelming to ignore. Traffic congestion stifles transportation networks. By design, building more capacity induces more development, which results in even more congestion.

This is a feedback loop that we can no longer afford. Since *Confessions of a Recovering Engineer* was published, the largest federal infrastructure bill in history was signed into law in the United States. Despite its enormous size, the federal spending does not even keep pace with the rate of decline. A decade from now, there will be more lane miles and bridges in a state of disrepair than there are today.

The centralized approach to transportation has also created the absurd situation where it is more convenient to drive miles than it is to walk blocks for routine errands. Throughout North America, highway design standards are routinely applied to local streets, making them simultaneously extremely expensive to build and extremely dangerous to navigate.

In *Escaping the Housing Trap*, we turn the bottom-up Strong Towns lens on housing, one of society's most complex challenges. The story has a familiar rhyme with the prior two books.

The pre-Depression approach to housing was far from perfect. It delivered abundant housing that was broadly affordable, but often of very low quality. The Great Depression saw American policy merge the attempts to solve the quality problem with programs to spur economic growth.

What came after World War II was a tremendous economic boom and an unprecedented expansion of the American middle class. The broad desire to sustain this magical moment has now trapped us in a top-down approach that relies on housing as an investment, making shelter broadly unaffordable.

Housing prices can't fall without wrecking the economy and the financial system. Housing prices must fall if people are to secure shelter and live prosperous lives. These are wicked problems.

The Strong Towns movement has grown to have thousands of members and millions of readers. We've done this not merely by having a more credible explanation of how we got here. The empowering vision of the Strong Towns approach is the assertion that we all have a role in making our places more prosperous. Each of us has an opportunity to move beyond the powerless frustration of complaining about distant, inflexible systems and into supporting meaningful, local change.

Each of us can, as we like to say, do what we can to build a Strong Town.

One of the most exciting developments since the publishing of *Confessions of a Recovering Engineer* is the explosion in Strong Towns Local Conversations. These are groups that form to promote bottom-up action in cities across North America (with some meaningful interest now forming in other parts of the world).

Even before the publishing of *Strong Towns*, we witnessed local groups form in our name. Many of them didn't do much beyond establishing a social media presence, but a notable number of them started to do things both extraordinary and meaningful. We studied these groups to find out what made them so special and then created a program—Local Conversations—to support their efforts and propagate their approach.

As of the publishing of this book, we have nearly 200 active Local Conversations with hundreds more in the formation process. If you read this book and are ready to do something in your community, go to strongtowns.org/local and see if there is a Local Conversation near you that you can join. If there isn't, consider starting one. We'll coach you and support you, as will hundreds of local leaders who have been where you are.

Another exciting Strong Towns program that didn't exist when *Confessions of a Recovering Engineer* was published is the Community Action Lab. We started this program at the urging of one tremendous Strong Towns advocate, Bret Jones of Lake County, Florida.

Bret approached us with a desire "to change everything" about how Lake County was approaching growth, development, and public investment. He was an active participant in the Strong Towns conversation, not just the books but the articles, podcasts, videos, and social media content we publish each day. His goal was to have his neighbors, along with the decision makers in his community, know what he knows.

We struggled to respond to this request, but Bret was persistent. Out of this came the Community Action Lab, a program to shift the culture of an entire community while training a local action team to implement Strong Towns approaches. We are now working with multiple communities through this program, sharing ideas and supercharging bottom-up change. Anyone can follow along with these exciting places, or enroll your community in the program, at strongtowns.org/cal.

With the publishing of *Escaping the Housing Trap*, we are working to expand the Community Action Lab to include more housing-related content and actions. Partnerships with the incremental developers mentioned in the book, along with others we have met along the way, allow us to grow an energized network of bottom-up developers. They are the vanguard of the bottom-up revolution we envision.

Maybe being an incremental developer or the leader of a Local Conversation is not your thing. That's just fine. We're all called to do what we can, and that will be different for everyone.

The one thing you can do right now is to tell someone. Share your thoughts on this book or anything you've picked up from Strong Towns with a friend or neighbor. At strongtowns.org, we publish more than a dozen new articles each week along with podcasts, videos, and social media messages. They are all free for you to access and share with others. Go ahead and start an informal conversation with others in your community on these ideas.

Then, do the most important thing: listen. With as much humility as you can, take the time to listen and understand, especially from those where consensus is difficult.

Strong Towns is a bottom-up movement that gains its strength from meaningful connections among people. A meaningful connection will transcend political affiliation, racial divisions, even class distinctions. Our movement can solve problems that others struggle to address because we have a commitment to working across these differences. We are willing to be humble listeners.

As Jane Jacobs wrote, cities have the capability of providing something for everybody, but only when they are created by everybody. Bottom-up change is, in some ways, more difficult because it requires us to work together with others. It sometimes feels easier, certainly more expedient, to look at some of our neighbors as the enemies who need to be defeated, those whom we empower distant leaders to thwart.

Yet, for our cities to work, for them to truly be prosperous places, they must be created by everybody. That creation is an ongoing process, one that begins anew each day. While neither author of this book is Jewish, we take inspiration from *Pirkei Avot*, an ancient Jewish text, which notes that "you are not obligated to complete the work, but neither are you free to desist from it."

Jane Jacobs was right; cities must be created by everybody, from the bottom up. There is no shortcut. We all have a role to play.

What is yours?

References

Andersen, Michael. 2019. "Oregon Just Voted to Legalize Duplexes on Almost Every City Lot." Sightline Institute. June 30, 2019.

Anderson, Dana. 2023. "Real Estate Investors Pull Back, Buying 45% Fewer Homes Than a Year Ago." Redfin News. August 31, 2023. https://www.redfin.com/news/investor-home-purchases-drop-q2-2023/.

Anderson, Dana, and Sheharyar Bokhari. 2022. "Real Estate Investors Are Buying a Record Share of US Homes." Redfin News. April 6, 2022. https://www.redfin.com/news/investor-home-purchases-q4-2021/.

Beito, David T., and Linda Royster Beito. 2016. "The 'Lodger Evil' and the Transformation of Progressive Housing Reform, 1890–1930." *The Independent Review* 20, no. 4 (Spring 2016): 485–508.

Bernanke, Ben. 2007. "Bernanke: No Recession on Horizon." *Money Watch*. CBS News. March 28, 2007. https://www.cbsnews.com/news/bernanke-no-recession-on-horizon/.

Bernanke, Ben. 2012. "Housing Markets in Transition." Speech at the 2012 National Association of Homebuilders International Builders' Show. Orlando, Florida. February 10, 2012. https://www.federalreserve.gov/newsevents/speech/bernanke20110210a.htm.

Black, William K. 2005. *The Best Way to Rob a Bank Is to Own One: How Corporate Executives and Politicians Looted the S&L Industry*. University of Texas Press.

Bowman, Sam, John Myers, and Ben Southwood. 2021. "The Housing Theory of Everything." *Works in Progress*. September 14, 2021. https://worksinprogress.co/issue/the-housing-theory-of-everything/.

Bui, Quoctrung, Matt A.V. Chaban, and Jeremy White. "40 Percent of the Buildings in Manhattan Could Not Be Built Today." The Upshot. *The New York Times*. May 20, 2016. https://www.nytimes.com/interactive/2016/05/19/upshot/forty-percent-of-manhattans-buildings-could-not-be-built-today.html.

Bush, George W. 2011. "Bush Shopping Quote. Clip of Presidential News Conference." C-SPAN. October 11, 2001. https://www.c-span.org/video/?c4552776/user-clip-bush-shopping-quote.

Carbonaro, Giulia. 2023. "Housing Market Crash Fears Rise among Americans." *Newsweek*. May 22, 2023. https://www.newsweek.com/housing-market-crash-fears-rise-exclusive-poll-1801788.

Choi, Jung Hyun, and Amalie Zinn. 2022. "Eighty Percent of Homes on the Market Aren't Affordable for Households Earning Median Incomes or Less." Urban Institute. December 7, 2022. https://www.urban.org/urban-wire/eighty-percent-homes-market-arent-affordable-households-earning-median-incomes-or-less.

Colburn, Gregg, and Clayton Page Aldern. 2022. *Homelessness Is a Housing Problem: How Structural Factors Explain U.S. Patterns*. March 15, 2022. University of California Press.

Congress. 2008. "Public Law 110–343." October 3, 2008. https://www.congress.gov/110/plaws/publ343/PLAW-110publ343.htm.

Congressional Research Service. n.d. "A Chronology of Housing Legislation and Selected Executive Actions, 1892–2003." https://www.govinfo.gov/content/pkg/CPRT-108HPRT92629/html/CPRT-108HPRT92629.htm.

Cortright, Joe. 2022. "The NIMBYs Made $6 Trillion Last Year." CityCommentary. June 4, 2022. https://cityobservatory.org/nimby_trillions/.

Demsas, Jerusalem. 2022. "Community Input Is Bad, Actually." *The Atlantic*. April 22, 2022. https://www.theatlantic.com/ideas/archive/2022/04/local-government-community-input-housing-public-transportation/629625/.

Dezember, Ryan. 2020. *Underwater: How Our American Dream of Homeownership Became a Nightmare*. Thomas Dunne Books.

Dougherty, Conor. 2020. "Build Build Build Build Build Build Build Build Build Build Build Build Build Build." *The New York Times*. February 13, 2020.

Dougherty, Conor. 2022. "Twilight of the NIMBY." *The New York Times*. June 5, 2022. https://www.nytimes.com/2022/06/05/business/economy/california-housing-crisis-nimby.html.

EDD. n.d. "Labor Market Information." Employment Development Department, State of California. https://labormarketinfo.edd.ca.gov/.

Edwards, John. 2016. "A History of Downzoning." *The Wedge Times – Picayune*. February 15, 2016. https://wedgelive.com/a-history-of-downzoning/.

Einstein, Katherine Levine, David M. Glick, and Maxwell Palmer. 2019a. *Neighborhood Defenders: Participatory Politics and America's Housing Crisis*. December 5, 2019. Cambridge University Press.

Einstein, Katherine Levine, Maxwell Palmer, and David Glick. 2019b. "Who Participates in Local Government? Evidence from Meeting Minutes." *Perspectives on Politics* 17, no. 1 (March 19, 2019): 28–46. https://doi.org/10.1017/S153759271800213X.

FED. 2018. "Household Debt-to-Income Ratios in the Enhanced Financial Accounts, Accessible Data." Board of Governors of the Federal Reserve System. Last updated January 9, 2018. https://www.federalreserve.gov/econres/notes/feds-notes/household-debt-to-income-ratios-in-the-enhanced-financial-accounts-accessible-20180111.htm.

Fischel, William A. 2005. *The Homevoter Hypothesis*. February 2, 2005. Harvard University Press. https://www.hup.harvard.edu/books/9780674015951.

FREDa. n.d. "International Monetary Fund, Interest Rates, Discount Rate for United States [INTDSRUSM193N]." Retrieved from FRED, Federal Reserve Bank of St. Louis. https://fred.stlouisfed.org/series/INTDSRUSM193N.

FREDb. n.d. "Board of Governors of the Federal Reserve System (US), Treasury and Agency Securities: Mortgage-Backed Securities (MBS), All Commercial Banks [TMBACBW027NBOG]." Retrieved from FRED, Federal Reserve Bank of St. Louis. https://fred.stlouisfed.org/series/TMBACBW027NBOG.

FREDc. n.d. "Board of Governors of the Federal Reserve System (US), Assets: Securities Held Outright: Mortgage-Backed Securities: Wednesday Level [WSHOMCB]." Retrieved from FRED, Federal Reserve Bank of St. Louis. https://fred.stlouisfed.org/series/WSHOMCB.

FREDd. n.d. "S&P/Case-Shiller U.S. National Home Price Index (CSUSHPINSA)." Retrieved from FRED, Federal Reserve Bank of St. Louis. https://fred.stlouisfed.org/series/CSUSHPINSA.

Fitch, Stephane. 2001. "What If Housing Crashed?" *Forbes*. September 3, 2001. https://www.forbes.com/2001/09/03/076.html?sh=46d3f803576c.

Goldenberg, Suzanne. 2008. "A Desperate Plea—Then Race for a Deal before 'Sucker Goes Down.'" *The Guardian*. September 26, 2008. https://www.theguardian.com/business/2008/sep/27/wallstreet.useconomy1.

Haynie, Ron. 2023. "After 15 Years, the Federal Government Should End Its Conservatorship of Fannie Mae and Freddie Mac." ICBA, Independent Community Bankers of America. September 6, 2023. https://www.icba.org/newsroom/blogs/main-street-matters/2023/09/06/after-15-years-the-federal-government-should-end-its-conservatorship-of-fannie-mae-and-freddie-mac.

Herriges, Daniel. 2016. "The Neighbor's Dilemma." Strong Towns. October 13, 2016. https://www.strongtowns.org/journal/2016/10/13/the-neighbors-dilemma.

Hertz, Daniel. 2016. "The Illegal City of Sommerville." City Observatory. June 6, 2016. https://cityobservatory.org/the-illegal-city-of-somerville/.

Hirt, Sonia A. 2014. *Zoned in the USA: The Origins and Implications of American Land-Use Regulation*. Cornell University Press.

Hung, S.-Y. K., and C. Tu. 2008. "An Examination of Housing Price Appreciation in California and the Impact of Alternative Mortgage Instruments." *Journal of Housing Research* 17, no. 1: 33–48. http://www.jstor.org/stable/24861452.

Jacobe, Dennis. 2007. "Will the 'Subprime' Meltdown Be Contained?" Gallup. May 21, 2007. https://news.gallup.com/poll/27631/will-subprime-meltdown-contained.aspx.

Jacobs, Jane. 1992. *The Death and Life of Great American Cities*. December 1, 1992. Vintage.

Joint Center for Urban Studies of MIT and Harvard. 1973. (Currently, Joint Center for Housing Studies of Harvard University.) "America's Housing Needs: 1970–1980." December 1973. https://www.jchs.harvard.edu/.

Katznelson, Ira (2006). *When Affirmative Action Was White: An Untold History of Racial Inequality in Twentieth-Century America*. W.W. Norton.

Klinkenberg, Kevin. 2021. "Mixing It Up in Midtown Tampa." Substack: The Messy City. November 21, 2021. https://kevinklinkenberg.substack.com/p/mixing-it-up-in-midtown-tampa.

Kronberg, Eric. 2021a. "Housing Atlanta's Future." Presentation given at Atlanta Regional Housing Forum, August 4, 2021. Slides 34–45. https://www.kronbergua.com/presentations-1; https://www.dropbox.com/s/dmbe42zmw3pg7u7/2021_08_04%20Atlanta%20Housing%20Forum.pdf?dl=0.

Kronberg, Eric. 2021b. Personal correspondence with Daniel Herriges. September 22, 2021.

Kuhn, Thomas S. 1962. *The Structure of Scientific Revolutions*. University of Chicago Press.

Lundberg, Ian, and Louis Donnely. 2019. "A Research Note on the Prevalence of Housing Eviction among Children Born in U.S. Cities." *Demography* 56, no. 1 (February): 391–404. https://www.ncbi.nlm.nih.gov/pmc/articles/PMC6358494/#:~:text=The%20most%20comprehensive%20analysis%20of,2018.

Lutz, James. 2011. "Lest We Forget, a Short History of Housing in the United States." Lawrence Berkeley National Laboratory. June 23, 2011. https://escholarship.org/uc/item/3jw1k5nc.

Mapbox. n.d. "54% of San Francisco Homes Are in Buildings That Would Be Illegal to Build Today." https://sfzoning.deapthoughts.com/illegal_homes.html.

Marohn, Charles, Jr. 2019. *Strong Towns: A Bottom-Up Revolution to Rebuild American Prosperity*. October 1, 2019. Wiley.

Marohn, Charles, Jr. 2020. "The Local Case for Reparations." Strong Towns. September 21, 2020. https://www.strongtowns.org/journal/2020/9/18/the-local-case-for-reparations.

McMorrow, Paul. 2014. "Sommerville Zoning: Sane at Last." *The Boston Globe*. June 17, 2014. https://www.bostonglobe.com/opinion/2014/06/17/somerville-zoning-sane-last/wuJFkpcQbw3DAeLk7oAWKL/story.html.

Molotch, Harvey. 1988. "Strategies and Constraints of Growth Elites" In Scott Cummings, Ed., *Business Elites and Urban Development: Case Studies and Critical Perspectives*. Albany: State University of New York Press, 1988, pp. 25–47.

National Alliance to End Homelessness. n.d. "State of Homelessness: 2023 Edition." https://endhomelessness.org/homelessness-in-america/homelessness-statistics/state-of-homelessness/.

National Archives. n.d. "Servicemen's Readjustment Act (1944)." Milestone Documents. https://www.archives.gov/milestone-documents/servicemens-readjustment-act#:~:text=Signed%20into%20law%20by%20President,WWII%20and%20later%20military%20conflicts.

New England Historical Society. n.d. "The Rise, Fall and Rebirth of the Triple Decker." https://newenglandhistoricalsociety.com/rise-fall-rebirth-new-england-triple-decker/.

NLIHC. 2022. "The GAP: A Shortage of Affordable Homes." National Low Income Housing Coalition. April 2022. https://nlihc.org/sites/default/files/gap/Gap-Report_2022.pdf.

Nolen, John. 1916. *Better City Planning for Bridgeport*. Brewer-Colgan Company, printers.

Oswego. n.d. Oswego Renaissance Association. https://www.oswegonyonline.com/.

Robinson, Kenneth J. 2013. "Savings and Loan Crisis." Federal Reserve History. November 22, 2013. https://www.federalreservehistory.org/essays/savings-and-loan-crisis.

Rognlie, M. (2015), "Deciphering the Fall and Rise in the Net Capital Share: Accumulation or Scarcity?" Brookings Papers on Economic Activity, Spring, 1–54. https://www.brookings.edu/articles/deciphering-the-fall-and-rise-in-the-net-capital-share/.

Rohrlich, Ted. 2022. "LA Loses Much More Affordable Housing Than It Gains." LAist. October 20, 2022. https://laist.com/news/politics/la-loses-much-more-affordable-housing-than-it-gains.

Rosner, Joshua. 2001. "Housing in the New Millennium: A Home without Equity Is Just a Rental with Debt." SSRN. https://ssrn.com/abstract=1162456 or http://dx.doi.org/10.2139/ssrn.1162456.

Schroeder, Pete. 2019. "Fannie, Freddie and the Government: It's Complicated." Reuters. September 5, 2019. https://www.reuters.com/article/us-fannie-freddie-hurdles-factbox/fannie-freddie-and-the-government-its-complicated-idUSKCN1VQ2Q4/.

Schumacher, E.F. 2010. *Small Is Beautiful: Economics as if People Mattered*. October 19, 2010. Harper Perennial.

Scott, James C. 1999. Seeing like a State: *How Certain Schemes to Improve the Human Condition Have Failed*. February 8, 1999. Yale University Press.

Shiller, Robert. n.d. "Online Data Robert Shiller." http://www.econ.yale.edu/~shiller/data.htm.

Shoup, Donald. 2019. "Parking Reform Will Save the City." *Bloomberg* CityLab. September 20, 2019. https://www.bloomberg.com/news/articles/2019-09-20/how-to-reform-your-city-s-bad-parking-requirements.

Smith, L.W., and L.W. Wood. 1964. "History of Yard Lumber Size Standards." NTRL, National Technical Reports Library. US Department of Commerce. https://ntrl.ntis.gov/NTRL/dashboard/searchResults/titleDetail/PB2006102557.xhtml.

Sperance, Cameron. 2021. "Saving the Iconic New England Three-Decker from Fire and Bulldozers." Boston.com. April 20, 2021. https://www.boston.com/real-estate/home-improvement/2021/04/20/saving-three-deckers-from-fire-bulldozers/.

Taleb, Nassim Nicholas. 2014a. *Antifragile: Things That Gain from Disorder (Incerto)*. Random House Publishing Group. Reprint edition (January 28, 2014).

Taleb, Nassim Nicholas. 2014b. "Small Is Beautiful—But Also Less Fragile." 2014 NYU Development Research Institute Annual Conference "Cities and Development." November 18, 2014. YouTube. https://www.youtube.com/watch?v=B0hMS4eUVV8.

Tuohey, Patrick, and Michael Rathbone. 2014. "Urban Neglect: Kansas City's Misuse of Tax Increment Financing." Show-Me Institute. November 2014. https://showmeinstitute.org/wp-content/uploads/2015/06/2014%2012%20-%20KC%20TIF%20Misuse%20-%20Tuohey_Rathbone_0.pdf.

Whittemore, A.H. (2013). "How the Federal Government Zoned America: The Federal Housing Administration and Zoning." *Journal of Urban History* 39, no. 4: 620–642. https://doi.org/10.1177/0096144212470245.

Woolf, Arthur G. 1987. "The Residential Adoption of Electricity in Early Twentieth-Century America." *The Energy Journal* 8, no. 2 (1987): 19–30. http://www.jstor.org/stable/41322257.

References

Index

Page numbers followed by *f* and *n* refer to figures and notes, respectively.